Adult Life

SUNY series in Contemporary Continental Philosophy

Dennis J. Schmidt, editor

Adult Life

Aging, Responsibility, and the Pursuit of Happiness

John Russon

Published by State University of New York Press, Albany

For information, contact State University of New York Press, Albany, NY
www.sunypress.edu

Library of Congress Cataloging-in-Publication Data

Name: Russon, John.
Title: Adult life : aging, responsibility, and the pursuit of happiness /
    John Russon, author.
Description: Albany : State University of New York Press, [2020] | Series:
    SUNY series, Contemporary Continental Philosophy | Includes
    bibliographical references and index.
Identifiers: ISBN 9781438479514 (hardcover : alk. paper) | ISBN 9781438479507
    (pbk. : alk. paper) | ISBN 9781438479521 (ebook)
Further information is available at the Library of Congress.

10 9 8 7 6 5 4 3 2 1

Dedicated to my son Theo,
whose future I hope these ideas will enrich,
and to the memory of
my mother Eleanor and my father Gordon,
from whom I learned many of the most important lessons.

'Tis impossible to be sure of any thing but death and taxes.

—Christopher Bullock, *The Cobler of Preston*

A man has nothing better under the sun than to eat, to drink and to be merry.

—*Ecclesiastes* 8:15

Contents

Part III.
The Content of Adult Life: Adult Occupations

Acknowledgments

I completed the final work on the manuscript for *Adult Life* in June 2019, shortly after my son's third birthday, whereas I wrote the initial draft of *Human Experience* over the summer months of 1996, just one year after starting my position as assistant professor at the Pennsylvania State University. In the twenty-three years between those two events, my life, predictably, underwent quite substantial changes. Because this work is largely an attempt to understand what happens in the context of an adult life, it is not surprising that the people who were involved with me in those personally transformative years have been most important for my efforts to understand the meaning of adulthood; consequently, my debts in this case are more personal than scholarly, though I have scholarly debts as well. I owe the greatest personal debts to my closest companions, friends and colleagues throughout those years: Patricia Fagan, Maria Talero, Kym Maclaren, David Ciavatta, Peter Simpson, David Morris, Bruce Gilbert, Caren Irr, Greg Recco, Peter Costello, Nate Andersen, Eric Sanday, Tara Gump Newhouse, Susan Bredlau, Ed Casey, John Stuhr, John Sallis, Vincent Colapietro, Rick Lee, Kirsten Swenson, Kirsten Jacobson, Ömer Aygün, Len Lawlor, Scott Marratto, John Lysaker, Ken Aldcroft, Mike Milligan, Nick Fraser, Chris Gale, Chris Banks, Tom Richards, Ethan Ardelli, Eve Rabinoff, Whitney Howell, Tristana Martin Rubio, Shannon Hoff, Greg Kirk, John Hacker-Wright, Laura McMahon, Siby George, and Pravesh Jung; and I am grateful for the companionship of my friends Joe Pernice, Andy Payne, and Kelly Gallagher-Mackay, who sat beside me almost every day at Ideal Coffee as I wrote these pages into existence. On the scholarly side, I am intimately aware with virtually every sentence that I write of my debts to Eugene F. Bertoldi, Kenneth L. Schmitz, Graeme Nicholson, H. S. Harris,

Joseph J. Owens, Francis Sparshott, Eva-Maria Simms, Robert Stolorow, Matthew Ratcliffe, Will McNeill, and, of course, many of those I have listed as more personally influential; and I am also especially grateful to Kirsten Jacobson, Jeff Morrisey, Laura McMahon, and Shannon Hoff, each of whom took the time to read the entire manuscript in draft and offer helpful, critical comments. And, finally, I would like especially to acknowledge my gratitude to Dean Pickard, who read and taught my books, and, on the basis of his interest, established a company to fund students to study with me; I am grateful for his friendship and humbled by his amazingly generous support.

Introduction

This book is an attempt to grasp what human adulthood is. When we study anything, though, we need first to have a reasonable sense of what the *phenomenon* is that we are trying to make sense of, and so, similarly, before we can dive into our *interpretation* of adulthood we need to have a rough-and-ready sense of what the basic phenomenon of adulthood is. For that reason, I will begin with three vignettes—three little dramas about real human situations. The narration of the three vignettes will bring forth, I hope, some of the most salient features of adulthood and help us to conjure up in imagination what it is like to live an adult life.

Vignette #1: The Generation Gap

Sitting in a coffee shop on a Saturday (actually, in *Coffee Matters*, in St. John's Newfoundland), I notice a striking difference. Some students, probably in their late teens, are talking animatedly with each other. Also, two women, probably in their forties, are sitting at another table, chatting with each other. The striking difference is between the content and style of the conversations in the two groups. I can overhear the students speculating excitedly—the table is virtually "bubbling over"—about which of their friends will be at some upcoming event, while the two older women are calmly discussing renovations to their houses and how much those renovations will cost. The dress of the members of each group is similarly different: the students are wearing a colorful mix of T-shirts, sleeveless blouses, ripped blue jeans, short skirts, and sweatpants, while the older women are wearing well-tailored, businesslike clothes. These two groups look, sound, and act like radically different *kinds* of people;

1

and that, furthermore, is not just how they appear to others—on the contrary, that is, presumably, how these groups look to themselves and to each other. The reason these differences are interesting, though, is that not that many years ago the older women looked and acted like the young students and not that many years from now the young students will look and act like the older women; in other words, though they *seem* like radically different kinds of people, each is, in fact, simply a version of the other.

This familiar scene draws attention to the phenomenon of age, by which I mean not just the fact that the different people involved have lived for different numbers of years, but the fact that those different numbers of years bring with them social, cultural, and behavioral meanings, such that being "eighteen" implies a recognizable lifestyle, and one recognizably different from the lifestyle of a forty-year-old. Presumably, this is something we all recognize easily enough, but it is a dimension of our existence that, though we ourselves live through it, we typically do not really comprehend. Indeed, the very fact that the eighteen-year-olds have no real interest in the forty-year-olds and, reciprocally, that the forty-year-olds have no real interest in the teenagers underlines the relative insularity with which we typically inhabit our "ages," for those in each group do not *see themselves* in the members of the other group.

Surely, we are all familiar with situations like this, and we can easily imagine that members of either group would attempt to explain their lack of interest in the other as a "difference in generations." This expression is no doubt correct, but perhaps not quite in the sense in which it is intended: the younger people likely attribute the boring appearance of the older people to the fact that those older ones like the things people liked in the '80s, and they imagine there is something objectively less interesting about the music, the dress, or the pastimes of the past, while the older ones reject the younger interests that they perceive to be rooted in the culture of the early twenty-first century, imagining there is something objectively less interesting about the music, the dress, and the pastimes of the present; the truth, however, is that each group likes what was popular in their own youth. In other words, while there may indeed be something that is more or less intrinsically interesting about those two historical periods, that is not really what explains the interest or lack of it that the members of each group experience.

It is not just the historical era that each group belongs to that seems alien to the other group; instead, for each group, the actual practices the other is engaged in seem boring, and this is the deeper meaning of the "difference in generations." The women in their forties are not excited to speculate about who will be at the mall and those in their teens do not find discussions of home renovation engaging. But though the "grown-ups" would not really want to deal with teenage conversations again, they probably are nostalgic for what they perceive as the lost vibrancy of their youth, and though the teenagers similarly would not really want to sit through the adult conversations, they nonetheless do anticipate such a future for themselves, and they find some excitement in imagining themselves as adults with families and careers. The difference in generations, then, is not so much a difference of historical era as it is a difference in the *time of life* in which the members of each group participate, and the difference *between* these different groups of people is actually a difference *within* the lives of the members of each group—the difference between their own younger and older "selves."

This typical scenario—the first of my three vignettes—is helpful, therefore, for reminding us of the pivotal change that happens in our lives, somewhere between the ages of eighteen and forty, that involves a fundamental change in our sense of who we are: it is a change in our interests and values, a change in our companionships, and a change in the worldly form of our activities. And one of the biggest aspects of this change, implied in the adult discussion of home renovations and finance, is the change from the openness of youthful expectation to the specificity of adult commitment.

Vignette #2: Worldly Engagement

Emma Goldman was born on June 27, 1869, in the city of Kovno, in what is now Lithuania and was then part of the Russian Empire. She was the daughter by a second marriage of an Orthodox Jewish woman named Taube Bienowitch who already had two daughters from her first marriage. Taube's marriage to Emma's father, Abraham Goldman, had been arranged by her family, and it seems generally to have been a site of unhappiness for Taube and especially for Emma. The family struggled constantly with poverty and throughout her young life Emma also struggled constantly with her father—and, indeed, with her teachers—as she attempted to get an education. In response to the limitations to her formal opportunities for education and because of her great emotional independence, Emma did her best to educate herself. Eventually, deeply frustrated with her social, familial, and personal situation, Emma, at the age of sixteen and against her father's wishes, emigrated to the United States.

In the United States, Emma lived initially with her sisters in the vicinity of Rochester, New York, and subsequently the rest of her family joined them, as they fled the threatening culture of Russian anti-Semitism that was developing around them. Emma took factory work as a seamstress, which she found stultifying. Though she married shortly after arriving in the United States, she divorced her husband within a year, and this resulted in her rejection by her parents. During this time, she became increasingly focused on politics and especially the activism that grew in response to the aggressive repression of workers and "anarchists" following the "Haymarket Affair" in Chicago in 1886, a public protest against the suppression by the police of labor organizing—a protest that resulted in the police openly firing into the civilian crowd, leaving eleven dead and more than a hundred injured. In the face of her parents' rejection of her, Emma struck out on her own and moved to New York City, where she met and became the close associate of Johann Most, who became her political mentor. Under the influence of Johann, Emma developed as a charismatic speaker, urging activism in response to the capitalist oppression of workers and the correlated domination by the state, and especially advocating for the persuasive power of violent acts.

Over the next fourteen years, Emma, who identified herself as an anarchist, was an active agitator for change, and she was involved in a number of prominent revolutionary activities. With Alexander Berkman, whom she met upon her arrival in New York City and who remained her close companion for decades, she plotted to assassinate Henry Clay Frick, the manager of the Carnegie Steel Company who had hired strikebreakers and private armed guards to oppose striking workers—a policy that resulted in armed conflict that left both striking workers and guards killed. Emma and Alexander had hoped that killing Frick would frighten exploitative industrialists and galvanize workers to resist them but Alexander's botched assassination attempt, on July 23, 1892, did not in fact win the support of the workers' movement. Alexander was sent to prison for twenty years for attempted murder and Emma was investigated as an accomplice, though no evidence was found and she was not charged. Emma continued to agitate for revolutionary social action and in the following year she was charged with "inciting to riot" after speaking to a crowd of three thousand people in Union Square in New

York, on August 21, 1893, urging workers to take action in resistance to the economic depression known as the "Panic of 1893"; she was sentenced to a year in prison. In 1901, the American president William McKinley was killed by a man named Leon Czolgosz who, under interrogation, claimed that he was an anarchist and that it was Emma's public speaking that had inspired him to action. Emma was again investigated for her possible involvement, though again no evidence was found to support charging her. Emma did not criticize Czolgosz's actions, however, and this led to her alienation from other anarchists and, though she was not charged in relation to the assassination, she was denounced in the press as a dangerous anarchist, and, subsequently, Theodore Roosevelt, who replaced McKinley as president, announced as his policy the suppression of anarchists and "all active and passive sympathizers with anarchists."

After the assassination of McKinley, and in the face of her denunciation by the press and anarchists alike, Emma withdrew from public life and took work as a nurse. Two years later, she returned to public activism, however, in the context of substantial public opposition to the U.S. government's new Immigration Act of 1903, which identified anarchists as inadmissible for immigration. Over the next ten years, she demonstrated her strength as an electrifying speaker to packed rooms across the country, and she simultaneously became progressively more involved in coordinating activities between different activist groups. She also wrote regularly on political themes—including anarchism, marriage, and women's suffrage—for *Mother Earth*, a magazine she had co-founded in 1906.

When the United States entered World War I, Emma and Alexander, who had recently been released from prison, formed a group resisting conscription. In 1917, they were both arrested after a raid on their offices and charged under the Espionage Act of 1917 with conspiracy to induce persons not to register. They were both found guilty and sentenced to two years in the penitentiary. In 1919, J. Edgar Hoover, then head of the General Intelligence Division of the United States Department of Justice, focused his attention on Emma and Alexander, whom he identified as "two of the most dangerous anarchists in the country"; they were both deported to Russia in November 1919. Though Emma was sympathetic to the principles of the Russian Revolution of 1917, once in Russia she found the government to be unresponsive and repressive, and in 1921 she and Alexander left, settling for a time in Berlin and then, in 1924, moving to London. In 1925, she married a Scottish anarchist in order to acquire British citizenship, which she used to travel to Canada and France. In 1936, in the context of the Spanish Civil War, she went to Spain to work with the anarchist workers' party, but after their brutal suppression in 1937, she returned to London and then, in 1939, moved to Canada, where she died in 1940.

I have included Emma Goldman's story as my second vignette because it demonstrates so powerfully the place of individual initiative and commitment in our lives, while simultaneously putting prominently on display the ways that the fabric of our personal lives is woven from worldly materials. Goldman's is a story of a unique individual, shaping her own life on her own terms, but this personal story cannot be told except as a story of her family life, the capitalist economic system and the political events of the day. Throughout the entirety of her life, she was oriented by the relatively simple goal of living her own life freely, but her circumstances made it clear to her that such freedom is possible only with the support of one's surrounding world, and she was in fact surrounded with inhibition rather than facilitation. Initially her family, that formative home base that we all depend upon to shelter us from adversity and to nurture our growth, was itself a force resisting her development: though she needed her family to support her, she also needed to escape her family if she was to have a fulfilling life as a free individual. The traditional views of her parents confronted her early with the oppressive and misogynistic dimensions of patriarchal culture, the values she came to fight against in her subsequent advocacy of free love and women's rights, and as she subsequently became aware of the pervasive and powerful roles that governments and business—like family—have for shaping our lives and of how these can be unhealthy and unjust, she accepted the responsibility, as an individual, for addressing these issues. Her story prominently demonstrates that individuals are not "uncontextualized," but are themselves *intimately* defined by the realities of family and society, and that individual agency is a matter of how we embrace these realities: Do we own up to the responsibilities intrinsic to them, and work actively to address the injustices we find around us, or do we passively acquiesce to the *status quo*, allowing ourselves the immediate satisfactions our circumstances afford while tacitly endorsing the continued supremacy of the existing power structures? Emma Goldman was surely more of an "agent" than almost any of us will ever be—indeed, the fact that she acted on the "world" stage is why we remember her as a historically significant figure—but though she is thus on a different scale than most of us, she shows something of the reality that is true for all of us and thus something of the possibility that defines all adult life.

Vignette #3: Mortality and Character

In the first book of his *Republic*, Plato (c. 427 BC–c. 347 BC) portrays a conversation between the Athenian philosopher Socrates (c. 469–399 BC) and Cephalus (c. 495–c. 420 BC), an immigrant to Athens who ran a prosperous shield-manufacturing business. At the time of the conversation, Socrates is a man of about fifty and Cephalus is on "the threshold of old age," that is, he is a man who is nearing death. In Plato's dramatization, Cephalus's son Polemarchus brings Socrates to his house, and Cephalus expresses his desire that Socrates visit more frequently for the sake of talking. Socrates responds:

> For my part, Cephalus, I am really delighted to discuss with the very old. . . . Since they are like men who have proceeded on a certain road that perhaps we too will have to take, one ought, in my opinion, to learn from them what sort of road it is: whether it is rough and hard or easy and smooth. From you in particular I should like to learn how it looks to you, for you are now at just the time of life that poets call "the threshold of old age." Is it a hard time of life, or what have you to report of it? (*Republic* I.328d-e)

Cephalus then describes his experience. First he notes that other friends his age lament their loss of youth, "reminiscing about sex, about drinking bouts and feasts and all that goes with things of that sort" (*Republic* I.329a). Cephalus himself, however, identifies a different reason for why one will or will not be happy in old age: the cause, he says, is

> not old age, Socrates, but the character of the human beings. If they are orderly and content with themselves, even old age is only moderately troublesome; if they are not, then both age, Socrates, and youth alike turn out to be hard for that sort. (*Republic* I.329d)

Socrates then challenges Cephalus's (self-)assessment:

> Cephalus, when you say these things, I suppose that the
> many do not accept them from you, but believe rather that
> it is not due to character that you bear old age so easily but
> due to possessing great substance. They say that for the rich
> there are many consolations. (*Republic* I.329e)

Cephalus grants that there is some truth to this perception, and affirms
that both issues—wealth or poverty and whether or not one is "a decent
sort"—are essential axes for determining whether one will be happy in
old age.

Finally, Socrates asks Cephalus what in particular is the greatest
good that has come to him through his possessing of great wealth.
Cephalus replies:

> What I say won't persuade many, perhaps. For know well . . .
> that when a man comes near to the realization that he will be
> making an end, fear and care enter him for things to which
> he gave no thought before. The tales told about what is in
> Hades—that the one who has done unjust deeds here must
> pay the penalty there—at which he laughed up to then, now
> make his soul twist and turn because he fears they might be
> true. . . . Now the man who finds many unjust deeds in his
> life often even wakes from his sleep in a fright as children
> do, and lives in anticipation of evil. . . . For this I count the
> possession of money most wroth-while [*sic*], not for any man,
> but for the decent and orderly one. The possession of money
> contributes a great deal to not cheating or lying to any man
> against one's will and, moreover, to not departing for that
> other place frightened because one owes some sacrifices to
> a god or money to a human being. (*Republic* I.330d–331b)

Their conversation does not continue far after this point, for Polemarchus
intervenes in the conversation and Cephalus departs. This short conversation, however, is quite rich in the further light it sheds on the realities
of adult life and the experience of aging in particular.

Cephalus's initial emphasis on the disappearance of sex, drunkenness, and festivity from old age underlines simultaneously the irreducibly
bodily character of our aging—specifically, the diminution of our bodily

powers—and, by implication, the otherwise prominent place of sex, intoxication, and playful celebration in a happy life. Cephalus makes an important point about the *place* of these pleasures in our lives, however: we do not all automatically adopt the same attitude toward them. Thus, he notes, whereas his friends are made unhappy by their disappearance from their lives, he remains content. What is at issue, in other words, is, as he says, our *character*. Whether or not we endorse Cephalus's specific views about what constitutes a good character, it is nonetheless clear that he has identified one of the most crucial parameters of adulthood: to a very great degree, healthy adulthood is a matter of developing within ourselves a *way of behaving well* in situations, and this healthy cultivation of character—*maturity*—is largely a matter of learning how to maintain a commitment to important values in coping with the challenging or tempting features of the situations in which we find ourselves involved.

It is not just the case that different individuals can have different attitudes *toward* pleasure and hardship, however; it is also the case that different individuals can face dramatically different situations *of* pleasure and hardship, whether because of issues of illness or disability, gender- or race-discrimination or poverty. Socrates's challenge to Cephalus's rather generous self-appraisal underlines in particular that being rich changes significantly the situations one faces as an adult and the resources one has for dealing with them; though Cephalus insists that, in his case, the significance of his wealth is subordinate to the significance of his character, we might nonetheless wonder whether his great wealth actually allows what is really a rather poorly developed character to masquerade as virtue. This last point is perhaps suggested in the final theme raised in this conversation, namely, the confrontation with death and the anxiety about "final judgment."

With his aging, Cephalus has been brought to recognize his mortality, and this recognition of his death—and the stories he has heard about a possible afterlife—has encouraged him to reflect upon his life *as a whole* and to assess its worth. His approach to this self-evaluation, however, sounds more like bookkeeping than morality: his wealth, he says, has allowed him to remain debt-free, and he includes in this his "paying off" of the gods through sacrifice. Facing one's mortality and trying to assess honestly the worth of one's own life is again a significant dimension of any adult life, though ideally we can imagine more profound ways to approach these matters than what Cephalus puts on display.

The Plan of the Book

Socrates's remark at the beginning of the conversation I quoted above is worth noting. It is interesting to talk with the very old, he says, because "they are like men who have proceeded on a certain road that perhaps we too will have to take." Old age, in other words, is not a fixed reality; instead, the experience of any person will be their taking of a path—a "way"—and though it is possible, it is not necessarily the case that their path will be ours (indeed, Cephalus himself implies as much in saying that his view of aging differs from that of others he knows). This point about aging is, I think, true of adulthood in general. For each of us, our experience of "growing up" and growing old is a kind of mystery and though the experiences of others definitely provide important guidance for us, we must, each of us, wait to find out for ourselves what our life will be like—we must find out *by living it*. Our own future confronts us, so to speak, with the ultimate "problem of induction," for this, our own most intimate reality, is never something the meaning and significance of which can be "derived" from any amount of evidence about the experience of others.

The experiences of others are nonetheless meaningful to us, though, because, however imperfect, the life of another gives one some kind of lens through which to reflect on one's own life. Indeed, perhaps this is why biographies are so popular and so interesting: the stories of others appear tantalizingly as if they held answers to the questions we are asking. It is for just that reason that I have included my three vignettes. Most broadly, these three vignettes—one an anecdote from everyday life, one a biographical sketch of a historical figure, one a scene from literature—put on display (vividly, I hope) recognizable truths about adulthood that transcend the experience of any particular individual but are characteristic of all of our lives; more specifically, they draw attention to the fact that adulthood stands in contrast to a period of adolescence, it is a time of accomplishment in a complex worldly environment, and it is inherently defined by its confrontation with death, a confrontation that draws attention to the meaningfulness of one's life as a whole and highlights the nature and significance of one's moral development. And, just as I have here tried to draw quickly some broad lessons from these vignettes, so will this book as a whole be a more systematic attempt to distill from the vast range of human experience—as that has been documented and digested in the history of psychology, sociology, anthropology, politics and so on—the fundamental parameters that are distinctive and definitive of adulthood.

This book, however, is not itself an empirical study in psychology or sociology as such, but is a work of philosophy. What this means is that, though it draws on the rich resources of these various domains of inquiry, it is not itself an attempt to add new empirical content to our already vast knowledge about human life; instead, it is an attempt to grasp that existent empirical material as an organized whole. It is an attempt, that is, to bring together those empirical details with an insight into the basic constitution—the "first principles"—of our distinctive character as human beings, and thus to *understand* those empirical findings in light of this insight.

What are the "first principles" from which we start? The first chapter, rather than this introduction, is the place to turn for the careful answer to that question, but I can nonetheless roughly sketch here the basic idea. The fundamental insight that orients our study is that our condition as human beings is primarily that we *experience*: we are not just natural beings *to* whom something happens, but we are subjective beings *for* whom something happens: we *find* ourselves situated in the midst of a happening and our experience is our ongoing process of coming to terms with this condition. The significance of this situation is helpfully captured, I think, in a saying attributed to the ancient Greek philosopher Heraclitus (c. 540 BC–c. 475 BC).

In his dialogue *Cratylus*, Plato portrays a conversation between Socrates and Cratylus, who was a follower of Heraclitus. Socrates there attributes a view to Heraclitus that has become one of our most familiar sayings, though no doubt we often do not think too deeply about its meaning. Socrates says that

> Heraclitus, I believe, says that all things pass and nothing stays, and comparing existing things to the flow of a river, he says you could not step twice into the same river. (*Cratylus* 402a)

What Heraclitus actually wrote is more likely, "On those stepping into rivers staying the same other and other waters flow" (Diels-Kranz fragment B12), but our familiar "you can't step into the same river twice" seems to capture the point well enough: the idea is that a river *is* only the flowing water, and that water is always changing, so the water you step in will never be the same water you stepped in before. Now, as a reflection on a river, that is an interesting enough observation, but probably not one that will grip most of us with its profundity. If we think of the river as a metaphor for life, however, we can perhaps see why this observation is so significant.

Our experience is of a constant passage, a "flow"—we call it "time"—and that flow is both the flow of our own experience and our sense of the unfolding of reality: neither "I" nor "it" ever rests in a simple, finished state, but each is instead a process—a "happening." On the one hand, this means that we experience ourselves at the center of a happening—it is *our* experience that is flowing; at the same time, however, that happening itself presents itself to us as having *its* "center" elsewhere, which is to say we find ourselves "caught up in the flow" of *reality*. The world itself is a "river," a changing, developing reality that we must always keep struggling to make sense of, and we ourselves age and grow, which means that we, too, never stay the same, and we must constantly be learning anew how to make sense of the changing form of our own experience. Our ongoing lives are the ongoing attempt to "catch up," so to speak, with both of these "moving targets" and especially to hold together coherently our sense of these two flows—the subjective time of our experience and the objective time of the world. It is because that is the defining character of our experience that, philosophically, we will only understand the real meaning of the empirical details of our experience if we grasp those details in light of both of these "temporalities."

The distinctive dual character of our experience is that it is thus defined both by the "form" of subjectivity and by the "content" of reality, and chapter 1 will focus on the careful description of this distinctive nature of our experience to define the project of studying adulthood in terms of our grappling with this need to realize an integrated and coherent sense of ourselves and the world. The simultaneously subjective and objective character of this goal entails that its accomplishment is a matter both of psychological health and of knowledge, and exploring the distinctive form that this, our definitive human path takes will be the subject of chapters 2 and 3, which study the themes raised in Socrates's conversation with Cephalus: character and aging.

In chapter 2, we will interpret adulthood in terms of our behavioral readiness to take up reality on its own terms. We will explore the fundamental attitudes and skills that human individuals need to develop in order to succeed at this, and, drawing especially on the insights of the ancient Greek philosopher Aristotle (384–322 BC), we will identify three fundamental "excellences" of character that are integral to a self-responsible engagement with the world: self-possession, courage, and co-inhabitation. Studying these developments of character will also make it clear that we can be "adults" to varying degrees and (as will become clearer in chapter 4) that there is significant difference between a minimal and a fuller cultivation of adulthood.

Growing up is not just a matter of psychological maturity, however; as we saw in the story of Cephalus, it is also a matter of aging, which is the philosophical focus of chapter 3. Aging is itself a physiological matter, of course, but also a matter of *how* we experience—a matter of *perspective*—and this side of our experience must be held together with the theme of our development of character. What it is to experience *as* an adult is not just a matter of the principles with which one engages with the objective temporality of the world at the present moment; it is also a matter of how one engages with one's *own* "objectively temporal" reality, that is, it is a matter of taking up one's own experience of the finitude, specificity, and mortality that is integral to the fact that one is a natural being. Each of us is a perspective *on* the world, but each of us is also a natural being *in* the world, a natural being that passes through a characteristic process of growth, development, and decay, and the *experience* of aging is the experience of grappling with the reality of this process.

Exploring the distinctive *form* our growth takes will lead us to what turns out to be the central theme of our study, namely, the distinctive *content* of our adult lives—our "occupations." Our study of the form of our experience will reveal that the process of accomplishing a coherent relationship of self and world is fundamentally a matter of dealing with other people, and we will see that the issues of adult life are most centrally defined by the parameters of the social world to which we belong. Specifically, in chapter 4, which is by far the longest chapter in the book, we will identify three essential forms of intersubjective engagement: intimate interpersonal relationships, economic life, and political community. The detailed exploration of our distinctive experiences of navigating intimate, economic, and political life—the essential domains of adult life—will help us to focus on the biggest issues that we face, both individually and socially, in our efforts to live happy and just lives.

Finally, beyond navigating the demands of our immediate natural and social world, it is integral to a well-developed adult life to grapple with questions of ultimate value—the sorts of questions that Cephalus grew concerned about only with his experience of the imminence of his death, but which others take much more seriously throughout their lives. Chapter 5 explores the meaning and nature of art, religion, and philosophy, the three distinctive human occupations that grapple with these ultimate issues. Each of these occupations has an essential role to play in the development of a healthy and full adult life, and each also has a long history, such that engaging with any one of them is on the one hand a matter of personal "calling" and on the other hand a matter of grappling with a highly developed body of work and highly structured institutional practices. Studying the relationship between the personal and the institutional meanings of art, religion, and philosophy will help us to understand what is involved in grappling with matters of ultimate value and to see why this is a matter of prime importance in both personal and social life.

This book is a complete and self-contained study, meant to be read on its own, but it is also intended as the concluding installment of a trilogy that began with my earlier books *Human Experience* and *Bearing Witness to Epiphany*. In studying the perspective of the adult, this work offers an important supplement to the understanding of our experience that is developed in *Human Experience* and *Bearing Witness to Epiphany*—which took their focus more distinctively from childhood and adolescent experience, respectively—just as those books offer insight into the essential context of personal development that is presupposed in adult life. Compared to those other two books, this book has a more fundamentally ethical orientation, whereas *Human Experience* was more epistemological and *Bearing Witness to Epiphany* more metaphysical in focus; these orientations are not ultimately separable, however, and so this work necessarily involves essential epistemological and metaphysical exploration as well. And, like those books, this is primarily a work of phenomenological philosophy, carrying on and developing further the methods and insights of Immanuel Kant and the other great European philosophers of the past two centuries; it is the founding insights of Kant, Maurice Merleau-Ponty, and Jacques Derrida that most prominently shape the philosophical method of this work, while Simone de Beauvoir and the American philosopher John Dewey are the thinkers who have most intimately informed the philosophical study of adulthood specifically. In these ways, this book is a scholarly study. That, however, is not the primary way that I want the reader to approach it.

I have pointedly tried to write this book in a way that is accessible to any average adult reader, and not just to scholars and specialists.

I have tried to write in as plain a style as possible, and the argument and analysis thus proceed only by referring to aspects of our world with which anyone can be assumed to be familiar and rely on reasoning of which anyone is capable; consequently, the work, like traditional works of philosophy, generally does not make specific reference to the scholarly work of others except in those cases in which I directly quote from other texts. (For the reader who is interested in pursuing further study, I have included an appendix with suggestions for further reading.) The reason for writing this way is primarily for the sake of making it available to any interested reader, but there is also a deeper reason.

More than anything else, this book is intended as a work that will speak to *you* personally and, ideally, transformatively. Philosophy is not primarily a matter of scholarship—it is not a matter of communicating "information" or of "proving" something—but a matter of wisdom: at root, philosophy is the attempt to attune us more deeply to our own reality so that we might live better, both individually and culturally. Accordingly, my writing is not an academic exercise in "knowing for the sake of knowing," but is an attempt to communicate what seem to me to be the deepest lessons our human culture has learned about living well. My belief is that anyone will benefit from taking the time to learn these lessons.

Part I

Human Experience and the
Meaning of Adulthood

1

Perception and Its Norms

We will begin our study by considering the distinctive character of our human experience; this will provide the "first principles" for our subsequent interpretation of adult life. This will accordingly be the most *abstract* portion of our study, for it is not dealing with any particular experience but with the very nature of our experience *as such*. Appreciating this distinctive character of human experience, however, is what will allow us to grasp the meaning of our concrete experiences, and it is precisely the *concrete* character of our experience that will be the subject of the remaining chapters; indeed, one could turn directly to any of the following chapters, each of which can be read on its own as a philosophical study of a particular aspect of our experience, but the discussion of the distinctive character of our human experience provides an essential key to understanding why our lives have the particular aspects they do have and how they are significant in our lives. In the interest, then, of establishing our fundamental philosophical orientation, let us begin by reflecting on the distinctive character of our experience of the world. We typically think of our experience as a matter of perception—being aware of what is around us—and a matter of action—pursuing our own projects within the world of which we are aware. We will begin by exploring the relationship between perception and action.

Perception and Possibility

It is because we are open to various perceptual possibilities that we can perceive something actually: we are able to perceive motion, we are able

19

to perceive distance, and we are able to recognize other people; consequently, we can perceive our friend waving to us from down the street.
We are in the world already anticipating certain sorts of experience, and
it is because we are thus alert for certain experiences that we can register
them when they happen. We are attuned to certain horizons and it is
our holding open of this field, being at the ready for engaging with it,
that allows specific occurrences to figure in our perceptual life.

In general, reality is meaningful to us in terms of how we can
or how we could engage with it, and the parameters of possibility that
define for us the field of meaning are thus fundamentally articulated in
terms of our human ways of behaving, and these, in turn, are themselves
articulated in terms of our bodies. Thus, I am open to recognizing
something red because I am open to the possibility of different colors,
and this is a possibility for me because (among other things) I have
eyes. Again, "rough" is an experience available to one who is open to the
possibilities of texture, and this is a being with sensitive flesh. Beyond
such sensory qualities, the things of our world are similarly domains of
practical possibility. The handrail in front of me, for example, is something I can grab, and something that has a firmness, a smoothness, and
an "other side" all of which are available as possibilities for my bodily
engagement, even though I am not actually engaged with any one of
them currently. The papaya, similarly, is given in my experience as
something I could pick from the tree, something I could bite and chew
(thereby releasing the flavors, juices, and fleshy texture I could taste and
feel), something I could carry, throw, smash, or rub. The handrail and
the papaya, too, are both situated among other things in domains—a
room, a jungle—through which I could travel, in which I can play, lie
down, or shout, and so on. The actuality I encounter emerges from a
field of possibility that is itself opened up to me by the capacities for
bodily engagement.

And beyond such specific spaces as the room or the jungle, space
itself, the horizon that stretches out beyond the local setting, is a significance for a being that can move, a being for whom "elsewhere" is a
possibility. It is through our motility—our bodily capacity for self-motion,
which requires, among other things, a body with joints—that we come
to "clear" for ourselves the concrete sense of our spatial setting, and
beyond the setting with which I am actually engaged is the farther space
through which I could travel, were I to walk or ride far enough. As a
moving being, this possibility for "moving beyond" is a significance that

shapes my experience of any particular space, and this possibility for my bodily behavior is what enables my experience of any specific place to be characterized by the sense of its placement in a farther space beyond.

Something similar, too, is true for the sense of "time." We are beings of possibility in that we exist as an openness to . . . , a readiness for. . . . It is as if we were constantly asking the world, "What next?" Our existence in the world is defined by a constitutive eagerness: a vulnerability and an enthusiasm in which we lend to the world our willingness to collaborate, our desire to participate, in an ongoing development that is simultaneously the process of the world and the process of our own experience. Such eagerness is the attitude of a being that experiences itself as a coherent point of reference through a changing experiential flow, a moving, changing subject who experiences herself and her world as situated in relation to a past and a future while she inhabits this present moment: someone who has a coherent sense of herself doing something. It is only such a being that is poised to act, a being that remains itself only in and through its process of engagement with what is beyond it, for whom this questioning attitude that defines the domain of temporal experience—"What next?"—is possible. It is because we are agents, beings who remain self-possessed precisely in and through our bodily interaction with the world, that we have an experience of time.

Our environment presents itself to us as spatial and temporal because we are moving, changing beings, agents who are open in principle to the coherent meaningfulness of a developing process. It is as such moving, active beings who exist as a bodily engagement with what is beyond them that we experience a spatial and temporal world, and it is our specific capacities for bodily engagement that set for us the primary parameters for perceptual possibility, such that the specific features of our world that we actually come to recognize are actualizations of these possibilities to which we are in principle attuned.

The ongoing enactment of our experience is the actualizing of perceptual possibilities, and the development of our experience is the development of these possibilities, their transformation into richer, more refined, more articulate, more complex attunements to our world. Knowledge and experience thus do not so much take the form of some new fact entering into our private domain, as if our consciousness were a container filled with contents. Rather, significances rise up within the already available field of the world. Thus, for example, the perceptual field that is the crowded city street at rush hour dramatically changes its sense for me when, to continue our earlier example, I suddenly notice a friend waving to me from down the street, a recognition I make in and by waving back and smiling, while my heart suddenly beats faster, my mood changes from grumpy and earnest to joyful and relaxed, and my thoughts turn away from the demands of my work day and turn to the activities my friend and I might engage in; this shift is not the introduction of some new entity into my perceptual field, but is a reorganization of the already existent whole of my relationship with my surroundings. We are constantly in the world, and within this field that our consciousness pervades, some localized setting or dimension becomes charged and draws our focus and we then witness the emerging, changing form of this aspect of our already available world, rather than having a new "fact" or entity somehow penetrate into our mental space. Our perception develops—we *learn*—when the features that draw our attention allow us to explore formerly unexamined dimensions of experience that, through their specificity, allow and encourage us to enhance and refine our grasp of what is possible. Our perception is thus a kind of dialogue—a process of mutual questioning and answering—in which the ongoing development of our perceptual powers reveals an ever-richer perceptual world that in turn elicits from us further perceptual growth.

As such a dynamic process of call and response, perception is thus fundamentally a *practice*—a matter of behavior. "Apprehend" is therefore a good name for what we do in perception, for we do not primarily perceive the world as spectators, but as agents who "grasp" the significance of our situation in and as a process of meaningfully acting within that situation. Our seeing (and hearing and touching and so on) is primarily a kind of doing, and something is apprehended by us as the eliciting from us of an appropriate, responsive action; thus, the experience of a dusty gust of wind is enacted in and through my raising of my arm to protect my eyes or again hearing the sound behind me is enacted in and through my turning to investigate its source. This "summoning up" of our action by what we are perceiving means our "agency" is typically experienced by us as a kind of passivity, rather than a deliberate forcing of our intentions into the world: it is a "being drawn along by" or "being drawn into" the development of a situation. Indeed, our action typically takes the form, precisely, of perception. Perception is thus not an isolated part of our lives, but is our very "being in the world." It is what we "are" as a whole. In all our actions, we are perceiving. All of our actions are our response to the call of the world, and to develop perceptually is ultimately to develop as an agent, to develop the abilities that will allow us to do what the situation calls for.

At root, then, "perception" and "action" do not name two different facets of our experience, but are two names for the same process, the same practice. In some situations, our sense of our self-directedness is more explicit and we are inclined to call it "action," while in others our sense of other-directedness is more explicit and we call it "perception." Our more careful observation, however, reveals that both are simply variant species of the same fundamental process, "perception" being itself a practice, an actualizing of possibilities for engagement, "action" being itself perception, a passive being-led by what emerges.

Reality and Maturity

Reality

This situation of approaching the world on the basis of possibilities to which one is in principle attuned is not unique to humans. It is because the cat is in principle alert to the possibility of prey that (what we call) the mouse scurrying through the grass can draw the cat's attention. It is because the thrush is alert in principle to the possibility of extracting the snail from its shell that it can take advantage of the presence of (what we call) the rock to break the shell. It is because the deer is alert in principle to having to flee a predator that it leaps and runs away in response to (what we call) the rustling in the bushes. Openness to possibility is the form of all perception, which is itself common, as the ancient Greek philosopher Aristotle noted (*On the Soul*, II.3), to all the living beings we commonly call "animals." What distinguishes us as humans is not simple openness to possibility, but is the particular form of our openness, which apparently differs from the perceptual possibilities of other organisms (though that is, of course, an empirical question), and thus the sorts of development for which we are prepared in principle.

The ancient Greek philosophers were particularly astute observers of nature, and it is again to them that we can turn—this time to Plato, in his dialogue *Phaedo*—for an introduction to the distinctive set of possibilities to which we humans are open. In the *Phaedo*, which is the dramatic depiction of the conversation Socrates had with his friends on the day of his death, Socrates's discussion draws our attention to three meanings that define the perceptual possibilities to which we are inherently attuned: truth, beauty, and the good. Indeed, it is only because we are already attuned in principle to these meanings that our attention can be drawn to them explicitly (the situation described in the *Phaedo* under the name "*anamnēsis*" or "recollection"). We are intrinsically alive to these *absolute* questions: "What is it in-itself, as opposed to how I see it?"; "Is it truly good or just something I value?"; "Is it beautiful or do I merely like it?" And to thus recognize the possibility of an absolute meaning is to recognize the limitation of our own perspective: it is to acknowledge, within our perspective, that there is a greater reality beyond our perspective. Our perspective is therefore inherently open to the question of itself qua perspective, and to recognizing itself as answerable to what is in principle non-perspectival.

It is this distinctive nature of our experience that we engage with whenever we ask the question of "being qua being" as Aristotle puts it—when, that is, we ask what the ultimate nature of reality is—and, indeed, whenever we consider something "as such" or "in itself." In these situations, we do not rest content with the specificity and the finitude of the specific, finite reality with which we are confronted, but instead we take up that finitude in relationship to an infinity to which we hold it—and ourselves—answerable. Though we only ever engage with specific actual realities, we can ask about "being" as such (and we then call the individuals "beings"): we experience the finite realities that we recognize as defined by an infinite that, in fact, we only ever experience through those very finite realities. Again, I can only ever see this or that side of your body, address this or that corner of the room, but I experience the presence of your body as such *through* that perspectivally limited side and I experience "the" room, which in itself is indifferent to my orientation, through my experience of the corner ahead of me to my right. I experience a thing through my apprehension of its finite features, and I experience the room as situated in an infinite space. In each of these cases, we experience the finite actuality as a realization of a more basic possibility, namely, the very possibility to be, to be somewhere, to be something. Ultimately, in other words, the possibility to which we are open, and which is definitive of our reality, is the very possibility of things—the possibility of existence itself: our definitive possibility is to be open to possibility as such, to possibility as possibility.

This "possibility as such," however, is only ever present as what is actual, that is, by definition it cannot appear "as such," since possibility can only appear as actuality—for what is actually appearing is always, by definition, the actual. In other words, possibility is not a specific "content" of perception beside the actual contents, but is precisely the unique dimension of meaning with which we engage through the actual. In Plato's dialogue *Timaeus*, the flow of time is referred to as the "moving image of eternity" (*Timaeus* 37d), and this expression captures well the idea that we experience the finitude of our everyday experience as the happening of the infinite, the making-present of a reality that can never be present as such—as non-perspectival infinity—but can only be present in and as perspectival finitude. We have seen that it is our "subjective" possibility for action—our "I can," as Edmund Husserl put it (*Ideas* II, 61)—that opens us to the "objective" possibilities of our perceptual field; but we can now see that, paradoxically, the "I can" that is the definitive form of the meaningfulness of our experience precisely opens us up to the meaning of the "I cannot," that is, our practical, finite experience reveals itself to us as defined in terms of a nonpractical, infinite meaning, a sense that is definitive of, but irreducible to, the very terms of practical engagement through which it is revealed.

Our nature as perceivers, then, is defined by its openness to a non-perspectival infinite that itself cannot be present as such. We cannot exceed our finite and conditioned experience, but—in the whole range of our experiences from spatial perception and mathematical calculation, through attraction to beauty, to recognition of moral, political, or religious duty—we can and do experience that finitude as defined by and answerable to the infinite and, indeed, we can see it as the appearing of the infinite, as the presenting of what can never be present "as such." We live our experience as the site for the appearing of the in-itself, of reality as such.

We cannot step outside our finitude—it is only as something finite and specific that we exist at all—and yet we simultaneously are the site for the happening of the infinite: we are simultaneously defined by our own perspective and by the non-perspectival onto which our perspective opens. Our experience thus always presents itself to us as rooted—simultaneously and incompatibly—in two different soils: on the one hand, our experience presents itself as rooted in our finitude, and on the other hand it presents itself as rooted in the infinite. This tension in principle that defines the very sense of our experience, the very sense of sense, also defines our sense of ourselves.

Mortality

In addition to having a sense of the world—that of which we have
experience—we also have a sense of ourselves as experiencers, and our
self-experience is thus importantly dual: we have a sense of ourselves
(1) as defining a perspective, as being the aperture through which reality as such appears, as the irremovable occasion for whatever it is that
appears to us; and we have a sense of ourselves (2) as defined by that
which appears to us. In other words, we simultaneously experience (1)
reality as happening within our experience and (2) our experience as
happening within reality. In relation to reality as such, we experience
ourselves as inessential, but, paradoxically, our own existence is essential
to our experience of our own inessentiality. Our sense of our own mortality highlights well this paradox and ambiguity that defines all "sense."

To any of us, it theoretically makes sense that we will die. We
are living bodies, organisms participant in the world of nature, and we
know of nature that it involves death, and that all living bodies eventually come to an end and decompose. This meaning however—this
perspective on life—is a perspective from the point of view of "reality as
such," a meaning that speaks only to one who can assume the position
of a non-perspectival spectator on the finite and evaluate it according
to the terms of reality as such. At the same time, however, it is only for
my actual perspective that this notion makes sense to me. Precisely the
sense we are thus entertaining, however, is the sense of the nonexistence
of our actual perspective: we are precisely entertaining the idea of the
disappearance of the perspective to which that disappearance of perspective
can be meaningful. The cessation of our perspective is precisely something
that cannot appear ("as such") to our perspective, and our death is thus
a constitutive blind spot in our existence. This is not just a theoretical
bit of logic, but a gripping existential problem.

We all, each of us, "know" that we will die, but we cannot conceive
what that actually means, and the "nonsense" of our own death, our
inability to grasp this meaning, in turn casts the entire meaningfulness
of our lives into doubt. Normally, we make sense of our lives—find
them meaningful—precisely in "worldly" terms, that is, we evaluate
ourselves by our popularity with our intimate friends, or by how well
we have succeeded in our careers, or whether we have completed work
on a particular project, or whether we have made a valuable contribution to our communities, or whether we have "cut a dashing figure" in

our public life. We draw our sense of worth and self-esteem—our very sense of self-interpretation—from the world, that is, we judge ourselves by "how the world would see us." We take reality as determining "what matters," and we then establish on that basis what matters to us. We are familiar, however, with popular sayings that challenge this approach to establishing self-worth in the terms of the world: "You can't take it with you," we say, for example, challenging the person who devotes their life to getting rich; even more forcefully, Ecclesiastes says, "Vanity of vanities: all is vanity" for "I have seen everything that is done under the sun and behold all is vanity and a striving after wind" (*Ecclesiastes* I.2, 14). The point of sayings such as these is that, with our death, nothing matters to us anymore. When we judge ourselves from the terms of the world, we essentially look back on ourselves from the point of view of the world after we have died, and evaluate "how we've measured up." But "the point of view of the world after we have died" is precisely *not* a meaning we can ourselves live with, that is, it is defined as a meaning that is not available to—not meaningful for—us. In that case, though, we are defining our lives in terms of a perspective from which we are in principle excluded; but if what I rely on to make my life meaningful while I live it is something actually meaningless to me, then surely this renders the whole of my life meaningless and points to a problem in this whole approach to finding meaning.

Our death, then, offers a lens through which to recognize the ultimate absurdity of trying to define ourselves in terms of the world. Such a worldly definition might mean something to the world—that is, it might mean something to others who outlive us—but it cannot be our meaning for ourselves. Our death, therefore, offers a lens through which to engage with the existential question of meaning, a lens for engaging with the sense that we must find for ourselves a way to make our lives meaningful for ourselves within the terms of our perspectival finitude. Our death poses to us the personal question, "What does my life mean *to me*?" or, again, "What am I living for?" Though the sense of "my death" presents this question in a specially clear and powerful way, this question lurks in all our experience, in all sense, in every aspect of one's life.

Our experience always presents us with two roots: the reality in which we are situated and the perspective in which reality is situated. There is no way for us to settle the question of which is ultimately primary—reality or perspective—because each, for us, depends upon the other. Grappling with the sense of experience—with the sense of our lives—involves grappling with this conflict between world and self, between infinite and finite for defining our sense of meaning. Both senses—both roots—are necessary and both are experientially compelling, that is, any attempt we make to live in denial of one of these roots will amount to a kind of dishonesty with respect to our own experience, an existential dishonesty that generates for us crippling problems in our experience. What we shall see is that the question of meaning—which is ultimately the question of a life—is how to integrate the terms of self with the terms of world. The practice of a life is ultimately the practice of grappling with this demand—a demand that it is ultimately impossible ever to fulfill—for the integration and reconciliation of these two conflicting senses of the ultimate terms of meaning.

Biologically, maturity is an organism's existing in its fully developed state, when its basic, constitutive form has been fully realized, "perfected." Existentially, on the contrary, maturity is successfully accommodating oneself to the inherent demands of "sense"—of *meaning*. We are human organisms, and become organically mature, like any other animal, when we reach a fully developed organic state in which we can reproduce and so on. Beyond being human organisms, however, we are also *persons*, and our maturity as persons—"adulthood," properly so-called—is not an organic development, but an existential accomplishment: it is precisely the process of establishing a lived reconciliation of self and world. At the same time, however, we are not disembodied minds, but animate bodies in behavioral, perceptual engagement with our material environment, and our existential development cannot be separated from this material condition, that is, it is this embodied individual who matures. Consequently, our adulthood, though not defined by our biology, is also not independent of it; we only describe human adulthood truly, therefore, if we recognize it as a reality accomplished at the intersection of existential and biological maturity. Adulthood is thus a phenomenon simultaneously of character and of aging.

Character and Aging

What is distinctive of our nature—of our constitutive perceptual attunement to our world—is our openness to the real as such, our openness to the absolute, to the definedness of reality from a point of view that is not our own. To know reality, then, will be to know it differently than as it simply appears immediately to our perspective. Our distinctive nature thus puts us in a position in which we are drawn to perceive reality differently from the way in which we "naturally" perceive it. The constitutive attunement of our nature precisely propels us to learn and to grow, to transform ourselves out of the terms of our natural perspective into a perspective that is oriented by its answerability to the norm of reality as such. This is what is distinctive of our nature, and it is why our maturing as perceivers is distinctively different from our biological maturing: our existential maturing—our fulfilling of our nature—is coming to recognize something, and coming to live by that recognition. Our existential maturing must happen within our perspective, or, more precisely, it is precisely the maturing—the transforming—of that perspective. We mature as we come to live from the norm of reality.

Perceiving things as "real"—perceiving according to the norm of reality—is a distinctive practical, bodily activity, like all other perceptual activities. To perceive the real as real requires that one develop various bodily, behavioral capacities. The real cannot be apprehended in its reality—we cannot discern "what is really happening"—except through the careful collection and organization of evidence, which involves careful observation, careful memory, the maintenance of a consistent point of view, concentration, patience, and more. To perceive reality as real, too, is to be "objective," that is, it is to recognize that one apprehends properly when one apprehends "as anyone would." Perceiving reality as real, then, is of a piece with the development of various bodily, behavioral, and intersubjective—personal, social, and political—abilities and attitudes. Our existential maturing will be accomplished in and through the cultivation of our bodily, perceptual practices: it is a matter of developing a particular sort of character.

First and foremost, then, the central significance of our existential maturing is our coming to replace what Freud called the "pleasure principle" with what he called the "reality principle" as the governing norm for our behavior (*Introductory Lectures*, 402–403). This development, which will be a development in our walking, our eating habits, our toilet practices, our desiring, our conversing, our plan making, and more—will be, in other words, a progressive shift away from thinking of the world of our experience as defined in terms of our perspective and a shift toward thinking of our perspective as defined in terms of the world of our experience—is essentially the development of a responsible character.

Responsibility is the first defining norm of adulthood, but it is not the only one. This is because, as we have seen above in our talk of the paradox of finite and infinite and of the need for their integration, this embracing of the "reality principle" that is the core of responsibility must be done without losing oneself, one's singularity. The embrace of the "reality principle" is a matter of orienting ourselves by the terms of the infinite time and the infinite space to which our experience is distinctively attuned, but the very condition of our access to infinite space and time is our ineffaceable rootedness in the necessarily finite space and time of our situated, animate bodies. Mature adulthood thus also involves an honest recognition of this distinctive reality of oneself as a singular perspective. That the singularity of her, his, or their perspective is ineffaceable—is of absolute significance—for each individual means that happiness is as definitive a goal for any human life as is responsibility.

And there is a second consequence of the ineffaceable singularity of perspective. This consequence is that, for any individual, happiness and responsibility are not matters of an abstract pursuit: happiness and responsibility are the defining norms of a life—the finite, actual life of single individual. A life, however, is the life of an individual who ages, an individual, that is, who experiences her-, him-, or themself as inherently temporal. Our study of adulthood will thus require us to investigate our experience of time, and especially the ways in which we experience ourselves as temporal: we must investigate the nature of aging.

Each of these three—aging, responsibility, and the pursuit of happiness—is essential to what it means to be an adult. Adulthood, then, is a reality and an experience that cannot be understood along any single axis. It is not a strictly biological notion (aging), nor is it a strictly personal notion (happiness), nor is it a strictly impersonal notion (responsibility). Instead, adult life is the navigation of the three separate but parallel domains. And, because each is of ineffaceable significance in our lives, the meaning of each cannot properly be grasped independently of the meaning of the others.

Part II

The Form of Adult Life:
Maturity and Aging

2

Character and Reality

In his discussion with Socrates at the beginning of Plato's *Republic*, Cephalus proposed that the most important difference between those who are happy and those who are not is to be found, not in the hardships they do or do not face, but in the ways they have developed for dealing with such issues: their happiness or lack thereof, that is, is primarily a reflection of their character. As I suggested in the Introduction, there are various aspects of Cephalus's position that seem to be open to criticism, but this remains an insightful claim. In this chapter, we will investigate more precisely the ways in which healthy developments of character are indeed integral to a flourishing and self-responsible adult life. To do so, we must return to the theme of our unique human experience of reality *as* reality and explore its dimensions more fully.

Exposure: Outer and Inner

Reality confronts us with its unrelenting surface. It demands of us objectivity, because it is going to go its own way without regard to our interests. This is typically what we mean by "reality": we mean that ultimate context of existence that answers to its own intrinsic norms, without regard to our subjectivity. This is generally what we refer to as the "causality" that the scientist, for example, studies: that inner law to which things answer in themselves. To a significant degree, the maturity of our perspective is coming to recognize this and coming to live in accordance with this recognition, whereas our immaturity is our living as if we did not have to acknowledge our answerability to reality's indifference to our wishes. Accomplishing our maturity is learning the terms of the real.

This learning is in part the familiar acquiring of "knowledge" about the workings of the real. We must, for example, learn how to manipulate the materials of the world to shelter us against the world. In the developed situation in which we live, this involves, for example, putting up concrete, wooden, and plaster walls to protect against the wind and rain. This process in turn has a longer history in that a similar process is presupposed in the very having of walls, concrete, etc. Originally, we (that is, our ancestors) had to learn to turn stone against stone to make a blade, which could then be turned against trees to make lumber, which could then be further cut and fitted or by other material means tied or connected, to make a palisaded compound, a wall, etc. This factual learning of the terms for interacting with material nature is one crucial form of our learning, necessary at the most basic levels of establishing for ourselves a livable environment: we must learn how to operate effectively with and within the (causal) terms of the reality that confronts us as our material environment. Failure to learn the terms of the real will result in our being overwhelmed by its unrelenting force.

We can, however, (and often do), overemphasize the importance of this "factual" learning. It is true that we must learn how the world does in fact operate, and we must learn to fit ourselves into those terms. The hardships with which the world confronts us, however, are not the only obstacles that threaten us. Our own reality as beings with a perspective—our "subjectivity"—is similarly a terrain whose terms we must learn to navigate. Though our subjectivity is what—indeed, who—we are, it is as much a "foreign" reality to which we are exposed as is "external" nature. Our subjectivity has its own "logic," its own principles—its own "causality"—and successful living is at least as dependent upon "learning the ropes" of being a person as it is dependent upon learning the way of the world.

Learning the ways of subjectivity, however, is not learning the rules of something else, but is learning about ourselves: it is more a matter of participation than of observation, that is, it is a matter of learning to be a subject, learning how to be ourselves. Our advances (or failures) in this learning are matters of how we live, are matters of who we are. Indeed, in order to learn the terms of external reality, we must first become someone who can undertake such learning. The education that enables our maturity, prior to being a matter of information, is a matter of formation.

This formation, too, has different aspects. One aspect, to be sure, is the mastery of our own physicality, in the sense that we must learn to control our limbs. In order to be someone who can interact effectively with the world, one must effectively inhabit one's own body: through practice, we must make our bodies our own, as we learn to walk and to sit, to sing and to speak, to hold tightly and to press gently. Again, though, more than simply learning the fixed, factual terms of an independently defined, physical reality, our becoming capable of engaging with the real as such is a matter of forming our attitude: it is a matter of character.

In fact, it would be a mistake to imagine bodily control and the formation of attitude to be separate matters. Learning to hold tightly is, to be sure, a matter of deploying the fingers and palm of one's hand, but it is simultaneously an intention to commit oneself to the exercise of force and to the maintenance of that intention over time. Learning to walk is a way of holding the limbs and trunk of the body in dynamic interaction, but it is simultaneously a commitment to pushing oneself beyond one's existing state into a new domain of behavior, a new domain of engagement with the world. Even at the most basic levels, inhabiting one's body is an irreducibly psychological matter as much as it is a physiological matter.

Rather than differentiating the bodily and the psychic, we might better think of their unity, and think in terms of "behavior." To embrace a way of behaving is simultaneously to adopt a psychic stance and to deploy one's physique in a specific way. Such a notion of behavior is especially illuminating when we consider more complex practices than "holding tightly," because the notion of behavior allows us to recognize the way in which the material conditions of our actions—the way our actions are embodied—are not exhausted by the terms of our simple organism, but in fact involve that organism in a sort of "networking" with the surrounding environment. This is already evident with the example of walking. Whereas making a fist involves only parts of my organism, walking involves my body in relationship to the earth: walking is not accomplished simply within my organic body, but is accomplished in and as a coupling of my body with the world. Progressively more complex couplings of body and environment provide the necessary "material conditions" for more complex behaviors.

Learning more complex ways of behaving is learning to live from more complex and elaborate couplings of body and world—more sophisticated situations. The development of one's character is the development of

the ability to inhabit progressively more complex situations: to live from
a more developed body-world relationship: a more developed relationship
that itself involves being—that requires one to be—a more sophisticated
person. Making a fist and walking are "attitudes" as much as they are
dispositions of bodies, and this is even more true of talking, playing,
listening, cooperating, being courageous, keeping one's word, demon-
strating self-control, and so on. Let us look at some of these "attitudes":
these developments of character that are ways of inhabiting situations.

Healthy Developments of Character

To be able to cope adequately with our world, one must be able to remain
committed to a project, even when it becomes difficult. One must be
patient. One must be able to follow instructions. One must be able to
respond to the needs and desires of others, even if they conflict with
one's own desires. One must be able not to express one's most immediate
emotional reactions, but to express a more subtle and sensitive responsive-
ness. One must be capable of reflective insight, intelligent self-criticism,
careful and systematic reasoning about intricate matters. These and similar
abilities are the abilities one must bring to one's situation if one is to be
able to cope with the demands of the real.

If, for example, one finds oneself stuck in a snowdrift while driving
on a country road—or, more seriously, trapped in a mine when a collapse
in the mineshafts has left the exit route obstructed—one will only be able
to extricate oneself from difficulty by working calmly and systematically
to move the snow or the stones. An attitude of panic—which might very
well be one's immediate reaction—will not address the material needs
of this situation at all; if one simply "freezes" and gives up, one will
get nowhere and, indeed, if one's feeling of panic leads one to act in a
panicked way (such as pressing the accelerator pedal and making the car
wheels spin, or aggressively and thoughtlessly clawing at the collapsed
stones), one might very well worsen the situation. The world, here, has
presented a difficulty, but it can be addressed; the panic, however, is not
an attitude that adequately addresses the terms the world presents and,
indeed, it presents a new problem of its own. Such examples of bodily
obstruction demonstrate that subjectivity needs to "measure up" to the
demands of reality, that is, our subjectivity needs to be properly developed to assume the correct attitude for collaborating effectively with the

world—it is not immediately or naturally the case that our subjectivity can take up reality on its own terms. Apprehending reality effectively—that is, answering practically to its terms—is not automatic. It is also not a matter of abandoning all perspective, that is, objectivity is not a matter of getting rid of subjectivity. Rather, what these examples point to is the fact that objectivity is achieved in the development of a particular stance of subjectivity: in order to be apprehended for the reality that it is, reality needs to be approached from the correct perspective.

Examples such as being stuck in the snow or being trapped in a mine, though, while correct as far as they go, nonetheless are insufficient models for understanding our full, human situation, for they make life appear as a matter of an individual independently struggling with a natural world. In fact, however, it is much more importantly true (1) that it is a personal, interpersonal, and social world with which we are engaged, and (2) that our engagement with this is not simply a matter of independent, individual action. In other words, we are not primarily individuals struggling with nature, but collaborators in a social world, and it is on these terms that we must understand the healthy formation of our subjectivity.

The world we inhabit is irreducibly intersubjective, from its most minimal to its most developed aspects. Think again of the example of making a fist. We typically do this in the context of a rich, interpersonal situation, and the action is either a gesture of resolve, a way of holding back an improper expression (as in the English idiom, "bite your tongue"), or, perhaps, the preparation for punching another person. Of course we can make a fist without these interpersonal projects, but the very fact that our fist making can function in these ways reveals that the basic way we live our hands is as media for engaging with other people. The very way, that is, that we experience our hands is that they inherently have other people "on their horizon," so to speak.

And this inherent intersubjectivity is surely evident, too, in the early childhood experiences of initially learning to make a fist. The infant grappling with the process of "owning" its own body takes this project up in a world that it shares with its parents: for the infant, the world does not neatly divide into our conceptual categories of "dealing with my body," "dealing with other people," "acting by myself," and so on. On the contrary, for the child these differences that we mark out are initially not differentiated, but are each and all constitutively interwoven dimensions of the fabric of its experienced world, and it will precisely

be the successful development of the child's perspective to come to mark
these distinctions. Indeed, for the child, its process of learning to inhabit
its own body is the very route by which it accomplishes an enriched
relationship with its parents (including the process of winning cherished
experiences of approbation, etc.) and brings to realization a relationship
to itself as an independent individual. Becoming an individual, inhabiting
its body, and developing its relationship with its parents are not three
separate activities, but three dimensions of the same practice. From the
start, the fabric of the child's world is intersubjective as much as it is
subjective and bodily.

In developing and enriching one's capacity for inhabiting the world—
in coming to inhabit more complex situations—it is skills of personal and
interpersonal navigation that one must be developing, as much as one is
developing skills of bodily control (whether of one's own organism or of
surrounding nature). In all our dealings, we are in fact grappling with
the "terrain" of our own subjectivity and with the terrain of the subjectivity of others, and our healthy self-development—our development of
adequate skills of coping "objectively" with, and participating effectively
in, our environment—will be measured by the level of our competence
in navigating these terrains.

The skills of managing our own nature are the "excellences" (*aretai*,
sometimes translated as "virtues") to which the ancient Greek philosophers
refer, and it is particularly helpful to consider two of the excellences they
identify: *andreia*, "courage" and *sōphrosunē*, which is often translated
"temperance" or "moderation," but which I prefer to leave untranslated
because the familiar connotations of the English terms can be misleading. In the *Nicomachean Ethics* (Book II, Chapter 7), Aristotle describes
courage as a mean between cowardice and rashness, that is to say, it is
a habit of acting from good judgment with respect to those situations
that one fears, but to which one is called to respond. He analogously
defines *sōphrosunē* as a similar mean—a habit of acting from a balanced
judgment—about matters of pleasure and pain, such that we do not take
our own pleasure and pain as sufficient criteria for governing our action,
but we are self-possessed in relation to pleasure and pain and respond to
them in an appropriate manner, rather as Cephalus indicated that we need
a good character for dealing with sex, drunkenness, and festivity. While
it is not my intention to engage in the study of Aristotle's position, I
draw attention to his analyses because these notions of the "virtues" of

courage and *sōphrosunē* are in fact essential—indeed, primary—aspects of our learning to navigate the terrain of our subjectivity.

Sōphrosunē

The notion of *sōphrosunē* as self-possession in relation to pleasure and pain opens up a particularly powerful direction for thinking. I invoke the language of "self-possession" to highlight the way in which we often find ourselves, in a sense, "dispossessed" by pleasure and pain. The fact that something is pleasing (especially highly pleasing) can seem to be—and, indeed, can seem *obviously* to be—a necessary and sufficient condition for pursuing it. We experience the intensity of this, for example, when we want to stick to our diet, with a goal of losing weight, but some tasty article of food strikes us as "too appealing to resist." In such cases, we feel that we are not choosing to eat the food, but that we have "lost our willpower": it is as if the pleasure itself compels us, stripping from us our own power of choice, our own agency. With pain, this experience of dispossession is perhaps even more clearly apparent. Pains can seem like something we simply "cannot endure," that is, our desire to retain our own self-directed path must be abandoned as the pain "takes over." It is probably the case that any of us would at some point succumb to this dispossession by pain or pleasure (though Epictetus the Stoic is said to have maintained his stance of tranquil self-possession even as his leg was being broken, and virtually all religious traditions have inspired some practitioners of ascetic self-discipline who have accustomed themselves to withstand the allure of very extreme pleasures and pains), but where the threshold is located at which we thus succumb is not automatically or naturally given, but is a matter of character: it is something we can shape through practice and habituation, and this is the core of the notion of *sōphrosunē*. If we now reflect on the distinctive nature of our existence as subjects, we can see the overwhelming significance of this notion for our lives.

Our own nature as subjects is something that presents itself to us: it is something to which we are exposed, rather than something that we make up on our own. To be born a subject is to be born with the sense of oneself as a center of experience, to find oneself taken over—"impressed"—with feelings: one finds out what it is like to be a subject. As the child develops, the character of its feelings develops: it finds itself the site of experiences of frustration, love, enthusiasm, sadness, anger, pleasure, effort, and more. That we adults were, as children, drawn to walk and to speak is, again, not something that we chose, but is the way we found ourselves developing. The nature of our subjectivity reveals itself to us as we live it: it reveals itself to us *as* "ourselves." This sense of self—self-feeling—that defines our living experience is a sense that locates us at the center of things: the one to whom, or for whom, whatever "is" appears. Our self-feeling puts us at the center of things, and the determinate feelings themselves are so many experiences of attraction and repulsion, so many ways this self is lived as an impulse toward or repulsion from aspects of its world. Our native disposition, in short, is precisely an emerging experience of self that is simultaneously a life of *dispossession* (a "heteronomy of the will," as Kant called it [*Groundwork*, 91], "polymorphous perversity," in the language of Freud, [*Three Essays*, 57]). Our emergent sense of ourselves as "selves" is largely constituted by our experiences of finding ourselves desiring, finding that we want.

We are centers of experience, but that precisely means that we are centers of experience "of." In other words, it is the very nature of experience to put us into contact with—to expose us to—an outside, a beyond. Our experience confronts us with a reality not of our own making, something that in its independent reality has a center of its own. We are, thus, de-centered centers, centers of the experience of a world that does not have us as its center. This "external" nature, like our "internal" nature as subjects, is something given to us, something we find, but, unlike our inner nature, this outer nature is not something we experience as "self," but precisely as "not-self." Inasmuch as our experience is always experience "of," we always experience ourselves as this given site of contact between self and not-self. Though this structure is implicit in all of our experience, however, the sense that explicitly predominates in our experience can tend strongly to one or the other of these poles.

Though we might initially experience our "selves" precisely in and as the experience of the allure of a particular place or the repulsiveness of something we are tasting, our maturing will require of us that we come to appreciate the independent reality of that place and that food, that is, we will have to come to realize that those "(un)desirables" are "things" that are not themselves defined by whether or not we like them. Though reality is "for us" in the sense that it appears to us, it appears to us precisely as that which is not "for us," that is, it is something "in itself," defined without reference to our perspective. The ultimate terms of our experience, then, are not the terms immediately presented to us in and as our "dispossession," but are the terms of an autonomous "not self"—terms to which we will have to come to accommodate ourselves. And our developing the ability to experience the world as thus *real* goes hand in hand with our development of a sense of one's *self* as not simply defined by the push and pull of pleasure and pain. Appreciating the independence of the object requires that I have a perspective that transcends the terms of pleasure and pain that define my desiring perspective: it requires, that is, an independent I that maintains its autonomy in the face of the dispossessing pressures of pleasure and pain. Thus, an "I" that is independently self-possessed is intrinsically correlated with an "it" that is independently real.

Developing the habit of *sōphrosunē*, then, is not just a matter of a well-formed individual learning to control its self-conscious desires. On the contrary, it names the core process of our development, the primary task of living from a sense of self that has accommodated itself to the terms of the not-self. It is the essential process of our development to use the powers made available to us through our subjectivity to shape and transform our relationship to this our very subjectivity. With the resources for being a self that we find ourselves given, we must transcend our simply given nature and cultivate a domain of self-possession: we must develop a sense of self that is not an "absolute" self that excludes or overpowers the not-self, but is a self that has defined itself in relation to the not-self, a self that is relative to the world.

We initially noted above that we must learn to accommodate ourselves to the unrelenting surface of reality. What we are now recognizing is that doing this is the same process as learning to navigate competently our own nature as subjects: learning to acknowledge the reality of the real is the same process as transforming our sense of "self," which is itself a process accomplished by deploying the powers afforded us by our subjectivity to transform the nature of our experience of that very subjectivity.

This self-transformative embrace of our subjectivity is equally the experience of our coming to experience ourselves as agents. Initially, our subjectivity exists as the givenness of dispossession, a fundamentally passive experience of oneself as given. The progressive development of our sense of self-possession—self-control—is the development of our sense of ourselves as active. As we come to define ourselves as relative to the independent not-self—the real world—we come to define ourselves as meaningfully capable of interacting with that world: we experience ourselves as selves who can act within that world, as selves who can accomplish a mutually preserving—a mutually *respectful*—integration of self and world. To exist with this sense of self is what it means to be an agent.

I experience myself as an agent when I experience my will to be what determines the form of things. In my immediate, organic body, it is my will that I experience as directly realized in and as the raising of my arm, or the making of a fist. This fist then interacts with an icicle, knocking it from the eavestrough of my house. The collision of flesh and ice is entirely an event of the world, entirely describable in the terms of physical nature, but I experience this event of the world as an expression of my will. To be an agent is to experience oneself as the reason why the determinacies of the world are taking the form that they do, and this is an experience of the integration of self and world. The world, in following out its course, confirms me in my sense of agency, confirms my sense of the reality of my will. If, on the other hand, I stare at the wall and "wish with all my heart" that I pass through that wall into the room on the other side, the world will not confirm for me a sense of the reality of my will, but will precisely reveal to me that my wish is not its command, so to speak. The wall does not bend to my will solely by my wishing; the wall bends to my will only if I approach it on the terms it accepts, through the mechanical and bodily acts by which a will, inhabiting a body, can integrate itself with the physical world. Only then will it confirm my sense of agency.

With this notion of confirmation, we see clearly the co-definedness of self and world. As an agent, my will is indeed decisive in determining the forms of things, but, equally, my will is decisive only by accommodating itself to the terms of the world. Learning to navigate competently the terrain of my subjectivity amounts to learning to be an agent, learning to inhabit my subjectivity in the terms that the world will endorse. Our experience of ourselves as agents, then, is of a piece with our experience of "being at home." We are at home in our bodies, in the sense that our will is directly realized as the movement of the body. We are at home in the world, in the sense that things are open to being shaped by our will, through the mediating role of bodily interaction. For the agent, reality presents an accommodating environment: an environment that operates on its own terms, but terms that are constitutively open to the appropriate ingress of subjectivity.

Agency conforms itself to the terms of the world, but it is not exhausted by those terms. With this notion of agency, on the contrary, we are precisely entering the domain in which we experience ourselves as original sources of meaning. In our simple experience of desirous "dispossession," our self-feeling is largely a matter of passivity: we find ourselves wanting in certain ways, and our "behavior" is effectively "drawn out of us" by the determinacies of the world that present themselves to us as inherently attractive or repulsive. In our developing experience of self-possession and agency, however, this sense of "having one's hand forced" is precisely what we are transcending. As we become self-possessed selves, we come to experience both ourselves as imaginatively creative in our ability to come up with ideas and expectations that exceed the given terms of our situations, and our situations as thus "plastic" in the forms of being taken up that they afford. To return to our discussion in chapter 1, we can say that, as agents, we experience things in terms of possibility.

Courage

For the agent, then, there is an important sense in which "it is up to oneself" to determine how the situation is to be handled. The excellence of courage specially draws attention to this aspect of our agency. When one is courageous, one is precisely conscious of oneself as the one who is in the decisive position, the one it is "up to" to determine what will happen. Courage is both the recognition of one's agency and the embrace of that agency, accepting to inhabit a position of transformative significance within one's situation. As with *sōphrosunē*, we again tend to think of courage as a virtue that pertains to well-developed adults in complex and demanding circumstances—as Aristotle notes (*Nicomachean Ethics* III.6), we most commonly associate courage with the behavior of soldiers in war—but in fact it is a much more basic and pervasively important human excellence, pertinent to every level of self-formation.

Growing up significantly involves experimentation—the throwing of oneself into situations with which one is inexperienced and for which one is therefore unprepared. Learning to walk, for example, requires of the child that it let go its familiar supports in its crawling engagement with the world and risk a new form of relationship. For the young child, the world offers so many horizons for exploration, each characterized by a mixture of excitement and danger unobservable to the adult for whom these terrains have long since become familiar. At a somewhat later age, making friends involves exposing oneself to new and challenging terrains of meaning and social experience that are both enticing and threatening.

In contemporary Western, North American culture, it is common for children to begin formal schooling at the age of five years, and this is a situation in which the child is suddenly confronted with a new and strong sense that she, he, or they is facing the world on her, his, or their own. Somewhere in the pre-teen years, a child will often participate independently in an extracurricular club or sports team, again embracing a new level of independent personal and social agency. The experience of growing up through the childhood and teenage years is very much a progressive exposure to situations that are more demanding of independent agency, and each stage of this exposure is an embrace of risk, an experience of having to take on responsibility for one's formative, participative impact on the situation.

In becoming initiated into and habituated to these experiences of risk, we are becoming initiated into and habituated to our self-experience as agents. Precisely because we are active participants in these situations, we will not all face and realize these situations in the same way. Because these are situations to be navigated, rather than "deterministic" settings that "force our hand," our agency in participating in these situations will reflect a strategy, a "way" by which we enact ourselves in such situations. Different individuals will develop different approaches to navigating their experiences of their own agency, approaches that can range from fearful to bold, defensive to aggressive, introverted to extroverted. Here, at these basic levels of learning to navigate the terrain of our own subjectivity—these basic levels of personality formation—we see the most decisive domain for enacting the excellence of courage: it is in these situations that we are determining the form in which we will embrace the reality of our formative and transformative agency.

Simone de Beauvoir helpfully uses Alexis de Tocqueville's notion of "an apprenticeship of freedom" to describe this formative experience of our initiation into and habituation to our own agency (*Ethics of Ambiguity*, 37). To say that we are free in principle, or by nature, is to say that we are able to be free, but how we will enact this freedom is precisely a matter of freedom, precisely up to us. Being free in the rich sense of having refined capacities and powers, living in relations with others that accommodate individual choice, being able to shape for oneself the path of one's life, and so on, is a matter of development—personal, interpersonal, and social development—and is not simply given, not our situation "by nature." These developed situations of freedom are human accomplishments, which means it is only in and through the history of human action that these have become real and meaningful possibilities for freedom. We learn to become free in these developed ways by initiating ourselves into these historically developed paths: we must "apprentice" ourselves to the ways of freedom.

For the developing, human individual, this apprenticeship most fundamentally amounts to practicing, in the way we might say one "practices" playing the sitar. We practice freedom by actually engaging in the practices of freedom, and repeating those practices until we become habituated to them and they become familiar and normal to us. In thus practicing, we effectively act from an identity we do not yet possess, in order eventually to enter into that identity: I act as a sitar player, which I am not yet, in order to become one, and similarly I act as a developed, free individual—basically, an adult—which I am not yet, in order to become one. The child apprentices itself to freedom by trying out the actions its older siblings or friends engage in, familiarizing itself with the new, risky terrains those actions open up, in order thereby to become the sort of agent its older siblings or friends already are. This apprenticeship is enacted through myriad specific activities, and progresses through many different levels. Overall, though, that to which the child is apprenticing her-, him-, or themself is precisely the experience of agency, the experience of embracing the risk of participating in the formation of a situation.

De Beauvoir's point in her discussion of this apprenticeship of freedom is that it has characteristically been the case that women have not had the same apprenticeship of freedom that men have had. Whereas boys are characteristically encouraged to throw themselves aggressively into situations, and are supportively taken through the experiences of habituating themselves to agency—to "courage," the Greek name for which, "*andreia*," literally means "manliness"—women are characteristically discouraged from such action, being directed instead to be passive and retiring—indeed, to defining themselves more as objects (for men) than as subjects. These different paths of upbringing result in fundamentally different experiences of "self" and correspondingly different experiences of the world: on the path of enforced passivity, one comes to experience oneself as not able to make a difference in the world, and, correspondingly, the world comes to be experienced as a relatively alien place in which one's self is not meaningfully implicated, whereas on the path of supported engagement—the apprenticeship of freedom—one comes to experience oneself as an agent capable of, and responsible for, shaping one's world, and the world comes to be experienced as a welcoming environment, malleably responsive to one's own aspirations and will. De Beauvoir's analysis (like Frantz Fanon's similar analysis in *Black Skin, White Masks* of the impact of being experienced as "black" in a white culture) is very significant for drawing our attention to the ways in which individuals live with quite different experiences of empowerment or lack thereof as a consequence of the expectations and interpretations put upon them in the context of family and social life because of their gender, race, ethnicity, and so on. Such an analysis makes clear both the social and interpersonal context of our capacity to establish an adult relationship to reality and the (potentially oppressive) political dimensions of this situation. In addition to being powerfully and importantly illuminating of the troubling ways in which the identities of men and women are constituted in our world, de Beauvoir's analysis very helpfully allows us to see the way in which the experience of agency is something that we must come into. It is not given how we will be agents, and this "how" will be shaped through our practical processes of initiation and habituation into this agency through our actions. This process is a matter of self, of world and, indeed, of our relations with others, in their role as supporters, inhibitors, models, and so on.

Courage and *sōphrosunē,* then, are very much definitive of agency: to be an agent is to be self-possessed in the face of the dispossessing tendencies of pleasure and pain, and to be self-determining by risking oneself in transformative engagement with one's situation. Becoming an agent is a matter of developing these excellences of courage and *sōphrosunē* through processes of habituation to progressively more complex and demanding situations in the context of the crucially supportive (or nonsupportive) role of others—or, said otherwise, becoming habituated to situations of the world that are, simultaneously, irreducibly situations of self-interpretation, where this self-interpretation is also simultaneously and irreducibly a situation of intersubjectivity. Let us now consider more directly this theme of intersubjectivity, and especially its distinctive relationship to the theme of self-interpretation.

Sugchōrein—Co-Inhabitation

We have noticed that others are on the horizon of every engagement with the world: all situations are implicitly intersubjective. This implicit intersubjectivity, however, does not entail that we acknowledge the constitutive role of others in our experience. On the contrary, it is precisely one of the definitive challenges of our development to learn how to acknowledge the weight of others, to learn how to act in such a way as to make our constitutive intersubjectivity explicit. We must learn to think of our actions not just as they immediately appear to ourselves, but as they figure in the world of others. Learning to perceive a situation from the point of view of the other's perspective is perhaps the most definitive aspect of our maturity, the most definitive aspect of our embracing our answerability to reality.

Again, we are especially familiar with these issues when we think of the characteristic demands of child rearing. Children are loud—energetic, boisterous, and vocal—and one of their major challenges is to learn to be quiet. Children, in other words, need to learn to experience the world they inhabit as a world in which the needs and desires of others must be accommodated as much as one needs others to make room for oneself. This is a demand that, among other things, requires learning how to control the volume of one's activities so as to be unobtrusive in the spheres of others who may be sleeping, thinking, talking, reading, or enjoying a still moment (though it also requires that children learn the legitimacy of their own acts of self-expression). These are not just children's issues, of course: it is precisely a matter of adult concern to act in a way that respects the perspectives of others, perspectives that will lead to others taking up the same material conditions that define one's own situation in ways that differ or even conflict with one's own projects. One must learn to inhabit the world of sound in a respectful, fair, and equal way, and one must similarly learn to inhabit space in such a manner. In addition to learning to control the volume of one's voice in a public place, or learning to move up and down stairs without pounding one's feet loudly, one must learn not to position one's body in a way that unnecessarily obstructs others' bodily movement in space: we must learn not to stand in doorways, learn to walk on a sidewalk in a way that makes room for others, learn to follow rules when driving on roads and to experience our driving as something that defines the driving space for others as much as it fulfills our own needs for transport, and, in a less mechanical way, learn to occupy a spatial environment in a way that allows others to feel welcome to do the same. There is another ancient Greek word that describes well this virtue of inhabiting one's place in a way that acknowledges and accommodates the need of others to do the same: *sugchōrein*. The ancient Greek word means, positively, to "come together" or, negatively, to "give way," especially in argument, and hence is used to mean "to agree," and in modern Greek it means "to forgive." Literally, its two component parts (*sun-*, "with," and *chōra,* "space") imply something like "co-spacing," or, we might say, "making way together," "creating a shared space," or "co-inhabiting." Though the Greeks do not themselves use the term in this way, I will use this term to name the excellence—the "virtue"—of practically acknowledging one's intrinsic intersubjectivity.

This virtue of *sugchōrein,* "co-inhabitation," is fundamentally a matter of living from a sense of the limitation of one's own perspective, internalizing a sense of the worth of the other, such that one embraces the other's perspective as one's own. *Sugchōrein* in this sense is thus fundamentally a matter of overcoming a selfishness of perspective. Whereas *sōphrosunē* and courage deal centrally with self-control vis-à-vis one's own "inner" nature as desiring, the being polite, being respectful and being considerate that characterize *sugchōrein* are matters that deal centrally with self-possession vis-à-vis the equal legitimacy of others to take up our locale in their own way. *Sugchōrein* is fundamentally a matter of habituating oneself to the practice of perceiving in terms of the possibilities of others, rather than perceiving one's situation exclusively or primarily in terms of the possibilities it offers for oneself.

The demand on our action, then, is that we act in such a way as to acknowledge the weight of the perspectives of others. What this means is that what is intrinsically at play in all our dealings with the world, all our actions, is our expression of our sense of others. Our actions are a commentary on the worth of others, whether or not this is what we explicitly intend our actions to be. In our earlier discussion of the correlation of the experience of oneself as an agent and the experience of being at home in the world, we identified the crucial "dialogical" character of the world in confirming for us our sense of our own will. In considering now the notion of our inherent intersubjectivity, we can see even more powerful dimensions to this structure of dialogical confirmation. All of our actions—and, likewise, the actions of others—are gestures, expressions of how the agent assesses the worth of the perspectives of others. Our actions work as a confirmation (or disconfirmation) of others' sense of themselves as agents and, similarly, others' actions work as a confirmation (or disconfirmation) of our own sense of ourselves as agents. Let us consider further this role of others' action in our efforts at self-interpretation. De Beauvoir's discussion of the difference in the typical trajectories of women and men through the "apprenticeship of freedom" points to this pivotal role that others play in our self-development through the encouragement or discouragement they offer us in our attempts to assume our status as agents. Let us look more directly now at the formative and transformative impact of the feedback we receive from others in the shaping of our sense of self.

We noted above that we live our bodies as media of intersubjectivity: others are always on the horizon of our bodies. Whether making a fist or crawling across the floor, the child is navigating its interpersonal world in the same practices in which it navigates its own bodily and worldly space. When the child crawls, it is doing that as an action within its shared life with its parents. It actions are thus implicitly intersubjective, and, indeed, its crawling, for example, can also very easily be explicitly an intersubjective gesture, when its crawling is a part of its playing with its parents, or a daring push into the farther reaches of space which the child ventures to risk on the basis of the sense of confidence it has in the supportive presence of its nearby parents, or, indeed, a transgressive and rebellious entry into a parentally prohibited household location. The child's sense of itself and its sense of its world are inseparable from its sense of its situatedness in the interpersonal world it shares with its parents.

In seeking the confirmation of the natural world, one must learn to accommodate oneself to the terms in which natural bodies function. The snow on the country road, the stones in the mineshaft, and the wall that obstructs our passage are bodies that must be addressed by appropriate bodily means. When they are approached in this way, however, these bodies are open in reliable and predictable ways to being formed by our wills. When approached in the appropriate bodily terms, natural bodies do confirm our agency. In seeking the confirmation of other people, however, we face a different challenge. The other person from whom we seek confirmation is another agent like ourselves, another will as an original source of meaning, a self who participates in transformatively defining its situation. Inasmuch as this other is thus free, it cannot be determined from the outside how she, he, or they will act on any given occasion. Simple, inorganic bodies automatically release their confirmation upon being approached in a way that respects the terms of their bodily nature; other agents, however, are free to give or to withhold their affirmation of us as they see fit. With natural bodies, the terms of possible approach are set; another agent, however, sets its own terms for how it will consent to being approached. In seeking confirmation in the domain of intersubjectivity, then, we are vulnerable to the will of the other.

We already experience these higher demands of confirmation when we deal with, for example, cats and dogs. The young child may find, for example, that the cat runs away whenever she (the child) approaches. Again, the dog may well demonstrate its independence and "willfulness" when it continues to sniff the tree after being called in for its dinner, despite giving clear evidence of having heard the call; though in other respects, the cat or dog may well express their dependence upon us, in these experiences they do not confirm a sense we might like to hold of ourselves that we are their "masters." In these familiar experiences of cat and dog, we already recognize the special domain of negotiating with the desire of another. Above, we identified the distinctive character of our perception as our ability to entertain the question of the "as such." The demands that the wills of such free agents bring extend even further than what we witness with the cat and the dog.

To experience ourselves as agents is to experience our will as formative of our situation. Our situation, however, is an intersubjective situation. For that reason, experiencing ourselves as agents involves experiencing ourselves as formative of our intersubjective world. Inasmuch as the others in our situation are agents, however, it is up to them to allow us to be formative upon them. In relationship to nature, simple bodily transformation—in such a way as to protect life, in the context of building shelter, for example, or even the more sophisticated interaction of growing crops—is by and large the medium for confirming for us our agency, but in the domain of intersubjectivity, it is only the transformation of the other's will that confirms our agency, and, further, such a transformation must itself be communicated to us. In matters of intersubjective confirmation, then, the materials of the bodily world function as media for the communication of will: their significance is not their bodily transformations as such, but those bodily transformations as signs of the will of the other. Our intersubjective confirmation can happen only in and as language.

Our need to experience ourselves as agents is the need for other agents to communicate to us that we have an impact upon them: that we matter. Inasmuch as the world we are always dealing with is intersubjective, this theme of having our "mattering" communicated to us by others is implicitly at issue in all of our dealings with the world. We live in the need to be confirmed in our intersubjective agency, and that entails that we are always asking of whatever eventuates in our world, "What does this say to me about my reality vis-à-vis others?" At stake in all our worldly dealings is our sense of our placement in the dialogue of intersubjective confirmation. Because we are agents, the meaning of the world for us will always be how it comments upon our mattering in the eyes of others.

First and most pressingly, this is an issue for children. Because children are so definitively engaged in the formative process of establishing their own sense of themselves—their own sense of freedom and agency—the interpretation of their agency communicated through their intersubjective world has a profound effect on their development. Parents are responsible to care for their children in various ways—supplying food, shelter, and protection, introducing the child to the natural and human world, inaugurating the child into language, and so on—but their most fundamental role is their communicating to the child the sense of the child's worth: this is how parents care for the child as a person. In her, his, or their dealings with the world, a world which, as we have seen, is essentially the medium of interpersonal communication, the child is fundamentally shaping her, his, or their sense of self. Parents—or their equivalents in the situation of children who are not raised by parents—are the voice of intersubjectivity for their children, that is, it is the parents who are primarily responsible for fulfilling the role of communicating to the children their intersubjective reality and impact.

In the development of her dealings with her body and with the world, the child is developing her sense of "I can," her sense of her abilities for navigating meaningfully within the world, and through her engagement with this communication from her parents, the child is developing her interpersonal "I can," that is, the child is learning how she can be an agent in dealings with other people. On this platform laid by the parents, interactions with other persons—siblings, relatives, and later teachers, friends, romantic partners, co-workers, students, and so on—in turn enhance the role of communicating to the growing child who she is, or, perhaps more basically, what she is. Indeed, the phenomenological "anti-psychiatrist" R. D. Laing describes what the child is establishing as "ontological security," that is, a fundamental sense of her very reality (*The Divided Self*, 39). It is only through being recognized as interpersonally effective that the child can have a sense of herself as an agent, a being who is responsible for having an impact upon the real. Our basic ability to have a sense of ourselves as agents—our basic psychological health—is something that must be accomplished, and accomplished with the support of others.

"Ontological insecurity," on the contrary, is Laing's name for the
failure to establish successfully a sense of one's interpersonal reality. If,
in our dealings with our important others, we find that our statements
of our own desire are negated ("you don't want that; you want this"),
that our views are not taken seriously, or, indeed, that our presence is
not acknowledged, then we are encountering an intersubjective world
that communicates to us our unreality. In other words, even as our own
self-feeling tells us that we are something, that we matter, our human
environment negates and denies this significance. Our interpersonal life
leaves us insecure in our ability to ascertain our own ontological status,
our own reality as agents. Such ontological insecurity is the opposite of
psychological health: it is the fundamental condition of what we call
"mental illness," the fundamental inability to establish an appropriate
"gearing in" of one's sense of self with one's sense of the real. The consistent
failure of parents or other significant persons sufficiently to acknowledge
the weight and worth of the child's presence in the formative stages of
its development of a sense of its place in the world—and comparable
failure at later stages by other important peers and associates—leaves the
developing individual with a core inability to participate comfortably and
healthily in the intersubjective world. And inasmuch as intersubjectivity
is integral to the very fabric of the real, this failure of acknowledgment
leaves the developing individual with a core inability to participate comfortably and healthily in the real.

Our intimate, personal others are thus integral to our own identity: we cannot have a sense of ourselves on our own, but establish a
sense of ourselves in and through how those others communicate to us
their sense of who we are. There are also impersonal dimensions to this
dialogue of intersubjective confirmation. We can notice this first if we
consider the terms in which our relationships of interpersonal confirmation
are established. The initial exchanges between the child and others are
enacted largely through touch, and also through taste, smell, sound, and
vision, in the form of nonlinguistic, nonconceptual engagement. These
exchanges normally grow, however, into linguistic exchanges. What will
grow up between parent and child will be exchanges that follow the
established patterns of the language in which the parents already participate, and also other established patterns of shared perception, ranging
from habits of "body language" to interpretations of "good manners"
and expectations about social roles. While exchanges between parent
and child may begin in quite primitive and personal matters of intimate

touch, they quickly develop into the reproduction of culturally established, customary practices of social integration. The terms in which our
intersubjectivity comes to be enacted, in other words, are not defined by
the persons who participate in that intersubjectivity, but are the impersonal terms for social interaction that one inherits from one's cultural
environment.

Our interpersonal relations take place in a language and in a set of
social customs that have been handed down to us. These traditions that
we take up are in principle available to anyone—each new child that is
born could have been born into a different culture, and any culture is
thus open in principle to any child who happens to be born into it—and
thus establish the terms of interpersonal relations as such, without regard
to the particularities of this or that personal situation. The inherited terms
of our intersubjective life are thus inherently impersonal, and it is precisely
because of this inherent impersonality that they are open to anyone. In
other words, just as these terms can be taken on by anyone born into
the culture, so are they equally open to anyone else—anyone "outside"
the culture—in principle. The very condition of our language—the terms
of shared perception—*being* language is its universal availability, its ability
to be a set of terms by which anyone can establish a shared perception
with anyone else. In inheriting a tradition, we inherit the impersonal
terms for recognizing each other, for acknowledging the reality of another
free agent as a free agent. Just as it is incumbent upon a parent to act
responsibly in fulfilling the role of "confirmer" for the child's sense of its
own reality, so is it incumbent upon social customs to fulfill responsibly
their role in recognizing the free agency of free agents.

We grow up simultaneously into the world of nature, into a sense
of self, into an interpersonal reality, and into an impersonal social reality.
These are not four separate processes we might engage in, but are four
facets of the single process we necessarily undergo/undertake in assuming
our reality as free agents. Healthy self-development is not simply learning
to respect the natural causality of bodily reality, but is also learning to
be self-possessed and self-motivated in embracing one's own "emotional"
nature as a subject, and learning to participate as a real individual in
one's intersubjective relationships. This last—our participation in our
intersubjective reality—like the learning of the ways of nature and the
learning of the ways of subjectivity, can be handled in a more or less
healthy way, but, inasmuch as this is a process we can only undertake
successfully through the help of others, the healthiness or unhealthiness

of this development is a matter that is substantially dependent upon the role of others—on the personal role of our intimate, interpersonal others, but also on the impersonal role of the terms of our cultural customs.

Our entry into our life as agents who "can" interact effectively with the natural world is inseparable from our formation as members of a family and a society, as accepted, effective participants in the shared world of our intimate and our impersonal others. Initiation into this intersubjective world is embracing the terms of that shared world as the very terms of our personal perception, the very terms in which we see the world. I do not, that is, separately act on the world first as a body relocating dirt and second as a daughter of a family in a traditional Greek society; on the contrary, my bodily moving of dirt is my way of carrying out my familial responsibility to uphold the laws of the gods by burying my dead brother, a situation paradigmatically portrayed in Sophocles's telling of the tragedy of Antigone. Antigone, a daughter of Oedipus and a member of the royal family of Thebes, has witnessed her brother Polyneices die in battle against the city of Thebes and has witnessed the regent of Thebes, Creon, rule that Polyneices, a traitor to the city, not be buried. Antigone defies the edict of Creon, burying Polyneices in the belief that the gods require all persons be buried (*Antigone*, ll 15–31). In Antigone's perception, burial is not an optional action that she undertakes as an independent body acting on an independent world, but is the very way she is called upon to enact her sense of agency, the very terms of her "ontological security." The very way Antigone perceives the earth is as charged with the weight of her engagement with her responsibility to the gods, itself interwoven with her love for, and her responsibility to, her brother, and all this in the context of her experience of herself as a participant in the community of Thebes, a participant responsible to make a public statement to that community about its responsibility. In similar ways, we all become agents by embracing an articulation of our perception of reality in terms of the inherited vision of reality that constitutes our shared perception. We develop an interpersonal "I can"—the ability to navigate competently our intersubjective space—by learning the "language" of our shared reality, becoming habituated to perceiving the real in these terms.

The terms of different cultural traditions, however, are not all the same, and are not all equally oriented toward recognizing the free agency of all free agents. Though the impersonal terms of our shared perception are universally shareable in principle, this is not always acknowledged in those very terms, in those very traditions. Antigone's own Greek tradition, for example, insisted on fundamentally different terms for those within her culture and those without, and, within her culture, on fundamentally different terms for men and women. Growing up into an embrace of the laws of her world involved coming to accept first that one "is" Greek and not barbarian, and that one "is" woman and not man (or vice versa). Accepting such self-interpretations is the route by which one comes to be recognized as a legitimate participant in the society, the way by which one comes to be recognized as "real," the way by which one comes to establish a sense of ontological security. (And, indeed, one of the ways in which Antigone faces difficulty in her carrying out of the course of action she feels called upon to follow—burying her brother and thereby defying the regent and chastising the city—is that her sister Ismene insists that Antigone's behavior is not the proper way for a woman to act [*Antigone* ll 46–51].) In order to assume our status as free agents, we must embrace a cultural discourse in which our own identity is established simultaneously with the establishing of the identities of others. These cultural terms of identity formation (which, it should be remembered, do not themselves automatically amount to a single coherent system, not least because language groups and social groups need not have exactly co-extensive membership or significance), however, can themselves be oppressive, can themselves be fundamentally inhibiting of our free agency or the free agency of others.

The demands of healthy self-development, then, entail successful development on a number of fronts, and each of these developments is governed by norms, such that it is possible to be critical of the ways in which this development is undergone. We must learn to respect the terms of nature, and act in accordance with the demands of causality; we must learn to navigate our own emotions and develop healthy habits of character; we must participate in healthy interpersonal relationships, a demand that we cannot fulfil on our own; and, finally, we must live on the basis of a social and political vision that is just in (among other things) its interpretation of individual agency. Healthy adult development entails healthy initiation into and habituation in each of these arenas of development and entails recognizing one's responsibility to all of these dimensions of agency.

Responsibility and Happiness

By and large, we think of the growth and development of plants as something automatic: given the presence of rich soil, water, and sunlight, and the absence of any particular hindrance, the healthy seed simply will proceed to become a mature plant. Human development, however, is not so automatic. On the contrary, we must lend our active support to our natural condition if we are to achieve a healthy and mature state, which is to say that we must cultivate certain forms of behavior if we are to be competent (and *a fortiori*, excellent), in navigating our situation. The foundation of this healthy agency comes through learning to respond to the real demands of "outer" and "inner" nature, by embracing the demands of objectivity, an accomplishment that is itself premised on the development of an appropriately courageous, self-possessed relationship to our own subjectivity. This is the accomplishment of the "I," the independent self-conscious individual who is capable of engaging in realistic projects in the objective world.

The ancient Stoic philosophers precisely recognized the essentiality of this experience of responsible self-consciousness, and the achievement of this "Stoic" self-consciousness is the essential foundation of adult life. The principle of Stoic life, as expressed by Epictetus, is, "Do not seek to have events happen as you wish, but wish them to happen as they do happen" (Epictetus, *Handbook*, ch. 8). This practical philosophy is based on drawing a fundamental distinction between what one can control (one's will) and what one cannot control (the natural and social world beyond oneself), and exercising that self-control to accept those things that one cannot control (Epictetus, *Handbook*, ch. 1). In a fundamental way, this Stoic philosophy names the basic principle of adulthood—the embrace of the "reality principle"—without which one cannot truly be said to be an adult, and the ethical writings of the Stoics—such as Epictetus, Marcus Aurelius, or Seneca—offer some of the wisest advice for adult life our world has produced. Stoic individuality, however, is merely the beginning of adulthood—its minimal realization—rather than its real fulfillment and flowering.

Stoicism as we have defined it here is fundamentally an attitude of self-control: it is, precisely, the limitation of one's desires by one's apprehension of reality. Control, however, is by no means the fullest recognition of the reality of our psyche, nor does it afford the fullest engagement with the reality of the world. While Stoicism is indeed a kind of *conditio sine qua non,* without which we would say the person is still "childish" or immature, demanding the world conform to him or her or them rather than acknowledging the primacy of the terms of the world, the experience of answering to the real takes many more sophisticated forms than the simple suppression of one's desires. There are, in other words, degrees of adulthood, and its full meaning is not sufficiently reflected in its first, minimal realization.

As we saw with the example of being caught in the snow or trapped in a mine, nature sets terms to which we must answer, but, more deeply, we must answer to the terms of our own subjectivity and the subjectivity of others; indeed, the Stoic principle of self-control is itself already a recognition that answering to reality must take the form of grappling with our own subjectivity. But answering to the nature of something is not simply a matter of controlling it: more fundamentally, it is a matter of recognizing its nature and aligning oneself with it: answering to the nature of something, in short, is care. And this is as true of answering to our own, "inner" nature as it is of answering to "outer" nature.

Indeed, approaching our inner life with a simple goal of control can be quite unhealthy. To see this, let us first recall the insight behind the Stoic orientation: nature is recognized as a force in its own right—as something one cannot control—and, consequently, to try to hold it within one's own plans will typically result in failure as nature shows its own character and transgresses the limits we have tried to set for it. In fact, our inner reality is no less potent than that outer reality, and though Epictetus begins with the premise that we can control our own will, this is in fact a misleading simplification. While we do have the experience of agency, such "self-possession," as we discussed in some detail in the second section of this chapter, is something won through negotiation with the forces of inner life that we discover to be our reality. In other words, our inner nature is just as "self-defined" as is outer nature: we must learn to give it its due just as we must learn that with the natural world outside us.

The embrace of the "reality principle" is a kind of revolution in experience, and learning to care for our subjectivity is analogously revolutionary. To recognize the essential and ineffaceable place of our subjectivity may initially give rise to experiences of scepticism, anguish, or nihilism, that is, embracing that idea that "how things matter to me" is of primary importance can make it seem that there is nothing "objective," that nothing "really matters." Indeed, the recognition of our existential subjectivity and the freedom it involves is something we typically associate with adolescence, and we might indeed call an adult "adolescent" who apparently denies the serious weight of objectivity—"the real world"—in favor of their passions and interests. But while it is true that a one-sided, "adolescent" attitude that fails to recognize the weight of reality is surely a failure of adulthood, it is precisely a healthy appreciation of the weight of subjectivity that is necessary to correct the equally unhealthy one-sidedness of an exclusively serious, "Stoic" attitude. Indeed, it is precisely the recognition of the weight of subjectivity that defines the terrain of happiness.

Responsibility in general is a matter of being "self-effacing"—objective—in the sense that we subordinate our relative viewpoint to the absolute viewpoint: we define our experience by the infinitude onto which our finitude opens. Happiness, on the contrary, is matter of being self-affirming—subjective—in the sense that we treat what is relative to us as of "absolute" worth for ourselves. Learning to care is as much a matter of caring about and caring for oneself as it is a matter of taking care of others and taking care of the world, and in embracing the ideal of care, it is important that we not live in way that implicitly construes our own existence as simply a means to the well-being of something else.

Caring for ourselves is not at odds with being responsibile, however. Sometimes we confuse happiness with selfishness, and imagine that caring for our own needs and desires is something done instead of acting in a way that is responsible to others, but that is a misapprehension of our character as subjects, and such an approach to happiness is fundamentally immature. As we noted above with respect to the situation of the developing child, our very sense of ourselves is inherently interwoven with our sense of being with others—our subjectivity is a matter of intersubjectivity—and this is just as true of one's own subjectivity as it is true of others'. Consequently, our fulfillment from the start thus involves taking account of the needs and desires of others. The pursuit of happiness, in other words, is the pursuit of fulfillment within the natural and human world to which we are otherwise responsible.

Being responsible is thus integral to being happy, both in the sense that our happiness requires us to be able to handle affairs in ways that presuppose responsibility—responsibility is thus a means—and in the sense that responsibility is a good in its own right, such that becoming a responsible person is one of the ways in which we are happy—responsibility is thus an end. But though learning to be responsible is the central process of adult development, responsibility is not in and of itself *the* goal of adulthood; the need to adopt this as a(n intermediate) goal, however, can often result in our forgetting that becoming responsible is something undertaken for the sake of living well. There is in particular a powerful tendency in our contemporary world to interpret ourselves more and more as component parts—"mechanical" parts—of a larger "machine" of society, and it is an ongoing challenge both personally to hold onto one's sense of one's own needs and culturally to promote a society structured in a way that recognizes the necessary place of happiness in social life.

That happiness is defined in opposite terms to responsibility, then, does not mean that these goals are opposed; rather, these goals, in a good life, must be made coordinate. We will go on now to look at the concrete terrain of adult life, the determinate domains within which we (both personally and culturally) must cultivate simultaneously both responsibility and happiness. We will begin with the most general "material" contours of our existence—time and space—and then proceed to the more specific arenas of our interpersonal, economic, and political life.

3

Aging

Adulthood is a matter of the values we have embraced and installed in our behavior; it is a matter of character, of maturity. It is, nonetheless, also a matter of nature, that is, it is inseparable from the biological reality of aging. We therefore cannot understand our experience—our reality—as adults without grasping our lived experience of growing older and hence our lived experience of time. As we experience ourselves getting older, we do not experience the passage of time as simply a quantitative matter ("five more years") but as a qualitative matter: our experience of our "time of life" cannot be separated from how we experience ourselves and this cannot be separated from how we experience our engagement with our world. As we investigate this "concrete" experience of time, we will see that it is intimately interwoven, as well, with our experience of space.

Time: Indifferent and Personal

The Present

To talk about our experience is to talk about what appears to us, to talk about what is present to us. At the most basic level, our experience is always present, and whatever it presents, it presents in the present: experience is always "what is actually happening now." The present, of course, is also always when "I" am: my experience is presented to me, and it is presented to my perspective. This is the reason why we often puzzle over questions of the "subjectivity" of experience, as when we

ask, "Is that how it really is, or just how it appears to me?" or, in a yet
more extreme way, "Is there a reality outside my experience?" Inasmuch
as my experience is only what is present to me, there is, it appears, no
reality as such in which we can anchor this experience.

The experience of reality precisely requires of us that we experience
what appears as not simply what is present to us: what is present must be
the presenting of what is itself beyond that presence. We must experience
our own present as *because of* a nature that is not simply subjective. Kant,
in his discussion of the "Second Analogy of Experience" in the *Critique of
Pure Reason*, sums this up well: when we have a fantasy, the sequence of
our experience is simply a reflection of our subjective will; to experience
what appears as reality and not as fantasy is precisely to experience the
sequence of appearance as answering to its own independent order, and
not as answering to our subjectivity. In short, we experience what appears
as reality when we experience the sequence of appearances as answering
to a causality independent of our own will: the sequence is objective,
not subjective. To have an experience of reality, in other words, will
precisely be to recognize an objective time, a sequence and directionality
of flow inherent to the nature of things that overrules the sequencing
of my experiencing, my "inner sense" of my own subjectivity (*Critique
of Pure Reason*, B233–34). Our experience of reality as such, then—our
embrace of the "reality principle"—begins with our sense that the object
of our present experience is itself a reality that exists independently of and
therefore prior to our experience. It is precisely with the recognition of
an "objective time"—a sense of time as a characteristic of objects—that
we participate in the domain in which our own maturity is a possibility.

Indeed, we do typically operate with such an "objective" perspective
and thus, like things and like space, time is typically imagined by us
to be an independent and indifferent structure of reality as such: it is
just "there," we are "in it," and it is marching on without regard to our
will. On this interpretation, our subjective sense of time is ontologically
irrelevant: how I "live" time—the concrete sense of how I experience
myself in relationship to my own past experiences and in relationship
to my own future possibilities, "how," in short, I experience the sense
of "the present"—is, *ex hypothesi,* not determinative for the objective
meaning of time as such.

This objective sense thus defines our subjectivity out of existence:
in objective time, we will die, and time will be unchanged. As we saw

in chapter 1, however, this sense of time with ourselves excluded is ultimately non-sense to us. We can have the objective sense of time only because we first have a lived sense of time, a sense of "concrete" time in which we are inherently involved. In our earlier discussions of our organic embodiment and of our participation in a community of gesture, language, and custom, we have seen ways in which we live from a sense of reality as "ours." In all these situations, we live from an engaged relationship with reality—a sense of the non-indifference of reality, a sense of reality as *home*—that precedes and makes possible our ability to experience reality as independent from and indifferent to us. Something analogous is true of our fundamental experience of time. It is only our non-effaceable embeddedness in a nonobjective time that makes possible our experience of our participation in objective time, at the same time as it makes that latter participation ultimately impossible.

We "live" time in the way in which we automatically experience each present as contextualized by a past and future. We do not first have an experience of the present and then subsequently learn of past and future. On the contrary, our experience is only ever given as temporally self-differing, as spread out between "already" and "not yet," as "on the way (from . . . to . . .)." Indeed, it is only because such temporality is already the given form of our experience that it is possible for us to have the experience of a reality "prior" to our subjectivity: were our experience not inherently temporal, we could never learn of the temporal distinctions upon which the distinguishing of "objective sequence" from "subjective sequence" depends. This is because "the past," the "already happened," is not simply another instance of "the present" (nor, *a fortiori,* is the future, which has not yet happened), but is an irreducibly, qualitatively different meaning: the repeated iteration of "present" could only produce a multiplicity of presents, but could never produce an experience of past or future. If all one had were the experience of the present, then, one could never learn of these "other dimensions" of past and future. And, indeed, the present itself would thus not be experienced as present, for the present is precisely "now," a notion meaningful only in the context of arising and passing away: it is not "now" unless contrasted with "then," not present unless recognized in contrast to past and future. Our experience, then, is always the experience of an unfolding meaning, a sense situated by its relationship to the further sense it anticipates and the preexistent sense whose own anticipations it fulfills.

Time of Life

The past and future that provide the context for the unfolding sense of our present are themselves specific: those things happened, and the present is the present of those things, as the future will be the future of this present. Past and future are not "ideas," not detached labels subjectively attached to things—time is not a "container"—but are the very form of the thing itself. This is especially clear in the case of the child, for whom the present is the unfolding sense of the very determinate engagement it has with (what we call) its body, its parents, its spatial environment, and, indeed, its own freedom. For the child, that body and those parents are very specific realities and, indeed, before being specific "things," they are specific histories, specific happenings that are the enacting of the determinacy that is the child's situation and of which the "now" is the continuing realization and development. For the child, "there is" no past other than these happenings, and, while it is true that it is only with its inherent openness to the sense of "past" that these happenings are able meaningfully to exist for it, it is equally true that it is only with these happenings that the past has become meaningful for it. For the child, its early experiences are inaugural: the actual experiences it has are its entry into the very possibility of meaningful experience. In such inaugural experiences, in other words, it is impossible to determine whether actual precedes possible or vice versa: while it is logically true that it is only by virtue of the subject's inherent openness that actual experience is possible, it is also true that only by virtue of actually experiencing that "there is" an experiencing subject—and thus "openness"—at all. These inaugural experiences present us with a reality that in its specificity makes available the meaning of "time"—and indeed, "self," "other," "reality," and so on—and makes it available as a significance that exceeds the meaning of this very specificity, as a domain of possibility, as a "universal." In such inaugural experience, the specific is presented in a way that is inherently meaningful—contextualized already in relationship to other possibilities—and the universal is presented in a way that is inherently embodied: this is the inherent "concreteness" of inaugural experience, a concreteness found also at other points in human life.

As we grow, we always experience time not simply "objectively," but also in terms of the unfolding of our own life. We experience ourselves as aging, and this does not simply mean that we "accumulate years," thus situating ourselves in a different spot on the "world clock," so to speak, but also means that we experience our own time as unfolding: we experience our own specific, local, embodied, embedded reality as unfolding its time, such that time has a style—childhood, adolescence, adulthood, old age—a specific, personal meaning, itself the continuing development of the sense of concreteness launched in the child's—our own—inaugural experience of temporality. In our experience of "being of a certain age"—the qualitative, not the quantitative, sense of this—we see the continuing experience of the concreteness of temporality, and the continuing way in which a nonindifferent, "personal" sense of time undergirds our participation in universal time.

Time, then, in addition to being experienced as an indifferent medium, is also always experienced as having a style and, indeed, a style that is my very reality. Our sense of time is thus always dual, simultaneously specific and universal, "personal" and impersonal, and, inasmuch as time provides the meaningful form of all our experience, the meaning of our experience—the meaning of our life—will thus always be a matter of grappling with the inherent significance of our own aging as much as it is a grappling with the indifferent and impersonal meanings of "objectivity." Indeed, "my life" will always be the meaning I am grappling with in and as my very grappling with the meaning of reality.

In this sense, then, time is always experienced as of me. Indeed, time *is* me. Time is the unfolding of the perspective that I am and, since this perspective is itself always embodied, always exists as the appearing of a world, the time of the world is always an aspect of "my" time. Countering, then, the way in which the unfolding of my life always exists on the clock of world time, the unfolding of the world equally always exists within the context of my time. For that reason, I will always experience the time of things as both on the clock of the world and as where they fit in relation to my aging.

On Aging

If we were to imagine the "aging" of a plant, we would mark out the different stages of its development, from seed to shoot to producing leaves to flowering and so on. When we speak of our own aging we are again imagining something like "stages"—the qualitative shifts in the style of existing—but for us these are changes in the form of experiencing: they are differences *that* we experience in *how* we experience. We also have many smaller-scale shifts in the style of our experience, which make us familiar with this basic sense of qualitative, experiential change. These are the changes that we undergo through the process of habituation, and considering the experience of habit can help us to appreciate the experience of aging.

Habituation and Aging

Whether in the development of a habit of an isolated practice—comfortably bowling a cricket ball, typing on a computer keyboard, flossing one's teeth, or wrapping one's sari—or in the transformations of our whole way of being in the world that we considered in our discussions of the development of "virtues," the establishing of a habit is the establishing of a new form of body-world relation that is equally a new form of perceptual appearing. Through becoming habituated to certain practices, I come to see the world in new ways, in terms of the new possibilities opened up by my enhanced and transformed "I can." Once I become, for example, an accomplished pianist, I become capable of and attuned to responding to the unique musical possibilities afforded by a situation, and I thus encounter and engage in situations that were not available to me in my earlier involvement with the world. Again, becoming a competent cyclist releases to my perception possibilities for travel and for the spatially distant activities enabled by that travel that were not alive to me in my former inhabitation of the situation. On the basis of this transformed and enhanced platform for engagement, my perception takes on a new style: the very style of my experience of the world is changed qualitatively.

In aging, we experience something similar. Our experience of aging is our experience of analogous transformations in the style of the world we inhabit. With respect to habits such as the habit of effective typing or cycling, repeated specific practices of typing or cycling result in our finding an enhanced ability released to us. Once we are habituated, we no longer need to struggle with that aspect of the world with which we are engaging such as the computer keyboard or the bicycle. Instead, we now engage comfortably and virtually automatically with it such that our perceptual and behavioral resources are released to attend now to the higher-level possibilities that are afforded by the situation of typing or cycling, such as writing a story or traveling to the market. With aging, it is not the repetition of a specific practice, but the accumulation of many years of many practices, that eventually precipitates a transformation in perspective. We find ourselves passing through stages in our life as we find the style of our relationship to the world transformed at a "global" level, such that we experience ourselves as at a "new stage" of our lives, a stage oriented around distinctive activities that are themselves correlated with a distinctive set of expectations, interests, and attitudes. These stages, though personally and culturally variable in how they are realized, are "objective" in the sense that they reflect discernible shifts in "embodied intentionality"—in the situated perspective that one is—that are broadly characteristic of the lives of persons, and thus our experience of aging is our experience of having our own "nature" revealed to us, in the sense that we discover about ourselves that we have now come to "this stage," so to speak.

This experience of stages is thus partially the experience of a given form of "reality" imposing itself on my experience, this time from the side of my self, rather than from the side of the world. In other words, adolescence and old age "are coming," whether or not one desires it. I do not, however, experience these changes simply as an alien imposition; on the contrary, though I am subject to them "against my will," so to speak, I nonetheless experience them as the establishment of my own reality, of my personal identity—in other words, they are "my will." These changes are the revelation of the global sense of "who I am," or "who I have become."

Through our years of acting as a child, or as an adolescent, we solidify patterns of behavior and forms of engagement with the world, and these established forms become the meaningful basis from which we live. Through repeated efforts at depressing the keys with my fingers, I become a typist; analogously, through repeated engagements with the world as "an active boy," or as "a Dutch girl," or as "someone who likes school," or as "a heterosexual," or as "a flirt," or as "someone liked," or as "someone threatened" (where each "as" is the effective sense of my behavior, whether or [more typically] not I explicitly intend it), I become such a person, and at a certain point I find myself as such a person, on the basis of a past history that I did not self-consciously live as such a person, but that effectively habituated me to this form of relating to the world, this form of being someone. The "stages" of aging are experienced by us as the unfolding of such an identity, itself rooted in the history of the actions by which we became habituated to particular forms of being someone. It is as such ways of experiencing, and not as sets of characteristics someone would establish from outside, that we shall reflect on life's "stages."

Childhood

There is, thus, an experience of being a child, an experience, that is, in which one lives from a sense of oneself as a child. The child is initially engaged in an ongoing experience of sense which has as part of its form that the child must "make sense" of it, that is, the child is involved in a process of development in which it aspires to achieve control of its body, its world, itself, its relationships. This process of sense-making is a progressive development of its sense of self as much as it is a progressive development of its sense of its surroundings. A significant dimension of the child's learning and development, then, is its coming to establish a way of recognizing itself.

This process of self-recognition, as psychoanalysis demonstrates, is a complex negotiating with the initial bodily parameters of sense (oral, anal, and so on), it has observable patterns of development (such as the "mirror stage," and so on), and it is heavily wrapped up with the child's negotiation of its interpersonal relations. The child's fixing of its sense of self, as much as it is a "discovery," is equally its establishing of the way it can integrate itself successfully in the dynamics of family interaction (or its equivalent). The child's sense of self will thus be inherently relational, inasmuch as it is understanding who it is in relation to these others, and this relational self-interpretation that the child develops will, of course, be fundamentally shaped by the interpretive terms—cultural, familial, and personal—projected by those significant others (the family members) with whom the child is negotiating its sense of self. Learning to recognize itself in relationship to the world of these others will, understandably, involve establishing a sense of itself as dependent and as largely ineffective in relationship to the world to which those others belong. Establishing some such sense of oneself is experiencing oneself as a "child."

We spoke above of establishing "ontological security," which we understood to involve, ultimately, a sense that one is real, that is, one is an effective agent. Inasmuch as one's sense of oneself as a child involves the sense of being fundamentally ineffective, we can understand that children often do operate with a sense of themselves as not fully real, at least not in the same sense that their significant others are real. Children, indeed, struggle with issues of separating reality from fantasy, being swayed, for example, by a sense that fantastical possibilities are plausible, even when the immediate engagement with the world is established on real terms; though the child has a local sense of the coherence of objective time, they might nonetheless anticipate the time, for example, "when I will go to ancient Rome," and though the child may well have a good local sense of the parameters of objective reality, they may nonetheless take precautions to defend against "a vampire in the closet." Children also very much work with a sense that they must await the day when they will really get "there" where the parents are, being "grown up" and fully real participants in the "real world," the world of serious affairs. Indeed, in many ways, this attitude of immaturity—of not yet being fully "geared into" reality—is the child's greatest strength, for this is the stance of openness to possibility that empowers the child to learn (and, indeed, sometimes to learn lessons that adults miss because of the rigidity of their habituated responses to things). To have a sense of oneself as a child is to have a sense of oneself as thus separated from the serious world, or, as de Beauvoir says, to have a sense of oneself as one who plays (*Ethics of Ambiguity*, 35).

Though the child is self-consciously not fully real in the sense that they interpret their parents and surroundings to be, issues of "ontological security" are nonetheless preeminently important here: if they are to have a healthy psychological development, the child must be respected for the reality that they are. The child needs to be treated (1) as one who matters, (2) as one who precisely is not accountable by adult standards, but (3) one who will be thus accountable. The child, in short, must be recognized as one who is appropriately and protectedly on the way to becoming an adult. And, indeed, though the child is not yet an adult and lives in the world of play, it is important not to underrepresent the myriad rich ways in which children do grapple with issues of responsibility, morality, and agency from the start. In short, the child thus experiences themself *as* a child when they experience themself as dependent, as one who plays, and as one who has the serious reality of adulthood in their future, and they experience this in a healthy way when this self-interpretation is confirmed by those around them.

Adolescence

There is a different experience that is the experience of adolescence. Whereas the child experiences her-, him-, or themself as relatively ineffective and irrelevant in the world, the adolescent begins to experience her-, him-, or themself as fully an agent, as one whose action makes a difference. The child's process of development involves a gradually changing self-interpretation as her, his, or their engagement with the world is developing and being practiced, a development that goes hand in hand with her, his, or their progressive development of her, his, or their bodily and other natural capacities and, of course, her, his, or their broader education into the ways of the world. Though the child begins her, his, or their engagement with the world with a sense of her-, him-, or themself as a child, that is, as a not-fully-serious or not-fully-real agent, the very process of living out this identity results in a change in this status: through her, his, or their childish practices, the child grows into a fuller sense of agency—grows into, that is, a status that is no longer that of the child. The child initially has a sense of her, his, or their dependence, her, his, or their own not-fully-accomplished agency, but the process of childhood development is the emergence of the fuller experience of individual agency.

This emerging sense of agency is certainly a matter of enhanced individual capacity, but it has as well an important interpersonal dimension to it. Simultaneously with developing a sense of one's individual self-possession, one experiences a development in one's sense of one's ability to—and one's need to—participate independently in social life as an equal and legitimate member. Like the teenagers I introduced in my first vignette, adolescents in contemporary Western culture begin to choose their own social groups, their own circle of peers, and in virtually any culture adolescence is a time of growing social responsibility and authority. A highly charged aspect of this social development is the emerging experience of romantic and erotic bonds, and adolescence is importantly experienced as the opening up of sexuality.

The young teenage body undergoes the transformations of puberty, and the changing sense of adolescent self-interpretation goes hand in hand with this changing sense of bodily capacity and, correspondingly, a changing sense of bodily self-identity. In early infancy, the child lives largely from the mouth and from the oral bodily bond with the mother's body, and the growing child's changing sense of self-experience is correspondingly a changing sense of their orientation within and orientation toward their body: how we locate ourselves "in" our bodies—the way what we might call our "bodily ego" is configured—changes as our organic bodies and our inhabitation of them develop, and the transformations of puberty dovetail with the social and sexual developments of adolescence to produce a new sense of one's bodily self. In addition to the changing ways in which the adolescent experiences "from the inside" the changing nature of her, his, or their bodily self, the emerging concern with the development of independent, erotic bonds brings with it as well a growing concern for oneself as a body-in-the-eyes-of-others, that is, the social developments of adolescent experience impinge upon the adolescent's self-interpretation in a particularly intimate way, as one comes to experience a highly charged sense of the identification of oneself with one's body.

Experiencing oneself as an adolescent, then, is an experiencing simultaneously of enhanced individuality and of enhanced sociality, and this is experienced as a matter of how one lives one's body as much as it is a matter of how one inhabits one's self-conscious, interpretive perspective on the world. Adolescence is when one's experience is "about" integrating this bodily individuality with the surrounding social world.

Modern North American and European societies have based themselves politically on the principles of liberal political philosophy so powerfully articulated by John Locke, and the cultures that these societies have developed present a strongly demarcated sense of adolescence. In these societies that cultivate both the political recognition of individuality and the experience of interpreting oneself as such an individual, the experience of adolescence is highlighted as the time for appropriating and developing this sense of individuality. Adolescence is the time for the emerging individual to wrestle explicitly with the experiences of individual self-definition, choosing one's own path in life, learning to live and think independently.

More traditional societies typically have not encouraged such a period of experimentation with individuality, but they nonetheless typically have various ways of marking a transition into proper adulthood from an earlier stage that is nonetheless not simply childhood. The Navajo (Diné) *kinaaldá* ritual for girls at the time of puberty and the Ojibwe dream-fasts for boys at the time of puberty are familiar examples from the indigenous peoples of North America; the Maasai (Ilmaasae) of East Africa practice a warrior-initiation ceremony for adolescent boys that includes the *Emuratare* (circumcision) ceremony, participation in the *Emanyatta* (warriors' camp), and ultimately the *Eunoto* (senior warrior) ceremony that allows the initiate to marry; and analogous rites of passage have characterized human societies from their earliest formation. Indeed, such formalized initiations into adulthood continue to be alive ritually in such traditions as "confirmation" in the Catholic church, the "Bat-" and "Bar-Mitzvah" in Judaism, and so on. Even if more traditional cultures do not encourage "experimentation with values," as we do in modern liberal cultures, they nonetheless typically recognize a period of "practicing" for adulthood, so to speak—a period, that is, in which one knows oneself not to be a child and not to be an adult, a transitional period in which one experiences oneself as learning to wear one's adult mantle.

Because one experiences oneself as on the way to adulthood, and as thus no longer a child, adolescence is typically an experience of a sense of one's independent power, one's detachment. One comes to experience oneself as a site of responsibility and authority, and, even in cultures that are not individualistic, adolescence remains an experience of individuality inasmuch as one comes to experience oneself as personally responsible for enacting the adult reality demanded of one. This is an experience of detachment, because one feels oneself, singly, to be no longer a part of the childhood world to which one belonged, and to be on one's own singular path of accomplishing the transition to adulthood. Successfully making this transition results in a later experience of reintegration, a growing sense (1) of the need to be involved with and answerable to the world (whether the local community or the broader world), and (2) of one's ability to be such. This is the emerging of the sense of adulthood.

Adulthood

Adult experience "comes on the scene" in the context of our aging. Adult experience arrives with one's coming to feel oneself answerable to the demands of self-responsibly living a life: one feels about oneself that one is at the stage when one has to "get real," as we sometimes say in contemporary North American slang. Whereas adolescent experience can be the thrill (or terror) of trying on this new "adult" identity, while still living in a largely protected environment, properly adult experience is recognizing the responsibility to measure up to this and to establish a life on its terms. Adulthood brings with it the sense that those earlier times (childhood and adolescence) are now past—and *essentially* past— and that one is now at the point where "it is really happening," and "there is no turning back from this." It is the fact and the weight of this recognition, presumably, that lies behind the common practice of young adults to revert to situations of adolescent behavior with their adolescent friends, trying to postpone defensively the passing of that protected time or to revisit it nostalgically. Adulthood as a self-experience emerges in this context of realizing that one must make decisions that will shape essentially and permanently the character of one's life and one's world.

As we grow up, we hear from others of this adult reality of responsibility, but as adults, we, like the forty-year-olds of my opening vignette, learn the reality of this responsibility by participating in it. Adulthood presents itself to us as a reality—indeed, our reality—the nature of which we have to learn through living it. We learn what it is like to be adults, gradually and progressively finding out what responsibility is really like, such that we can come to say, "I made that choice and now, five years later, I see its real weight as I see the real consequences it had for me and for others." This kind of experience is notable both for its relationship to responsibility and for its relationship to time. We learn the nature of responsibility through these choices, as we discover that our actions do matter; we learn that, for example, our own careless—or even careful but immature—approach to relationships has had a disastrous effect on the life of another, or that our shortsighted approach to education has left us unable realistically to pursue the career to which we had aspired. We also learn that matters of choice are intrinsically related to matters of time, and it is characteristic of adult experience to come to have a sense of time different from what one had as a child, inasmuch as one can now look back on projects undertaken over periods of time impossible for children or adolescents: a ten-year relationship, seven years spent in a job, twelve years spent in university, eight years living in a city, sixteen years raising children, and so on. Finally, these choices make "who one is" more and more determinate: whereas as children, as adolescents, and even, indeed, as young adults, we live from a sense of our possibilities for shaping a life, our adulthood is the experience of the actuality of shaping a life, the reality of revealing to ourselves and the world "who in fact we are," a reality that might or (more likely) might not correspond with how we had imagined ourselves. The growing sense of responsibility, coupled with the growing sense of "no-way-back" and the growing sense of having become someone specific continues throughout the whole of adult life. This is the very nature of aging and our maturing largely has to do with comprehending this process of human aging.

Though the lives of different individuals will take different forms, and though the expectable shape that aging takes can vary between different cultures, there is nonetheless a generally predictable pattern of changing self-experience from early to mid- to late adulthood.

Early Adulthood

There is a time when we start to think of ourselves as "adults," recognizing about ourselves that we no longer belong to that "time" of adolescence. Often, our self-interpretation as "adult" will happen in specific contexts, rather than being a wholesale transformation of our self-experience. Perhaps it is at the office, or in meetings with a supervisor, or in taking responsibilities for economic matters at the family home, or in shopping for groceries when living independently, or in setting up a home with a spouse: any of these, or many others, can be contexts in which we start to live from a self-conscious sense of responsibility, a self-conscious sense of adopting the stance of engaging with the real as such. As we go through the transition to such adult self-experience, there will typically be sectors of our lives in which we retain our adolescent identity. Perhaps I live as an adult at work, but on the weekend I socialize with former schoolmates, and together we enact a collective experience of adolescence, or perhaps when I return to my parents' home I reassume the adolescent self-identity I shed at work. Gradually, though, these returns to adolescence carry with them a sense of nostalgia, and one truly makes one's home in one's adult sense of self.

In this early adulthood one can feel like a ship that has just cast off its mooring lines and is setting sail. Early adulthood is a time of embarkation, as we let go the lines of protected dependency that have defined us throughout childhood and adolescence and launch a life that is—that will be—properly "our own." The unique character of this time of life is powerfully exemplified in the story of Dorothea Brooke, the protagonist of the novel *Middlemarch* by George Eliot (Mary Anne Evans), who leaves the home of her uncle and guardian to marry the middle-aged scholar Edward Casaubon, imagining (wrongly) that she will find happiness and fulfillment through supporting him in his research; it is exemplified in the story of the young Siddhattha Gotama (the Buddha), who, according to Buddhist tradition, left his father's home to embark on an independent life of study with the great spiritual leaders in the urban centers of ancient India; and it is exemplified in the contemporary experience of Dolores Huerta (1930–), who met and married her first husband while attending the University of the Pacific in Stockton, California, to earn a teaching diploma, had two children, and began a career as an elementary school teacher, surely with no sense that she would soon divorce her husband and quit her job to embark on a life of political activism and ultimately become one of the co-founders of the United

Farm Workers' Association. In early adulthood, people commonly take on long-term jobs, establish an independent residence, marry, begin to raise children—all matters of laying down the planks that are to be the platform for later life. The experience of this time can be a matter of keen excitement, a sense, perhaps, of "finally getting there," or a matter of terror, as if one were now called upon to leap off a cliff.

In modern Western culture, public portrayals of generic adult life typically rely on images of people in this stage of life—people beginning to embark on an adult career, still "young," still "on their way" to their life and career goals. The result is that we have inculcated into us quite a distorted image of adulthood, for there is much more to adult life than these beginning stages. Coming upon the later stages, and discovering that life is not simply the way we had imagined it based upon such images, can be quite an existential challenge.

Middle Adult Life

Dante begins his *Divine Comedy*, his famous tale of spiritual crisis and resolution, with the following lines:

> When I had journeyed half of our life's way,
> I found myself within a shadowed forest,
> for I had lost the path that does not stray.
> (*Inferno*, Canto 1, lines 1–3, trans. Mandelbaum)

Dante notes that it is the midpoint of life that is the occasion for his spiritual crisis, and this is not at all an uncommon phenomenon. Somewhere around the age of fifty, it is common for one to notice that one is past what is likely the quantitative "halfway point" of one's life, according to the presumption that one will live a life of an "average length" of between eighty and ninety years. Rather than being a merely quantitative matter, however, this situation can bring with it a unique—and challenging—change in one's perspective. There can be a qualitatively distinct character to middle adult life that one could not easily anticipate (except perhaps conceptually) from a younger age. This perspective is evident in a number of areas—career, family, other intimate relationships—all of which can take the form of announcing to one one's finitude. These culturally underlined aspects of middle adult life are major contributors to the experience often referred to as a "midlife crisis."

As a young adult, for example, one has projects and aspirations—I want to be a social worker and make a difference, I want to be a famous musician, I want to be rich, powerful, and respected, I want to be happily married with a family, and so on—and the process of life largely takes the form of working on these projects. What characterizes middle adult life is that, typically, one has now largely accomplished—or failed to accomplish—what one set out to do (or simply dreamed about). This has the twofold effect of (1) leading one to experience oneself as accomplished and capable rather than "in training," so to speak, or at least judging oneself by this standard, in cases where one feels oneself a failure, and (2) allowing one to find out "so that's how successful I in fact turned out to be." Of course it is true that at the age of fifty, for example, one's life is typically not over and one can expect still to accomplish a great deal more. What is nonetheless true, however, is that it is a general characteristic of life in our culture that our ability to establish our "impact" on the world is largely determined between, say, the ages of twenty-five and forty-five.

This experience of this shift can happen in the context of one's career. A jazz musician, for example, will likely study music in their teenage years and enter the professional arena in their early twenties. Through their twenties and thirties, a budding saxophone player or bass player will gradually be developing a professional profile; by their late thirties, however, it will usually largely be settled how deeply into the profession they will penetrate, such that at the age of forty, for example, they would commonly have the realization, "I guess I'm never going to make it into the big leagues," or something similar. In some domains, it is precisely older adults who are exemplars of success—statesmanship is a striking example, with important political figures such as U.S. senators or U.S. presidents commonly reaching this position of power only in their sixties, and Gertrude Stein, for example, had her life as a great, recognized artist begin only in her sixties—but generally speaking the temporal "arena" in which our level of professional success is definitively established falls somewhere around the forties. Indeed, for the many individuals who take on "nine to five" jobs, working for a wage in someone else's business enterprise, by their forties it can become apparent that their life "amounts to" a constant struggle from which they can never really get free. In all of these situations, one can find that the quantitative midpoint of one's life brings with it a new—and troubling—experience of oneself and one's relationship to the career to which one had initially turned to make one's life meaningful.

These issues that arise in one's career can also arise in one's family. For many, for example, middle adult life will be a time when their children will be old enough to begin developing independent lives of their own, such that the life of "establishing a family" has now happened and passed by (though in contemporary North American culture it is becoming more common for the raising of children to begin at later ages than in former generations). Such so-called empty nesters may find this experience liberating, of course, but they can find that they had pinned the meaningfulness of their lives on their family life with their children and, in the new absence of those children, they find themselves practically, emotionally, and spiritually adrift.

By midlife, too, we can find ourselves interpersonally "defined," and these issues can thus arise as well in our most intimate and personal relationships. Having lived in varied relationships with others throughout one's life, for example, one experiences one's reality as embodied in and through them and, whether or not any one of them remains one's "love interest," they define who one is, that is, they are one's "significant others" whether one desires that or not. Indeed, the fact that they are past partners may mean that one actually feels uncomfortably alienated from one's own life inasmuch as one's single reality is no longer empowered to inhabit with them those ways of being-in-the-world that one established as definitive of oneself. Of course it is true that even an older woman of, say, seventy-five whose partner dies can marry again, and this establishing of a new partnership can be wonderful and fulfilling; nonetheless, it can never "take the place of" the lifelong marriage, for that marriage precisely was the unique—the one and only—process of her establishing her fundamental inhabitation of the intersubjective world. Even though the new relationship "is" her life, it remains true that that earlier marriage is fundamentally definitive of "who" she is in a way that cannot be reenacted by the new relationship. While at "midlife" the possibilities for redefining one's life are significantly greater—and, indeed, it is not uncommon for the response to the midlife crisis to be a radical change in one's relationships, career, or lifestyle—it is nonetheless similarly true that by this age one typically finds oneself interpersonally "defined," and this means that the world of one's experience presents a different face—a more fully "actual" face—than did the world of one's younger life.

In all of these ways, one has the experience of finding out, "So this is what I have become," both in the positive sense of having developed powers and capacities and having made significant accomplishments, but also in the possibly negative sense that "I am only this." Middle adult life is the time when we can experience the "metaphysical balance" in our life shifting from the primacy of the infinitude of possibility to the primacy of the finitude of actuality. It is the experience of this shift from being a person defined by possibilities to being a person who has become "actually" someone specific that can take the form of a "midlife crisis."

In the perspective of middle adult life, the world, which had formerly seemed to be infinitely demanding, the very context that defines what is and what is to be done, suddenly is *only* the world, only this world that can appeal to nothing beyond itself to justify itself. The world of one's life has become fixed in a way that was not possible earlier, and this "settledness," inasmuch as it can come with a sense of accomplishment, can equally bring with it a sense of sterility. Indeed, beyond even sterility, the world of middle adult life can have the sense of finality, a sense that "it's done," with no chance of starting again. In this sense, the meaning of the world is intimately woven with our own sense of mortality—the finitude of our lives and the imminence of death.

Whereas for the child, adolescent, or young adult, death typically can appear as only an alien intervention into life—something that really "could happen," but would be an unexpected and untimely interruption of one's life—for the adult of midlife, "death" can suddenly come to appear as an anticipatable event that is ever nearing on the horizon. Of course, as we have discussed above, death can never be an "event" "in one's life," for one's death is precisely the "no longer" of events—not something that happens within time but the elimination of temporal happening altogether. Nonetheless, the external, quantitative approach to measuring one's life—counting one's years against what is statistically likely for a person—can commonly have the effect that the reality of death becomes experientially salient at midlife. This sense that one is now on the path to one's own death couples in an experientially potent way with the sense of the finishedness of one's world such that, as one experiences one's own mortality, one experiences the split of one's subjectivity from the substantiality of the world. This is the experience that it is our own reality, and not just the reality of the world, that is the Heraclitean river in which we cannot step twice.

One's subjectivity can seem split from the substantiality of the world inasmuch as the world no longer offers one the fertile environment for the cultivation of one's aspirations, but rather seems like a solid terrain that dictates to one what one can and cannot do, both in terms of the limited routes for action that it offers and the responsibilities that it puts upon one. In contemporary Western culture, at least, there is considerable "objective" justification for this perspective, that is, this perspective is not just an arbitrary "subjective" opinion, but is in fact a well-motivated apprehension of the realities of one's situation. This is, first, a matter simply of the nature of choice.

We are beings who make the choices that shape our situations, but to choose something is to be bound by it, which is to say the initial experience of subjectivity—"It's up to me"—brings in its tow the experience of objectivity—"This is the life I have chosen." It *is* the reality of the choices one made as a younger person that one must deal with now, that is, the determinacy of one's life at midlife is "who one is," and these are the responsibilities to which one committed oneself. This intrinsic reality of choice is also underlined and exacerbated by the characteristics of contemporary culture.

Whereas we broadly expect individuals in their twenties or even their thirties to be launching their careers, and there is considerable social infrastructure in place to support this, we do not, as a society, expect individuals in their fifties to be beginning their careers, and we have neither the policies nor the attitudes that support such behavior. And, indeed, as Plato's characters prominently note in the *Republic* and the *Laws*, individuals typically can practice only one "art," that is, inasmuch as it generally takes many years of study and practice to bring into being a meaningful career, it is a "material" truth that one life does not easily allow one the resources to have a second career. With interpersonal relationships, the situation is similar: whereas teenagers and young adults are often in settings—most notably, schools—that surround them with other individuals at a similar stage of life who are "eligible" for developing romantic relationships, adults at midlife have no easy access to such socially rich environments; hence, the popularity of internet "dating sites." And with relationships, the "material" conditions are perhaps even more restrictive than are the conditions of developing a new career, for the partners of a new relationship begun at midlife will not be the fresh and open individuals who launch themselves into interpersonal life in their twenties but will be individuals with "baggage": they will be, that is, individuals who bring with them richly developed worlds of existent responsibility and, perhaps more important, already well-developed characters; and, while this can mean these individuals have the psychological and behavioral resources to take up relationships with a greater depth and maturity than they could have as younger individuals, it also means they come with "hangups" and rigidity rather than the psychological openness and flexibility of someone developing the interpersonal practices of relationship life for the first time.

In these ways, then, the world at midlife does not offer the fertile environment for cultivating one's hopes and plans that it does in young adult life. The adult at middle life, in other words, is to an important degree assessing the situation correctly in seeing her, his, or their world as an environment that is not inviting of a "new beginning," and this sense of the split of subjectivity and substantiality is the "embodied intentionality" of midlife, the perspective that reflects the substantial reality of one's developed, situated temporality.

The middle adult life experience of oneself as "determinate" and "settled" can thus be the source for significant anxiety. The external and "objective" view on oneself can bring the sense that "life is over" or the sense that "all I have to look forward to now is decay," and the internal and "subjective" view on oneself can' bring the sense that, since the possibilities of the world are now exhausted, one must now live one's life in lonely isolation, grappling with psychological and existential issues that will no longer be reflected in transformations of one's world. No doubt, this anxiety can be evaded and ignored, but in its form it is a call to change. In our familiar clichés, we imagine individuals who deal with this call to change by various actions aimed at "revitalizing" a "youthful" life, whether by launching new projects, changing careers, or developing new intimate relationships. No doubt such responses can sometimes be positive and worthwhile. In its nature, though, the call to change is a call to transform one's own relationship to meaning.

The crisis of middle age is, at root, the nature of our embodied temporality making itself known as such, and the most honest response to this is to own up to our aging. In other words, the crisis of middle life is the nascent recognition, emerging naturally within our experience, of the very themes we have been studying here: it is the call, emerging naturally within our experience, to "own up" to the distinctive nature of our freedom. Just as adolescence is our opening onto the possibilities for self-responsibility and is fulfilled in the deepening of our sense of our unique existential reality as human beings, so is midlife our opening onto the actuality of our aging, and it is fulfilled in the embrace of the distinctive realm of meaning that is opened up to us by virtue of our mortality. The midlife crisis, in other words, is an opportunity to live as someone who dies and to live in a way that finds meaning in the world without the (immature) presumption of infinite possibility. It is the opportunity to identify oneself with the life one has made—the choices, for good or for bad, that have made oneself and one's world the determinate reality that each is—and to accept to live within this life rather than to live from the (impossible) dream of another.

Old Age

While all ages of life bring with them experiences of loss, old age is uniquely defined by this reality. Middle adult life, as we noted above, is marked by the experience of a split between the substantiality of the world and one's own subjectivity. Old age is a further step in this direction, for it is marked by the experience of one's world disappearing. Just as we are aging, so are those intimate others with whom we have made a life, and the consequence of this is that, the older we get, the more those companions die. And, just as our friends die, so does the social and cultural world we established with them disappear as the world around us takes its shape more and more from the activities and interests of the generations that have come after us. At some point the older individual will have to give up the practices that constitute her, his, or their career, with the corresponding loss of the engagement, stimulation, accomplishment, and novelty that those practices offered through earlier adult life. And contextualizing all of these losses will be the deterioration, whether gradual or rapid, of one's bodily powers and, indeed, of one's organic (and possibly mental) health. These various aspects of the deterioration of the world of the adult in old age bring with them an increasing experience of dependency.

We always depend upon others, but in old age, as in childhood, this dependence becomes definitive of our perspective—we experience as dependent beings—whereas from adolescence through middle adult life, it is our independence (sought, enacted, or realized) that defines our perspective. We experience ourselves as old when we encounter our world against the meaningful background of these various dimensions of loss and, in light of that, we recognize about ourselves that we are fundamentally and irremediably in need of the support of others to allow us to carry out our lives. The primary loss that defines old age, then, is this loss of independence, contextualized by the disappearance of friends, activities, career, bodily health and powers, environment, novel input, interests. We depend on support from a world that, on its own, is disintegrating, a disintegration that is often accelerated by the dismissive attitude of the surrounding, younger culture.

This broad set of stages—the immediate bond of self and world in the protected time of childhood, the splitting of self and world in the adolescent sense of emerging agency, the challenge of the objective world in early adulthood, the split of subjectivity and substantiality in middle adult life, and the loss of world and independence in old age—admits, of course, of much richer analyses than these short sketches provide. And, of course, these stages presume a "normal," healthy development for the individual, and so the experience of any individual can be quite different, due, for example, to abnormal organic, psychological, or cultural conditions. A young woman grappling with the probable imminence of her death from cystic fibrosis, for example, will likely experience her emerging, early adulthood rather differently than the young woman who experiences this time as the presumptive start of a long life; a schizophrenic man in his forties might have largely missed the experiences of objectivity that define adulthood; and an extremely wealthy man in the ninth decade of his life might be able to avoid many of the experiences of dependency that so define the experience of others, as we noted in the Introduction with the story of Socrates and Cephalus. Nonetheless, this analysis is not simply an idiosyncratic account of the experiences of an arbitrary set of persons. On the contrary, this is an analysis of the intrinsic "rhythm" of our human temporality: it is the changing pattern of accomplishment and loss that corresponds to our developing perspective and displays the changing relations of self and world that are intrinsic to us as embodied beings, rather than being alien circumstances that befall us.

The Spatiality of Adulthood

The basic experiential meaning of each of the different life-stages—the "temporalities" we described above—is also intimately intertwined with a "material" reality: a concrete, body-world relationship. In other words, having each of these forms of experience—of "embodied intentionality"—is not just an isolated cognitive matter, but is a matter of embodied, situated practice—a situated practice that has organic, spatial, interpersonal, and political dimensions. Let us now describe how adulthood in particular (and the aging that comes with it) is a concrete matter of body-world relationship: how it is situated.

Spatial Environments

We draw our resources from our places: things and their structured situatedness in our places are like our limbs in that it is with them, through them, and by them that we carry out our projects. They supply the meaningful atmosphere that nourishes our motivation; they define the terrain and terms of our interaction(s); they are the material medium for the realization of our intentions. They support our resolve and they support our practices.

We house ourselves, of course, for the obvious reason that we need protection from the threatening aspects of the natural environment. If we cannot presume an environment in which we can stay warm and dry on cold, rainy days and in which we can rest, confident of our safety, we will be fundamentally inhibited in our ability to realize our capacities, to develop and enact our "I can." Not having such assured protections is, of course, the lot of many individuals, whom we typically designate as "homeless" (but who might better be called "houseless"), and has also, of course, been the lot of many peoples historically. It was a major human goal—a major adult occupation—to develop such shelters through centuries of developing technology all around the world, as ancient Russian hunters, for example, developed their tents of mammoth-hide, as the Greenland Inuit developed igloos, and, in subsequent centuries, as advanced forms of insulation, plumbing, electrification, windows, roofs, air conditioning, and so on were gradually developed to allow a reliable and comfortable home life. This developing of more supportive and more satisfying shelters is not just a technological, material matter, however. The shelter we need is also a psychological sense of confidence in the reliability of our protective environments.

Restaurant owners, for example, commonly recognize some aspect of this psychological power of environments. How the chairs and tables are placed in the restaurant, the character of the light, the wooden or tiled floor—these features will determine whether I can "settle in" and work here, or whether you and I can have an intimate conversation. Some rooms are cozy, some cold. Some rooms stimulate imagination; some encourage concentration; others are sterile or stifling. It is common for us to have a similar experience in our familiar dwelling places. We feel "at home" in our houses, and we find certain rooms or certain pieces of furniture welcoming. We find some of our household locations conducive to working, some conducive to sleeping, some conducive to lively conversation, some to dining, and, conversely, it feels "wrong" and uncomfortable to take up certain activities in certain settings. Indeed, rearranging the furniture can often be the route to establishing for ourselves a more comfortable psychological environment. In all these situations, we are recognizing the ways in which our carrying out of our projects is accommodated (or not) by the character of our places.

Friedrich Schiller, in his *Letters on the Aesthetic Education of Man*, wrote that artworks offer to us unique and irreplaceable routes for psychological development. He writes of artworks—works of architecture, of music, of painting—that they "soften" or "tighten" us (*On the Aesthetic Education of Man*, Letter 16, 110–15). We are familiar with the metaphor of one's being "too tightly wound" or "uptight," and we can recognize the value of "loosening up"; similarly, we can imagine someone who is "slack" or "too loose" in their approach to things, and we might encourage that person to "tighten things up." "Looseness" here has the sense of giving ourselves over to passive immersion in the immediate flow of the particularities of life, "tightness" the sense of active, self-directed, intelligent detachment from the immediacies of experience in favor of a self-conscious concern for some deeper purpose. Without much further exploration, we can see the sense of these notions of tightening and loosening, and of the idea that either can be present to too high a degree in a person, and equally that each can be a valuable corrective to an excess of the other. We can be so preoccupied with our rational concerns that we never appreciate the inherent worth of immediate circumstances or, alternatively, we can be so wrapped up in the myriad specificities of the moment that we fail to adopt any wise overview or to develop any larger, effective plan of action. We might think of our living environments on something like Schiller's model of the artwork.

I spoke of the extremes of cozy and cold environments, and this pair roughly maps onto Schiller's "loose" and "tight," respectively. Though my language of "cold" might seem to imply a denigration of environments with this character—and surely sometimes this is a negative term—this quality, like Schiller's "tight," is often, in fact, positive. The issue that decides this is that for which the space is an environment. Sometimes one wants very much not to be in a cozy, homey room, perhaps at a job interview or while undergoing an academic examination. Indeed, it is just for these reasons that we do design such things as offices, school buildings, lobbies, highways, and so on. In considering our forms of inhabiting space, we need to recognize the role they play in articulating our perspective, and, similarly, in considering our perspectives, we need to recognize the way they are articulated through our forms of spatial inhabitation. In chapter 2, we considered the psychological and inter-personal parameters of growth, and this growth is equally a matter of our participation in specific environments. The formative "forces" that encourage or inhibit our development include the articulated spaces into which we are initiated, and in which we make our homes, and we can study these "cozy" and "cold" characteristics in relation to our growth into adulthood.

We commonly recognize that a child needs a home in which to grow up: the child needs a supportive environment. For a child, the appropriately supportive environment will include spaces matched in size to their limbs, for, beyond mere "protection," it will be a space for experimenting with new practices and investigating new things. Thus, the legs and seat of what an adult construes as a chair may well, for the child, define instead a fort into which she can crawl; "stairs" may be a challenging and thrilling site for practicing climbing; and a door, rather than fitting in the door frame, may fit with the wall in defining a hiding space. Furthermore, the appropriately supportive environment will offer psychological shelter for engaging with these thrilling spaces for imagina-tive growth. In other words, the appropriate home for the child will be a "cozy" space that "fits" the whole range of the child's needs, from the simply mechanical parameters that address a child's small body through the more dynamically practical and intimately emotional dimensions that define the experience of a growing child. When considered in terms of the mechanical issues pertinent to size, the supportive home can appear merely as an indifferent, external frame; when considered in terms of emotional support, however, it is clear that the home is not a disposable scaffold, but is the very substance of the child's life, that is, the home is the interpersonal world in which the child is (becoming) a member. In other words, the child will grow up both in and into a home that is both a material medium and an intersubjective reality, and having such a home is essential to the child's healthy development. The need for a home does not end with the child, however.

Whereas for the child the home is the space in which they grow up, our growing up typically requires that we must leave this home and go out "on our own." This independence and autonomy that we (rightly) associate with adulthood can lead us to imagine that "home" is no longer a necessity for the adult. Or, more exactly, though we acknowledge that, as adults, we will indeed "make a new home for ourselves," we can easily misconstrue this existential need as a mere practical necessity. In order to grasp the distinctive character of the adult's existential need for a home, let us reflect on the role of confirmation in our identities and specifically on the distinctive character of this need in adult life. For the child, as we saw in chapter 2, the support it requires is the support that allows it gradually to assume the identity of "agent." Our adult identities are such accomplished "agent" identities, however, and, consequently, rather than looking to our parents, we look to the broader world for confirmation of this "agent" identity: we need a world, that is, that "fits" and confirms our self-experience as agents.

The Space of Adulthood

We saw in chapter 2 that adulthood is largely a matter of "being realistic," and one central aspect of this "realism" is, of course, how we conceive explicitly of our world. Being logical in reasoning is an instance of this, and grasping space "objectively" is another. To introduce this notion of objective space, a children's book, for example, might encourage the child to notice the "space between" bodies. Now, in fact, in the situations thus pictured, there is, of course, always a body of air between the dog and the tree or the grass and the wall, that is, there is in fact no "space between" bodies. The book can be pedagogically useful nonetheless, however, because the transparent character of the air allows us, so to speak, to "see through" it to recognize the spatial context that is coextensive with, but not reducible to, all things; indeed, as Husserl puts it, space is not a separate "thing" but is "co-seen" with each thing (*Thing and Space*, 223). To grasp space is thus to grasp the "container" of all things; a container, however, not in the sense of a separate thing but as the infinite, unending, indifferent expanse of possible locations, any location open to any possible thing such that, simply by virtue of its bodily nature, that thing is able to be somewhere. Grasping space objectively is a matter of recognizing that the answer to the question "Where is it?" is to be answered from the perspective of this ultimate context, rather than from the perspective of oneself; indeed, from this perspective, where one is oneself is defined by the terms of space, rather than being that which defines the terms of space.

At some level, our healthy development always involves some such "decentering" of our own perspective, that is, we need to speak from a perspective that is more universal than, and that is indifferent to, our own. To speak from the perspective of the family house—"I'm in the bed-room"—is already an advance over simply saying, "I'm here," because one is recognizing a context that defines one's "where" rather than presuming that the context is defined by where one is. Recognizing that the house is at "2636 Wascana Street" or that we live "in North America" pushes ever farther away the defining parameters of spatial perspective. Indeed, it is surely a similar advance in perspective to shift our grasp of our earthly situation from a "geocentric" to a "heliocentric" perspective, recognizing that the earth itself is part of a spatial situation the orientation of which is indifferent to "our" position. These parameters, however, each define only a *more* universal and a *more* indifferent perspective: they remain relative rather than absolute spatial contexts, for each is still fundamentally local, that is, though the frame of reference is stretched quite far, it is nonetheless still defined by some specific place and, indeed, a place relative to our perspective. In fact, most of us will never go beyond this to explicitly grasp conceptually the ultimate spatial horizon of space as such—a space that is not relative to any perspective. Comprehending such "absolute" space—a spatial frame of reference utterly indifferent to our place within it—is, however, a powerful development of our minds, a powerful advance in our ability to relate to reality objectively, and, inasmuch as it is integral to objectivity, this ultimate "cold" space is thus integral to the distinctive environment of adulthood.

Whether or not any one of us, individually, recognizes absolute space, our world is significantly shaped by this perspective. Specifically, this interpretation of the nature of space was integral to the "scientific revolution" of the Early Modern period, which has in turn been highly formative of our contemporary culture. This spatial interpretation was launched by Kepler (1571–1630), Galileo (1564–1642), and the earlier Islamic astronomers and mathematicians whose work laid the foundations for their investigations, such as Naṣīr al-Dīn al-Tusī (1201–1274) and Muʾayyad al-Dīn al-ʿUrḍī (c.1200–1266), and it was ultimately systematized by Newton (1643–1727) in his *Mathematical Principles of Natural Philosophy* (1687). This interpretation of the ultimate nature of space challenged the interpretation of space that Aristotle (384–322 BCE) developed in *On the Heavens*, an interpretation that posited an inherent orientation to space and a non-indifferent relationship between natural bodies and the space "proper" to them, and it brought with it a revolutionary interpretation of the motion of bodies, an interpretation that massively unleashed the potentiality for human harnessing of "the power of nature" by justifying an indifference to the specific forms in which natural bodies occur in the interpretation of natural causality. The development of airplanes, of nuclear weapons and long-range missiles, and of the communications satellites upon which our telephones, internet, news services, and more depend, all have their history in this revolution in spatial interpretation and its corresponding reinterpretation of the nature of natural bodies. Consequently, even if we do not personally reflect on or imagine such matters, we nonetheless live lives that fundamentally do depend upon such reflection, inasmuch as we rely upon technological developments in our world that presuppose such reflection. In using our cellular telephones and in relying upon the cultural prosperity that is a byproduct of the military domination of much of the world by the United States, in other words, we are implicitly enacting—implicitly living from—an interpretation of our experience in terms of this Early Modern revolution in spatial understanding.

It is in experiencing space as objective that, in part, we have our identity as adult subjects—as agents—reflected back to us, and to a large extent it is our recognition that we live in a world in which the perspective of the physical sciences has authority that we have such an experience of objective space. Thus, in finding ourselves "at home" in the world of cell phones and airplanes, and in appealing to scientists and technicians to "take care of" these things for us, we inhabit an environment that implicitly announces for us our identity as adult agents; whether or not we explicitly study Newton's work, that is, we are "interpellated," in the language of Louis Althusser, as "objective" subjects—that is, we are "called" to such a self-experience—by our very environment ("Ideology and Ideological State Apparatuses," 173–77). This "interpellation" that is embedded in the technological parameters of our modern environment is even more pronounced in our social structures.

Just as there is a modern scientific conception of space as an indifferent site for any body, so is there a modern political conception of space as an indifferent environment for any person. In the modern world, we live with a sense of space as a neutral domain, inherently open to anyone. Indeed, we understand space—public space—on the model of something like a (modern) road, which is a space not for someone specific going somewhere specific but for anyone's going anywhere: a space of travel. Modern public space, similarly, is a space through which anyone can (and must) pass in carrying out their life activities.

This conception of "public" space is not, however, simply the given, inherent nature of space, but is a historically developed, militarily defended, culturally specific interpretation of our spatial experience—an interpretation carried out behaviorally and intersubjectively, rather than in the explicit theoretical consciousness of an individual. It is not given experientially that any space is "not mine" or "not yours," for either of us can live with the sense that it is our own; indeed, we have seen in our description of the child's experience that our original establishment as subjects requires that we treat at least some spaces as our proper places. To apprehend space as publicly neutral, then, presupposes an overcoming of the original partiality of our proprietary perspectives: it presupposes that we have come to a shared perception, a lived agreement, about how we will occupy space, about what "we can" do with this environment. Inhabiting space as neutrally public is thus inherently a modality of what we called above *sugchōrein,* of "co-inhabiting."

This historically accomplished sharedness of spatial perception involves as well a particular interpretation of human nature. It is not new that communities live from a shared perception of the nature of space—indeed, such *"sugchōrein"* is a necessary condition of their being communities—but it has not always been the case that space has been cooperatively interpreted as publicly neutral. In the traditional class and caste systems of Indian social life, for example, there is a shared perception of space enacted, but this is a perception that recognizes fundamentally different privileges and duties for spatial inhabitation for different "types" of person. Space is not anyone's space, but is rather an organized system of places—a system defended by military, political, cultural, and interpersonal force—some of which are proper for these, some proper for those, and it is not given that there is a neutral public domain through which all can pass without interference. Interpreting space as thus neutrally public goes hand in hand with an interpretation of humanity as inherently equal. The modern spatial co-perception is rooted in an essentially "democratic"—liberal and individualistic—interpretation of human reality.

Precisely because we can live from different interpretations of the nature of space—because anyone can live any space as his or their or her own, because we can participate in a social perception of space as differentially organized and apportioned, because we can interpret space as a neutral social environment—any such interpretation of space is in principle a matter of opposition and controversy: living from any interpretation will involve "taking a stand" against someone else's appropriation of that same space. Because a lived interpretation of space is a sense of being accommodated, however, we precisely experience such spatial interpretation not as interpretation but as something given: in experiencing space as accommodating our identities, we experience it as not an object in need of an active response (such as "interpretation"), but as something whose nature is simply to yield automatically to our perspective. This self-concealing prejudice inherent to our spatial perception is further able to be maintained—we do not have to encounter the prejudicial and controversial nature of our spatial interpretation—because we participate in a broad social movement that similarly interprets space (that is, we live in a culture that shares our perception) and we have a military system that enforces our "right" to thus interpret space by using its force to oppose competing cultural perspectives. The "global" interpretation of "the" world as a single economic domain—the contemporary interpretation of space as inherently "public" that shapes contemporary capitalist culture—thus presents itself as a natural perception of a fact, whereas in truth it is a militarily enforced perception that actively suppresses alternate conceptions of space—indeed, precisely suppresses the interpretation of space as a site of or for "alterity," of or for alternative ways of being.

Thus, whether we self-consciously intend it or not, by coming to be effective participants in our social world, we become collaborators in the reproduction and enforcement of a form of cooperative living that involves an implicit interpretation of the nature of our sociality. The very way we inhabit space—the very way we develop habits of moving our bodies from place to place—is implicitly an intersubjective gesture, and the way we treat space is implicitly a way of construing the privileges and duties of other people. In more traditional societies, one must grow up into responsible movement by learning to respect the differentiated social status of elders and children, for example, or of women and men. Perhaps I, as a woman, am responsible for walking always three steps behind my husband (a structure embedded in the very case-endings of words, for example, in the Tabassaran language of the Northern Caucasus), or perhaps I must move aside or lower my eyes when a wealthy citizen walks past. In modern society, on the contrary, we are responsible to move in space in a way that respects the equal rights of all other individuals to do the same.

We can see further the "placement" of this modern political vision. In North America of the twentieth and twenty-first centuries, we have come to accept as an ideal and as the norm the notion of the "detached, single-family dwelling." At many other times in history, and in many other areas of the contemporary world, it is accepted as normal that people live in closely packed apartments or houses, but in Canada and the United States the detached house with its own yard and automobile garage is taken as the way one should be housed, and one measures one's success, at least in part, by whether one has achieved this level of spatial inhabitation. Such a conception of housing brings with it a perception of human relationships as well: such an approach to housing encourages conceiving of the "nuclear" family in detachment from the extended family; it encourages thinking of home life as a retreat into seclusion, rather than as a negotiating of a shared social space; the typical division of the house into separate bedrooms for each person (except for the shared bedroom for wife and husband) encourages thinking of oneself as an individual, destined to detachment from other family members and destined ultimately to occupying the shared bedroom with one's spouse when one marries and has children oneself; it encourages a sense of a private, proprietary relationship to land—"our" yard—in which one is at liberty to do as one desires, without interference; and, of course, it establishes an essential connection to a "mortgage," according to which one turns a substantial portion of one's earnings through the whole of one's working life to the acquiring of this home, and to the banking system that controls such mortgages and the interpretation of finance that that involves. And that relationship to a mortgage also implies that, though the dream of the "detached, single-family dwelling" is in principle intimately connected with the conception of the equal rights of single individuals, it is in fact a meaningful dream only for the members of a wealthy and privileged class, a class that also expects a neighborhood populated by similar people, and not by the members of excluded social and racial classes, who are kept out of sight in ghettos, in segregated neighborhoods or on reservations.

And something analogous is true when we step outside the house. Outside the family home, we in North America go to schools with indoor classrooms in which we sit facing forward in desks arranged in straight rows and columns; we travel down city streets that are arranged in neat, geometrical grids, all with clearly defined directions for the sanctioned movement of automobiles, ensuring a smooth, predictable flow of traffic; we live in cities that are themselves connected to other cities by a well-maintained, public system of roads, which can carry us to carefully defined and demarcated "parks" that offer us a controlled dose of "nature," and which collectively reflect a sense of the country (simultaneously a spatial, a political, and a linguistic identity) to which we belong. This is a world tightly controlled, in which participation is premised on the recognition of boundaries and the commitment to keep everything tidily in order. Both within and outside the home, then, we can see, in other words, how the very forms of the spatial articulation and interpretation that one accepts as "normal" in coming to live in this society involve a social and political vision that is of a piece with the individualism and "rationality" (the uniformity and mathematical regularity) of modern, bureaucratic liberalism.

When we thus consider the political dimensions of the articulation of our spatial environments, we can see that space as a phenomenon—space as we experience it—is very much not just an indifferent container, but, as sites of intersubjectivity, our environments cannot be separated from or defined in independence of the specific forms of intersubjective life they house. A form of social life and an interpretation of place are covariant, each inseparable from the other, and even the supposedly "neutral" inter-pretation of space as objective is not in fact intersubjectively neutral, but is the behavioral realization of a particular interpretation of humanity, a particular manner of *sugchōrein*. Our maturity involves adequately living up to the demands of our social co-inhabitation—becoming compe-tent in the navigation of this space, such that one "can" function as a participant—but it also involves, ultimately, owning up to the political responsibilities implicit within this *practice* of spatial co-inhabitation. We are always in fact taking a political stand (to employ again the very metaphor of spatial inhabitation), and it is incumbent upon us to rec-ognize this and, indeed, to be self-responsible and thus self-critical in our practices of inhabitation.

Our healthy adulthood will be embedded. We have seen that, on the one hand, our adulthood involves growing beyond our ecologically embedded singularity as a child and becoming a self-reliant, "stoic" adult, as we noted at the end of chapter 2. Inasmuch as our adulthood thus requires the development of a "tight," stoic sense of self-possessed agency, we depend on a world of spatially indifferent locations, a "cold" world indifferent to subjectivity, and the modern development of the institu-tional—military, scientific, economic, architectural—interpretation of space as thus indifferent is therefore a crucial development of our freedom, a crucial establishing of a collective inhabitation of space that enables our healthy maturation. This stoicism, consequently, is not a neutral condition but is an embedded social accomplishment: we can be such free, "stoic" individuals only through the intersubjective support of others, only through laws and customs that articulate an appropriate conception of the human person, and only in and through material environments that are themselves structured in terms of this vision of the person. Acknowledging this embeddedness, however, entails recognizing, on the other hand, that our adulthood is an interpersonal, social, and environmental phenomenon as much as it is a personal accomplishment, and that our becoming adult is thus a matter of establishing a living "dialogue" with appropriate personal, interpersonal, political, and spatial environments as much as it is a psychological matter of individual choice. As we also noted in chapter 2, however, these recognitions precisely challenge the adequacy of the "stoic" interpretation of the person, and thus the interpretation of space that supports our stoic self-identities, while necessary, is insufficient for accommodating the needs of our freedom, insufficient for housing our adulthood. Becoming adult involves our developing and participating in a world that reflects back to us our adulthood, and our healthy adulthood ultimately requires an articulation of space that goes beyond the "objective" and "public" conception of space that corresponds to stoic individuality; healthy adulthood depends on the articulation of a richer sense of "place."

The notion of space as indifferent is inadequate because our very ability to be in the world at all rests on the non-indifference of space: we are able to be selves experiencing a world only because space first and foremost offers itself to us as an accommodating home, a non-indifferent location that is precisely for ourselves. Space in this sense is experienced by us—livingly interpreted by us—as our proper place, as our natural environment. Most immediately, this necessary environment for our self-experience is found in our accommodating body, and then, beyond that, it is found in the bodily realities beyond our immediate organism with which the body couples as it becomes capable of progressively more sophisticated action. With the intersubjective developments of our agency, the accommodating character of our places becomes especially important. As we noted above, becoming adult involves "making a home of our own," but this homemaking is not simply the acquiring of a "single-family dwelling"; it is a matter, more broadly, of taking our place in the world, of coming to experience ourselves as active (co-)participants in the happening of the real. Like a road, space interpreted as indifferent is only meaningful—only livable—if it is contextualized by an engagement with the real that does not have this spatially indifferent character. We take a road from our place of settledness to our place of engagement and back again, but both of these places—where we settle and where we work—do not have the indifferent and alien character of the road. The road is important and effective, not in and of itself or absolutely, but relatively: it is important and effective because it mediates between the place of settlement and the place of engagement. Similarly, the indifferent sense of space in general is important to life not absolutely but precisely because it is relative to those domains that are important in and of themselves, the domains of the world lived as home and as the site of engagement.

Space and Aging

During early adulthood, it is understandable that one experiences the world as essentially a "road," because one experiences oneself as embarking on a (life's) journey and a life's work. Middle adult life, on the contrary, is precisely a situation in which one is no longer simply "going" somewhere, but one has, rather, become someone and one is thus established, settled. The spatial inhabitation definitive of adulthood involves the "objective" recognition of the impersonality and indifference of the world, but also involves the sense that one comes to belong in one's world. One cannot, in other words, simply inhabit space indifferently, but one must, instead, "lay down roots." One's growing sense of accomplishment—or just the quantitative passage of time in which one feels the desire to be "getting somewhere"—goes hand in hand with the a growing sense of one's embeddedness in a place: one's belonging somewhere (or the need for such, if one finds it lacking). We become "of" a place as we become more and more responsible to it and more responsible for it, and our maturing into a developed, self-responsible identity typically goes together with the reality—or at least the expectation—of holding a position of responsibility and authority in some place. We expect to be respected in our work environments, where our long history of involvement is known and is translated into the respect we have earned from our colleagues; we expect to have our lifestyle respected and protected in the neighborhood where we have built a life among and with our neighbors over decades; we expect to be honored for the years of work we have invested in our studies or in our contributions to the development of our field. Our aging brings with it the expectation precisely that we are making a home in the objective world to which we have answered as adults, and we expect the world to reflect back to us the reality of our accomplishment. And, indeed, even beyond the limits of our own lives, we hope for our worth to be remembered. Consequently, we also depend upon generations—upon a future that "takes the torch" from us. All of this is the natural expectation of our aging, the inherent trajectory of our embodied, adult intentionality.

The interpretation of public space as indifferent—the interpretation that defines and is enacted and enforced by the institutions of contemporary social and political life—does not, however, recognize the sheltering role that space plays in housing communities and hence the essential role that sheltering plays in allowing the healthy fulfillment of adult life. Indifferent space is instrumental space, and there are powerful forces in our society—forces of capitalism and technology—that have a strong vested interest in the instrumental interpretation of the world; human life, however, requires that we be able to interpret space as "home," as a site with which we are intimately and not just instrumentally involved, which means being able to treat spaces in their singularity and their particularity—"places"—as of intrinsic value. Consequently, we need our human world to be governed in a way that accommodates this interpretation of space, not a human world that is governed in such a way as to strip the world—strip space—of human qualities.

Thus, for example, we necessarily inhabit spaces as neighborhoods: our meaningful experience of "where" is rooted in the irreducible personal space of our singular bodies, but, because we are interpersonal beings, it is simultaneously rooted in the irreducible interpersonal space of our intimate communities, and we thus "live from" the local place where we belong. In our contemporary legal and political culture, however, such spaces are not maintained as neighborhoods. Governments responsible for urban planning—whether at the national, the regional, or the municipal level—commonly support the interests of business, and this generally means allowing urban space (or rural space) to be treated as a site for commerce. Prioritizing the economic interpretation of urban spaces, however, has a significant dehumanizing effect, especially evident in the context of growing old. Imagine, for example, the situation of an aging Italian immigrant man in "Little Italy" in Toronto who lived through the emergence of an Italian community over the space of sixty years, from the 1930s to the 1990s, only to experience its replacement by a generic, commercial "entertainment zone" for young, affluent professionals. Initially, such a man would have witnessed the development of the neighborhood inhabited by "his people" as the area grew in size and wealth and a flourishing Italian community developed, a community that was maintained even when many residents moved to other areas of the city. Around the age of retirement, however, this man would have witnessed the almost complete disappearance of the culture and the families he knew from the neighborhood as it was transformed into a "hip" center for nightlife, with the opening up of bars and nightclubs, and the transformation of traditional Italian shops and restaurants into businesses that catered to the tastes of young North American professionals. Such a man would feel his place taken from him: "This is not where I grew up; this is not where I live." Our human condition makes it clear that we need governments that protect our places in their role as homes, but attention to human issues of, for example, aging are typically not given significant weight in contemporary urban planning.

The distinctive needs of the aged to experience space as home is not just an issue at the level of the city, but can be seen in relation to the space of a whole culture—a country. Consider, for example, the experience of dislocation that characterizes the life of an aging Iranian woman who was one of the many who emigrated to Canada as a reaction against the Iranian revolution of 1979. Such emigrants, though opposed to the theocratic regime, nonetheless left their home in a Muslim culture to make a new home in Christian North America, often emigrating in the hope of offering their children a brighter future than they would have in Iran. As such a woman ages, she finds herself away from "her people" and "her culture" in a modern, liberal environment that maintains, among other things, a very different attitude toward family and toward the public appearance of women than did her Iranian culture; she experiences her children as belonging to this North American culture and thus to a different world than she does; and she has few of the cultural supports and points of reference that she grew up expecting. For this woman, as for the Italian man, but for different reasons, she experiences her world as not offering her the home that it should, and her aging is an experience of alienation and anxiety rather than an experience of belonging.

These problems that such immigrants experience in their environments are in fact simply magnified versions of the problems that aging in general brings with it. Though not all experience the loss of their home world as starkly as do such Italian and Iranian immigrants, all of us will experience our old age as a time when the world in which we made our home has changed. And, indeed, just as we have seen that our "being at home" is originally a matter of inhabiting our body and the primitive couplings of body and world, so does the transformation of the experience of home in old age touch on our embodiment as well as on our built environments. Organic deterioration in the bodies of the elderly leaves them unable to inhabit the "I can" of their younger life, and they lose their sense of being at home in their bodies. Indeed, just as amputees can sometimes experience a "phantom limb" where there is no actual limb present, so can the elderly live from a sense of their home in their bodies and in their worlds that is no longer actual such that they constantly search in the world for a support it will no longer offer. What such experiences reveal is the fundamental way in which our adult identities are inseparable from our sense of being at home in the world, and thus that the ways we make our homes are the ways we make ourselves.

Adulthood appropriately brings with it a political imperative to recognize the public character of space, and hence the experience of "indifferent" space that is integral to contemporary "globalism" is essential to the needs of adult life; but though this is a necessary condition of adult spatial co-inhabitation, it is not a sufficient condition. The political recognition of the equal rights of others to occupy space must be coupled with the political acknowledgment that indifferent space must be contextualized by inherently local space—by the inherent specificity of "place." The examples above of immigration and old age thus make explicit what is in fact implicit in all adult experience. Adulthood rightly brings the need to recognize "objective" space, but that is a one-sided adulthood; we must also recognize a continuing need for home.

This integral role of place, and the shaping of place, in the forming of our identities points, then, to the essential role that caring for our places has in the caring for our psychological health. Making a healthy adulthood involves making a healthy home in the world, and this means developing an intimate relationship with place—developing a place for intimacy. Inasmuch as our contemporary world lives with an ethos of institutionally recognizing space only as inherently indifferent, we have institutionalized a world that denies for all of us the possibility of being at home. We have a world that makes a space for the indifferent and instrumental relationships—for economics—but fails to make a place for people. Let us now look more fully at the roles of intimacy and economics in the making of an adult home, and at the essential role of government in this context.

Part III

The Content of Adult Life: Adult Occupations

4

Domains of Settlement
and Engagement

We have so far studied the way in which our adulthood is not something that simply befalls us through the simple passing of objective
time, but is an identity we must assume, an identity that is called for
by our characteristic development, but to which we must lend our own
agency. Becoming an adult, then, is something we do—it is a way of
living. Specifically, it is living in reality *as* reality: it is living in such a
way that our behavior and the developed engagement with the world
that it enacts is an effective acknowledgment both (1) of the self-defining
autonomy of the real, of its independent normative power, and (2) of
our own participative role in this reality: it is acknowledging both the
normative character of reality and our own responsibility to it. Finally,
it is the acknowledgement (3) of the autonomous demands of our own
finitude, which is to say, it is the need to answer to our own exclusive
reality, to be happy. These tasks—identifying the inherent normativity of
reality, being responsible to it, and being happy—are each infinite and
inexhaustible. These are not tasks that will be completed, but the horizons of meaning that are definitive for adult participation in the world.

Participating in the real in real terms is, effectively, not living under
protective illusion, not living in a way that requires someone else to
"buffer" us. The child lives under the care of others (adults) who "take
responsibility" (or, at least, who should do so) for addressing the world
on its own terms, while the child is free to play, and to live with the
comfortable presumption that its needs will be met. The adult perspective
is the one that recognizes it cannot simply live with this presumption,

but must "take responsibility" for itself. Though there is no one who can "complete" this task, and we will thus all ultimately be less than fully autonomous, the extent to which individuals accomplish this adult perspective varies greatly.

A relatively small number of individuals fail to embrace the adult perspective in an almost total way, and, though organically "mature" and old in years, they live as largely incompetent individuals, highly dependent on the care of others to keep them from suffering disaster at the hands of the impersonal and interpersonal world. Most individuals, however, accomplish at least a minimal degree of self-reliant competence in taking on responsibility for living their own lives. There is a great deal of difference, however—the difference, indeed, that largely marks out the fundamental character and quality of different lives—between those who accomplish merely this minimum and those who embrace the demands of reality more deeply. These differences have an impact, as should be expected, in the domains of responsibility and happiness, and these two as they pertain both to others and to oneself.

We have seen above that there is the answering to reality that is enacted in mathematics and natural science—the adulthood that results in one's being able to calculate expenses accurately or get out of the collapsing mineshaft successfully—as well as the answering to reality that is enacted in developing the virtues of courage and *sōphrosunē*—the adulthood that results in being able to choose one's own behavior successfully. Beyond the "indifferent" reality of the world of mathematics and mineshafts and the personal reality of one's individual "soul," however, there is the reality of the social and interpersonal world. It is this domain that is the primary arena for the meaningful pursuits that define the bulk of our lives—this is the domain in relation to which our competence in managing nature and our competence in managing our own soul primarily matter—and it is in this domain that we see the most important arenas for our developing adulthood. It is adulthood with respect to social and interpersonal matters that is ultimately most decisive for shaping our lives, it is in these arenas that we most fundamentally make an adult "home," and it is this arena of adulthood in which we see the most significant differences in the degree to which different individuals "own up to" the reality of their situations.

We studied above the way in which our establishing an experience of agency goes hand in hand with our establishing a sense of being "at home" in the world, and, in particular, we investigated the necessity of becoming at home with other people who reflect back to us a sense of our agency, our reality. This feedback happens at different levels, as we have seen: it happens at an explicitly interpersonal level, when we deal with particular others with whom we have personal dealings, such as family members and friends, and it happens at impersonal levels, through the vision of human life and identity that is projected in and through the social institutions that structure our living together. As we turn now to study the social and interpersonal dimensions of reality directly, we will see that there are in fact three basic domains, each essential and each distinct from the others, that always characterize our being-with-others (and that, therefore, are the essential dimensions to our *sugchōrein*). These three dimensions are intimacy, economics, and politics, which are realized most fundamentally as the family, the "market," and government. Now, to be adult is to participate in reality as reality, which means not to be managed by a caretaker, but to engage in the ultimate context oneself. Inasmuch as human reality is always defined by intimacy, economics, and politics, adulthood requires one to take up one's identity as participant in—as defined in terms of—family, market and state.

Intimacy: The Family

As children, we develop our sense of ourselves through developing a sense of belonging with our intimate others—our parents, grandparents, siblings, or whatever other primary caregivers and primary associates there are with whom we spend our lives—and a child's development is fundamentally crippled when such intimacy is absent in early life. This sense of belonging with specific others with whom we have developed personal relationships is not merely a matter for children, however. The sense that we belong with others who care about us personally—companions, friends, family—is perhaps the most essential component to our healthy and happy adulthood.

We very often think of ourselves as single individuals, and, indeed, to a large extent, establishing an independent individuality is the core of adulthood. In fact, however, we always occupy this position of self-possessed detachment only on the basis of intersubjective support. As individuals, we make our accomplishments in the broader public world, but we seek support and recognition from our intimate companions. Though we may well have concerns for the well-being of humanity, world justice, and other such global matters, we also characteristically have distinctive concerns for those specific individuals with whom we have established personal bonds. Ultimately, it is these local bonds that give us our "root" in the world, establishing the terms of our home—indeed, making the world "homey" for us, and not just vast and indifferent. This feature is particularly thematized in the experience of old age, when our lifelong companions, one by one, die, and we are left more and more alone in, and alienated from, a world in which we no longer experience ourselves as participating (and, hence, it is easily understandable why grandchildren can give one a sense of a vicarious link with the future, a continuing relevance or participation in the world). The need for a sense of interpersonal belonging is an essential dimension of meaning in human life, and living as an adult entails responding to this essential dimension of meaning and answering to the need to make an interpersonal home.

Adulthood is living in reality as reality, and, inasmuch as our reality is thus inherently interpersonal, adulthood involves a behavioral recognition of this. Adopting an adult perspective, that is, involves recognizing that one must take up one's position in the domain of interpersonal relationships, establishing through companionship an interpersonal home. It is certainly possible to be organically mature and of adult age, but to live in denial of the need to cultivate an interpersonal home: though "quantitatively" an adult, "qualitatively" we can maintain an adolescent relationship to matters of companionship.

Sexuality and Adolescence

In the modern Western world, at least, it is common in adolescence to experience the wonder and thrill of establishing intimate and erotic relationships with others. On the one hand, we here experience our desire to be with others; simultaneously, though, this adolescent erotic life can be very much an expression of our desire to be independent and individual. Our establishing of erotic relationships does indeed affirm our enthusiasm for our partners, but it is often more fundamentally our individuality that we affirm by showing ourselves to be independently able—able, independent of the family—to develop new relationships.

"Intimate relations with specific others" thus opens up for us as a field, a domain of reality that we can explore and in which we can develop a distinct history and identity, rather as a geographical domain opens up to a traveler or a disciplinary domain opens up to a student. Societies more rooted in tradition than the modern West often enforce what sociologists call "narrow socialization," in which the life path of individuals is substantially decided without their input, and in which young individuals thus find themselves "practicing" the occupations of their adult lives from a relatively early age. This is true of personal relationships as well as of matters of work, and in such societies individuals typically find themselves committed to marriage from an early age. In such social circumstances, individuals can feel that their participation in the new field of "intimate relations with specific others" is stifled and truncated, that they have had no chance to "explore" or "experiment" and to establish their own relationship to this field. Whereas in this traditional situation, one can feel that one's exploration has stopped as soon as it has started, in the contemporary Western situation adolescents can typically dwell in the experience of "beginning," and can experience the thrill and the opening of possibilities that comes with launching a new relationship without automatically embracing the commitment to make a home in that relationship. One can imagine many reasons why this "noncommittal" relationship to relationships is valuable and healthy. Like virtually any other domain of reality, the domain of interpersonal relations has a nature of its own, and it takes time and practice to develop an insightful and powerful engagement with its complexities, needs, possibilities, and implications. For the purpose of understanding adulthood, however, we must also consider what the "price" of such "experimentation" is.

We have seen above the distinct character of interpersonal relations: the space of interpersonal life is a space made available only through and only as the collaboration of individual wills. Though the many media of advertising—and the ubiquitous presence of pornography—work hard to convince us that sexuality is simply a matter of the manipulation of a body for the sake of pleasurable feelings, it is important for us to recognize, on the contrary, that sexuality is fundamentally a matter of engaging with the subjectivity of another, that is, it is the experience of having one's perspective "touched" by another perspective. Consequently, in order to have sexual experience, we necessarily rely upon another: the reality of another person's perspective is required for, and presumed in, the possibility of our own sexual experience. For this reason, we can ask of our sexual practices, "Is the way I undertake this practice honestly responsive to its dependence upon another person?" Non-adult experience is experience that does not "own up" to its own reality, and sexual experience that does not adequately acknowledge its dependence upon another person is an example of such non-adult, or immature, experience. This suggests two ways in which we can live out our adolescent sexuality in ultimately unsatisfactory ways.

In sexual situations, one is in fact engaging with the will of another, but one can act in such a way as to deny or disrespect this, and this is the first way in which one can mishandle one's sexuality. Rape is the paradigmatic example of this sort of wrongly enacted sexuality, for the attempt to force sexual interaction is the attempt to deny the essentiality of the other's consent, that is, it is to pursue an inherently interpersonal relationship with the dishonest (and performatively contradictory) interpretation that one is not interacting with another subject. Such sexual violence is evident at less manifest levels too, however. In relationships that are manifestly relations of mutual consent, one partner can nonetheless relate to the other in a way that is degrading, humiliating, dismissive, belittling, and so on. We can take up our interpersonal situations with a project of dominating or mastering the other (perhaps, indeed, as a defensive response to experiencing the threatening character of the uncontrollable nature of the other's will), implicitly disempowering the other's will even as we explicitly acknowledge its legitimacy. Such practices of domination, furthermore, are often part of a paired practice in which the other partner enacts a stance of submission, and so we should note that there is an equally dishonest set of practices in which one partner worships, fawns upon, or otherwise excessively emphasizes the superiority of the other partner; while it is importantly true that individuals who adopt a subordinate role in a degrading or oppressive relationship commonly do so under duress, it is also true that such a submissive role can be a role autonomously enacted by an individual, and this, too, is a dishonest approach to relationships that unfairly saddles the other partner with an unhealthy role projected upon her, him, or them. All such practices—of domination, submission, or other forms of inequality of status—are fundamentally unhealthy and irresponsible practices of interpersonal relating because they do not honestly own up to the inherent demands of enacting an experience of shared subjectivity. One demand of adulthood, then, is that we learn how to enact our sexual, interpersonal relationships in a way that is honest in its appreciation of the subjectivity of the other with whom we are related. (Indeed, it is precisely the need to develop such a mature relationship to sexuality that is ultimately facilitated by a culture that treats adolescence as a time to learn how to handle interpersonal life through a graduated practice of involvement with it, though this culture may equally encourage the opposite.)

Unequal treatment of one's partner is one way in which we can fail to "own up" to the interpersonal domain upon which we depend. There is also a second way in which we can draw resources from this interpersonal domain without acting in a way that does justice to that domain. Basically, we can draw upon the "nutrition" of this field without recognizing that we depend upon it, falsely thinking, for example, that we are individually self-sufficient, or, again, we can underappreciate what this field requires in order to be cultivated in a healthy way.

In the case of falsely thinking ourselves to be individually self-sufficient, we can, for example, treat romantic life as simply a pleasant diversion. In taking up our interpersonal relationships in this way, we can fail to cultivate, for ourselves or for our companions, the healthy interpersonal life we need by drawing from our relationships only short-term pleasures. By failing to enter into those relationships with the care and commitment necessary to make something long-lasting, we can take the seeds of intimacy and subvert their growth, producing, ultimately, a sterile interpersonal field.

In the case of underappreciating the requirements of the field of interpersonal life, we can actually live in a way that openly and explicitly recognizes the importance of interpersonal life, but we may be immature in how we handle its needs. With the examples of being stuck in the snow or being trapped in the mineshaft, we saw the way in which we are able to participate "beyond our means" in nature, that is, we can participate in nature (simply by traveling along the road or through the mineshaft) in a way that can involve us in situations we are not competent to handle and our maturity involves learning how to handle the demands of this reality in which we participate. We can similarly participate in interpersonal life "beyond our means." We can, that is, develop relationships with others that are meaningful and important without ourselves being competent to care for these relationships or to cope with the various developments that ensue within these relationships. Like objective nature, subjective interpersonal life presents us with resources and demands that we must learn how to navigate. Let us consider what it takes to be mature in handling the demands of interpersonal life.

Intimate Relationships

Interpersonal life entices us with the allure of exciting new connections, the interest of seeing into someone else's life, and the thrill of the risk of linking one's experience with another's whose actions cannot be predicted. Another person is initially an unknown: precisely because the other is a perspective, the nature of that other cannot be known from the outside—we can get to know the other person only with that other person's help. When we are attracted to another person, it is commonly this "unknown" that is attractive: we are drawn by the promise of what lies outside our grasp, by the appearance of a reality in which we are not yet involved. Entering into a concrete relationship with another, however, typically involves transforming this very character that was initially appealing to us.

Though in important ways another person with whom we are involved will always remain "other," and thus "unknown," to us, it is nonetheless normally the case that becoming involved with another literally amounts to "getting to know" that person. The other initially appears to us as the possibility of a reality in which we do not yet participate, but our engagement with that person transforms that possibility into actuality, and we come to learn the actual character of that formerly unknown reality. Entering into a relationship, then, can be fulfilling or disappointing—or both—inasmuch as the actual is both more and less than the possible: more, in that the actual "really is" something, whereas the possible is only a nebulous promise waiting for its realization in the actual; less, in that the real is "only this," always underrealizing what was possible.

When we approach another solely as the unknown possibility of another world, we are largely free to imagine whatever we like within that world (and, indeed, people can often feel, when they begin relationships, that they are negotiating with the other person's projections of whom they wanted or whom they expected). It is a challenge to measure up to the actuality of another person, in contrast to the mere imagination of another, which we can generate or change as we like, without resistance. For that reason, people can often feel antagonistic to the relationships they develop, either becoming resentful of the other person for not conforming to their imaginations, or becoming overwhelmed by the demands of the other's actuality, or in general being disappointed by the disappearance of the "thrill" of discovery and its replacement by the predictability that comes with familiarity. For reasons such as these, one can develop a practice of repeatedly starting new relationships, but withdrawing from them once they are no longer new.

While it makes sense that people might initially have such a response to relationships, reveling in the thrill of the "new" and turning away from the work of developing a concrete relationship with the actual, this is not ultimately a mature way to engage with relationships, and this for two related reasons, one negative and one positive. The negative reason is that what makes possible those experiences of thrilling beginnings is in each case the reality of the other person. Implicitly, one depends upon the support of the other in order to indulge in the pleasure of this experience, and it is ultimately a matter of exploitation to use the other to produce results without caring for the reality of that other. The other person intrinsically calls to be treated as an end in her-, him-, or themself, and not solely as a means to one's own pleasure, but to treat the other as an end is to hold oneself accountable to answering to that other's needs. The adult engagement with relationships, in other words, must "own up" to its interpersonal dependence, and embrace the demands of responsibility and care that come with entering into a relationship with another person. Negatively, then, the exclusive pursuit of new beginnings is immature because it is exploitative. Positively, it is immature because it does not allow partaking in the transformative richness of experience that comes through responsibly and caringly developing interpersonal relationships.

Through developing relationships of mutual caring, in which we transform our own practices of living to accommodate the practices of another and thereby establish a kind of shared, interpersonal "equilibrium," we enter into the most intimate, the most fulfilling, and the most distinctively human domain of experience. It is through the cultivation of intimate bonds that we practice "being there together" in the way that touches us most fully and immediately. The threshold of interpersonal life is a domain of excitement, possibility, and risk; crossing this threshold opens up for us the field of shared experience, the field of companionship, the field of love, the field of establishing a home with another.

Making a Home

A home is not an optional or detachable component of our existence but is, rather, the context for and fabric of the ongoing enactment of our experience: it is part of who we are. In developing a home with another person, one is not, then, simply adding a feature to one's existing life; on the contrary, one is entering into a new, shared identity. Developing intimate relationships, in other words, is personally transformative. Whereas, as we noted in our discussion of adolescent relationships, one is typically initially attracted by something superficial about another person that is at best a hint of the other's reality, the development of adult intimacy becomes an embrace of the substance of the other person and the subsequent sharing of one's life with that of another becomes the very platform and character of one's ongoing life. Indeed, unlike adolescent relationships that one sheds with the season, as it were, adult intimacy can never be shed: one can change one's relationship to one's established relationships—in divorce, for example—but one cannot change the fact that they have become one's reality.

This shared reality of intimate life is the experience of commitment. One gives one's life to another, adopting a sense that the needs and the concerns of the other will be one's own. Initially, this is a matter of promise: as one enters into such a relationship, one hopes and imagines that it will continue and that it will become a truly shared reality, but this promise needs to be carried out and this, like aging, is both a quantitative matter of the investment of time and a qualitative matter of actually coming to share a way of life with another. Indeed, though, like aging, it is to a certain extent automatic that two people will grow together simply by virtue of living together for a long time (hence the "success" of traditional, arranged marriages), the deeper realities of true intimacy will come only if the individuals involved are reasonably compatible in their manners of existing and if they actually try—are committed—to live in a unified, mutually sympathetic fashion. When we try, though, we do learn about each other, and this is true both reflectively—that is, we explicitly notice things important about ourselves and each other—and, more importantly, behaviorally—that is, we gradually "gear into" each other through our continued practice of *sugchōrein*. And thus, together, we establish a reality where each of us feels we belong—and, inasmuch as each of us belongs there, each of us also belongs to it. In this way, making a home with another is a matter of giving away our exclusive, singular autonomy and becoming part of something bigger.

Developing such an intimate co-inhabitation is deeply fulfilling to our most constitutive human needs for companionship, collaboration, and co-inhabitation and, consequently, for many people throughout history and in many cultures today, the family defines the primary sphere of meaningful life. For many people, this shared life with another—marriage—defines "what life is about," and provides the context for other life activities, which themselves serve as cultivations and enrichments of this shared life. Thus, one might recognize the need for engaging in gainful employment, paying taxes, and obeying laws, but these matters of economic and political life are experienced and interpreted as the necessary contextualizing conditions that enable one's household life. Similarly, one will deal ongoingly with many people beyond one's primary partner, but these, again, are experienced and interpreted in terms of that primary relationship: other relationships that run the range from intimate and substantial to pleasant but instrumental—friendships—are organized into this shared life with another in such a way that those relationships embellish and enhance the shared reality one has with another but do not challenge the defining centrality of the primary relationship. And this centrality of the primary relationship is often underlined by embracing it as a platform for "having a family," that is, for raising children. In thus "having a family of one's own," a couple enriches and deepens its self-defined "world," solidifying and developing the reality of the bond that has come to define, for each, "who" they really are.

The raising of children is itself a unique and profound domain of human fulfillment. Children begin in utter dependence upon their parents for the fulfillment of their needs, the most serious of which, as we have noted above, is precisely the need for supportive intimacy. Embracing the reality of family life is for many the opportunity to experience the fulfillment of taking on this great responsibility of nurturing the life of another. In further contrast, then, to the relatively superficial relationships of adolescent life, the marriage that ushers in children becomes one of the very deepest experiences of responsibility. Indeed, whenever one enters into intimate life—in adolescent sexual experiences or in a serious romance—one is engaged with another person and one's actions are thus actions on behalf of that other, whether or not one acknowledges that responsibility; in giving birth to a child, however, this "acting on behalf" is total. The activity of giving birth to another brings into being that other as a vulnerable, moral being, and thus having children is a matter of giving birth to responsibility, so to speak. For this reason, having children, perhaps even beyond the experience of marrying as such, can appear to be the ultimate fulfillment for persons, a responsibility that uniquely attaches to a couple, inasmuch as only a couple is able to give birth to a child. The experience of giving birth to and raising children is thus a powerful reason for interpreting family life as the primary domain of human happiness and fulfillment.

This interpretation of one's family as the ultimate goal of adult life is itself an interpretation of human life that can be a culturally enforced value and not simply an individual perspective. In ancient Greek culture, the notion of the *polis*—the city or the state—was pointedly cultivated in opposition to the *oikos* or household, and in our modern Western culture we encourage the political and cultural development of individuality apart from family identity, but in many other cultures past and present, these are not the definitive values. Indeed, in many cultures, these Greek and Western values can seem alienating and dehumanizing. Thus, in ancient Vedic culture from around 3000 BC, for example, the household was assumed to be the fundamental unit of human life and this basic value still strongly colors the contemporary culture of India that remains significantly attached to these Vedic roots. Similarly, the family was the presumed unit of human life in the Arab world in which Islam first arose in the 600s AD, and it preserves much of its presumed, primary status in contemporary Muslim culture around the world. Again, the principles attributed to Confucius (K'ung-fu-tzu) express the similar commitment to the primacy of the family in ancient China, and these values continue to be of substantial import in contemporary Chinese culture. Indeed, in virtually all the world's cultures that retain strong roots in what anthropologists call "traditional societies," the family is generally taken to be the primary platform for any developed human life, and individuals apart from their families are thus viewed as "abstractions," that is, the individual is only a partial human reality that is completed and fulfilled only in family life. And, even in the more individualist, Western culture, the notion of "family values" continues to be commonly appealed to (both sincerely and rhetorically) when matters of public policy are discussed.

Such a commitment to the family involves the recognition by the family members themselves of the importance of generations, that is, the embrace of the primacy of the family involves the embrace of the "naturalness" and propriety of the distinct roles of parent and child, for example, and also of ancestors and descendants, the "rules" of which are expressly articulated, for example, in Confucianism, or in what is commonly identified as the fifth of the "Ten Commandments" of the Hebrew scriptures (Exodus 20:1–21, Deuteronomy 5:1–23), "Honor thy father and thy mother." The fundamental idea here is powerfully expressed in the Catechism of the Catholic Church:

> The family is the *original cell of social life*. It is the natural society in which husband and wife are called to give themselves in love and in the gift of life. Authority, stability, and a life of relationships within the family constitute the foundations for freedom, security, and fraternity within society. The family is the community in which, from childhood, one can learn moral values, begin to honour God, and make good use of freedom. Family life is an initiation into life in society. (*Catechism of the Catholic Church*, §2207)

We noted above that entering into a substantial intimate relationship is a matter of finding one's place in a reality that is bigger than oneself, and embracing this familial interpretation of one's experience means finding one's place in the material and interpersonal realities of immediate and extended family, with all of the responsibilities toward other members and toward the family property that come with that and, correspondingly, all of the rewards: children in such cultures are generally "brought up" into such a world of family values, and their acceptance of their subordinate status with its attendant responsibilities for working within and caring for the family's world will become, in their adulthood, the assumption of a position of authority and the inheritance of the family's wealth. Whether or not this is the dominant system of values expressed in a culture, it is a very common set of values adopted by individuals in any culture at any time in history.

This experience of family membership is undeniably a profound reality in human life in general and thus defines an essential terrain with which anyone must contend in becoming an adult, but the commitment to family life as the primary domain of our fulfillment is an interpretation and it is easily possible to live one's life otherwise. There is an adolescent attitude toward relationships that has not yet appreciated the real weight of intimacy and companionship, but rejections of the primacy of family life are not limited to this immature perspective. It is very much possible to appreciate the weight of our needs for substantial relationships with intimate others without accepting that this requires marriage in the traditional sense or the embrace of the extended family with all of its organizing principles and norms.

Nontraditional Relationships

Rather than assuming the simple opposition of "spouse versus friend," for example, an individual can develop rich and varied intimate relationships with a number of different individuals such that no one of those is strictly a unique life partner, while all are "more than just friends," in that these interpersonal relationships all reflect a depth of commitment that exceeds the easy but alienating presumption of clear limitation that is typically involved in the notion of friendship. Aristotle, in the *Nicomachean Ethics*, distinguishes three types of friendship—friendships of pleasure, of utility, and of virtue (*Nicomachean Ethics* VIII.3)—and his distinction can help us to understand this point.

We commonly populate the world beyond our intimate romantic life with "friends" with whom we interact either because their company is "fun" or because our involvement with them is in some way useful or important to the ongoing enactment of our projects. Friends of both sorts—of pleasure and of utility—are easy to keep at a distance precisely because they have not impinged upon the intimate sphere of our lives. And, indeed, these friendships typically come and go over time, with no significant change to one's life. We typically have some true friendships, though—friendships of virtue—and these are friendships based on each friend's recognition of and care for the goodness of the other person, a commitment to who that other person is. These are friendships that we experience as more important, more long-lasting, and more defining of ourselves.

Such friendships of virtue, though, because they are substantial and intimate, precisely demand—like romantic partnerships—to be embraced on their own terms, that is, we must give ourselves over to them if we are to be true to them. But the more honest we are about the integrity and weight of these friendships of virtue, the less are we able to distinguish them from romantic relationships and thus to hold them apart emotionally and practically from the intimate core of our lives. Thus, in fact, even many who interpret themselves as living by the traditional norms of married, family life in fact demonstrate otherwise inasmuch as they live from "divided loyalties," so to speak, just in the richness of their embrace of deep, meaningful friendships with significant others (and, indeed, to some significant extent this is put on display just in the fact of normal parental intimacy with children, as the emotional and behavioral lives of the parents become invested uniquely and deeply in the lives of individual children, drawing their focus away from their original and exclusive bond as a couple). It is possible, however, to be honest about this reality, and to embrace a life of romance and companionship that accepts this inescapable multiplicity of commitment that informs a healthy interpersonal life. This, then, is not an adolescent blindness to the reality of interpersonal commitment but, on the contrary, an adult acknowledgment of its nonformulaic complexity.

Inasmuch as engaging with another intimately amounts to allowing oneself to be transformed by the unique demands of the life of another, any truly intimate bond will have a self-defined shape, whether it is contained within the pattern of monogamous family life or whether it is more interpersonally open-ended. Thus, again, the model of traditional marriage is somewhat disingenuous to the extent that it portrays the fulfilling form of interpersonal intimacy to be specifiable "from the outside." This is pointedly put on display in relationships that "formally" are marriages, but that interpersonally are situations of mutual alienation. In other words, while traditional family life can be very fulfilling and while the simple fact of enduring proximity will typically bring about some meaningful intimacy between partners, it is nonetheless true that the simple fact that one's life corresponds outwardly to the format of traditional marriage is no guarantee that one has established any sort of intimate bond whatsoever. If one, then, is truly to embrace the demands of interpersonal intimacy, the true form of one's interpersonal life cannot be specified in advance, either in relationship to a single person who is one's life partner or in relationship to multiple others who are intimate companions. And this recognition of the unique demands that each individual brings to the domain of intimacy also requires us to recognize that not all individuals will experience traditional family life as desirable. For some individuals, living alone is not a matter of loneliness or lack of interpersonal opportunity but is the most satisfying material arrangement. Such persons, like all persons, have a profound need for intimacy and companionship, but fulfilling that need does not have to take the material form of sharing a bedroom or a roof with some particular other or others. Without denying the substantial import of intimate interpersonal commitment, then, fulfilling adult relationships can take forms that are both more and less than the form of traditional marriage and family life.

And these nontraditional forms of intimate life are also paralleled by nontraditional forms of bearing and raising children, the other central dimension of family life. There have, of course, always been single parents as a consequence of "illegitimate" pregnancy, untimely death of a spouse, and so on, and the social imperative to care for "widows and orphans" has been a standard dimension of traditional societies that advocate the primacy of the family. Single parenthood, however, need not be thought of as a lesser or unsuccessful situation of child rearing, but may very well be a deliberate and fulfilling way of life. Modern institutions for organizing the adoption of unwanted or orphaned children and modern medical technologies for facilitating pregnancy make it possible for the normal existence of nontraditional families—single parents, same-sex couples with children, and so on—thereby offering ways of fulfilling the desire for those forms of intimacy and responsibility, which have traditionally been reserved for monogamous heterosexual couples, that do not require embracing those traditional family values.

These challenges to that interpretation of our lives that insists on the primacy of traditional family relationships all emerge from within the domain of intimacy, that is, they are ways in which our actual experience of the needs of intimacy reveals the limitations of the traditional forms we have imposed on our attempts to address those needs. Challenges to this traditional interpretation of our lives also come from other sectors of our experience as well. While intimacy is a crucial dimension of our fulfillment, it is not the only dimension of our fulfillment, and there are other ways that we interpret our lives that draw attention to these other essential dimensions and domains of experience.

Economics: The Market

Though our reality as subjects is not exhausted by our being organic bodies, it is nonetheless the case that it is only as organic bodies that we exist as subjects. For that reason, our ability to be subjects is inherently dependent upon our ability to satisfy the basic material needs of life. As Marx writes, near the beginning of his *German Ideology* (Part I, 181), "men must be in a position to live in order to be able to 'make history.'" The simple fact of one's continued existence as a subject depends upon one's relating bodily to the organic world in such a way as to appropriate from this world, common to all, something that will be used exclusively for oneself. Because the maintenance and care for our subjectivity depends upon the maintenance and care for our body, our lives will always be intertwined with relations of bodily appropriation of nature; because that nature is the same nature with which all subjects must engage in such bodily appropriation, this caring for our material needs will always implicate us in negotiations with others who, metaphysically, have exactly equal "rights" to this natural world. Our reality, then, is inherently "economic," and our adulthood will involve developing a responsible relationship to this facet of our reality.

In general, our adulthood will involve taking responsibility for our own economic well-being and, likely, for that of our dependents as well (whether children, parents, spouse, or others). To deny the need to embrace the demands of appropriation is fundamentally unrealistic—it is a denial that one is a body—and it is fundamentally immature to live in denial of the complex development and structure of the social forms in which this economic reality is presented to us. To own up to our economic nature, we must accept to make our way within the world by negotiating the demands of contemporary economic life.

The imperative of this economic reality is reflected in the familiar image of parents telling their lackadaisical teenage daughter or son that she or he needs to "enter the real world" and "get a job." This imperative to "get a job" does, indeed, seem like the familiar mark of adulthood. Getting a job is opposed to a number of immature possibilities. It is opposed to continued dependency on the financial support of one's parents. It is opposed to living by theft, a parasitical exploitation of the work of others, powerfully dramatized as a lifestyle, for example, by the famous American armed robbers Bonnie Parker and Clyde Barrow. It is opposed to the life of destitution faced by those who live, unemployed, on the street. It is opposed to an unfocused drifting between temporary employments that do no more than satisfy the immediate needs of the day. The imperative to get a job is the imperative to adopt a life-practice of caring for one's long-term economic needs, accepting that work will be a substantial and essential dimension of life and committing oneself to a long-term program of gainful employment.

There is, then, something certainly adult about getting a job. And, indeed, being able to get—and hold—a job is a practice that itself requires many adult skills, for one must be consistent in arriving on time, have the endurance to carry through a full day's work, be able competently to carry out the required tasks, be able to take and follow instruction and do so with an appropriately cooperative demeanor, and so on. Such an approach to economic participation, however, is only a minimal embrace of the demands of adulthood. Finding employment in this way typically means integrating oneself into the already established system of economic life by finding the already established position into which one can insert oneself. In such a situation, one takes for granted the existing terms of the economic world and the possibilities it offers, whereas it is possible to be more radical in one's embracing of one's economic reality.

One can "make a living," not by "getting a job," but by creatively making one's own way into and through the realities of economic life. Whereas most people will be content to accept one of the ready-made options presented by various already established economic enterprises— getting a job as a cashier at a department store, as a teller at the bank, as a driver for a trucking company, as a nurse at the hospital, as a salesperson at an insurance agency, as a biologist at the distillery, as a chemist at the pharmaceutical company, as the receptionist at the local real estate office, as an accountant at a medical office, or as a programmer at an advertising firm, and so on—those economic enterprises themselves were not brought into being by this same approach. Those economic enterprises, on the contrary, were brought into being by entrepreneurs who sought to define for themselves a path into economic participation. Those who try independently to "make their own way" through economic life engage with this domain more actively than those who rely upon others to provide them with work opportunities, and this more direct participation brings with it greater vulnerability than does the "buffered" route, which counts on the security provided by others who manage that direct economic engagement.

Reliance upon others to construct a functioning economic domain for us is both a boon and a risk. It is a boon because it exempts us from the challenges of struggling directly with the demands of the economic world: we can do the work if given the job, but someone else will be responsible for ensuring that there is a job available for us. We have seen above that we are always establishing habits that, by accomplishing for us a comfortable relationship to some sector of our experience, allow us to disregard the demands of that sector and focus our attention elsewhere. Having others define our economic world for us similarly releases us from the challenging demands of struggling with the marketplace, as someone who opens a new restaurant, for example, might find her whole waking life for years to be devoted to making the enterprise succeed. The boon, then, of having someone else run our economic affairs for us is that we can focus our energies on other matters that we care about, such as, for example, the family that we discussed above. The risk of such an approach to economics, however, is that we will not be well cared for by those who shape our economic reality.

Early in Plato's *Republic*, Socrates asks his aging interlocutor Cephalus whether he has earned or inherited his wealth, noting that, in his own experience, those who earn their wealth are more attuned to the need to care for it, whereas those who have inherited it tend to spend it freely without any real sense of its weight or worth (*Republic*, I.330c). We can see a similar distinction between earning and inheriting in relationship to our experiences of comfortably taking it for granted that some sector of our experience is "under control." When we develop a habit, we have "earned" a relationship to some aspect of reality, and we can now live on the fruits of that initial labor. When we allow our parents to care for our needs, however, we have not earned through our own efforts what they deliver to us, but have rather "inherited" it, and we are reliant upon results that we did not and could not achieve for ourselves. The way in which we comfortably rely upon the successful functioning of our economic life when we count on others to supply us with "job opportunities" is an example of the second kind of reliance: we inherit our economic position from others, without ourselves being capable of establishing on our own such an economic reality for ourselves.

One of the most troubling dimensions of the phenomenon of contemporary adult life is this childish approach that most "adults" have to economics. We all grow up in a world in which there is private property, there are banks, there is money, there are trade agreements, taxes, labor unions, insurance companies, and stockmarkets, and we take these for granted as normal and regular structures of reality, without truly understanding what they are: we do not even ask (let alone answer!) where they come from, how they work, or whether they are good. Indeed, even the enterprising individuals or collectives that "make their own way" by establishing their own businesses are still participating according to the received parameters of the economic world and, though more self-active than those who get their jobs "off the rack," so to speak, they are still operating within and relying upon the terms of the economic system without taking up those terms in their own right and establishing for themselves what is happening in economics, what is happening in one of the most basic and formative dimensions of their own and everyone else's lives. As we turn now to study the basic meaning of contemporary economics, we will see that it is the phenomenon of money in particular that we must understand, and understanding this will require us to work through a number of dimensions of contemporary government and banking in some detail. Before we get to this point, though, we must first grasp the first principles of economic life.

The Division of Labor

Economic activity is, of course, as old as human life, inasmuch as humans have always had to interact with others in appropriating aspects of the shared world to satisfy the material needs of their lives. Ibn Khaldûn's *Muqaddimah* (1377), Adam Smith's *An Inquiry into the Nature and Causes of the Wealth of Nations* (1776) and Karl Marx's *Capital: Critique of Political Economy* (1867) study thoroughly and effectively the history of human economic practice and its role in forming the character of modern life. Perhaps the most important observation that each of these thinkers makes is that economic life is largely a collective affair, that is, it is societies that are the basic "agents" who grapple with the demands of economics, rather than individuals: individuals, that is, deal with their economic well-being by participating in an economic system, and that system is an integrated network of differentiated activities, shaped historically and distributed across society. We deal with our economic needs in a systematic way, and *I* am able to deal with my own economic needs only on the terms established for me (or others like me) by this system.

This notion that "we" deal with "our" economic needs is the basic sense of what Smith and Marx refer to as the "division of labor." Coping with the world so as to meet the material demands of living has always been a collective affair: indeed, the very fact that we refer to "hunting and gathering societies" or "agricultural societies" points to the way in which the very form of life of a society is shaped by its collective mode of defining and addressing its economic needs. In hunting societies, such as the ancient whale-hunting society of the Thule Inuit or the more recent societies of the Plains Indians of North America, hunting and gathering are socially shared tasks producing the socially shared "wealth" of food and materials for clothing, tools, and so on, and, corresponding to the practical demands of carrying out such a life, these societies tend to be small and family-based, and, in hunting societies at least, there is typically a division of labor between those who hunt and those who care for domestic matters, a division that typically falls along gender lines. In pastoralist ("shepherding") societies such as the Maasai (Ilmaasae) of

East Africa or the ancient Hebrews in which the tasks and the fruits of herding are typically shared, the life of the society is typically based upon the demands of the herd, and these societies, too, thus tend to be small and family-based. More sophisticated agricultural societies, by collectively harnessing the powers of the earth, began to develop societies in which substantial accumulation of wealth first became a meaningful possibility (a possibility that, in turn, gave rise to the possibilities of trade and, later, the industrialization and finance that define modern economies). In these societies, a settled life is both possible and required, unlike hunting and gathering or pastoral societies, which tend to be nomadic, and social structure tends to emerge on the basis of the issues that arise surrounding ownership of land; further, a greater economic differentiation emerges, as the need to farm is complemented by the need for the manufacture of tools and, commonly, by the need for trade. In all such situations, individuals do not "fend for themselves" against a challenging nature, but take on distinct roles—hunting, cultivating the crops, making tools, caring for the household, managing the religious affairs—each of which alone would not satisfy all the needs of life, but which, cooperatively and collectively, produce a standard of living that is higher overall than the sum of individuals each operating singly could accomplish. The satisfying of the material needs of human life has always been a collective endeavor in which social groups have systematically pursued an economic course in which individuals play small, specialized parts in the production of the social wealth, and in which individuals survive on the portion of the overall wealth of the society as it is distributed (not necessarily equally or fairly) to the members of that society. In short, as economic beings we are always interdependent: our work is effective only because of its integration into a larger economic system that defines a role in which that work is useful, and we have resources for our own personal, private consumption only because of the socially enacted distribution of wealth that allots some portion of the social product to us. We can neither produce nor acquire on our own: our participation in the economic system, from start to finish, is mediated by the social system of production and distribution that makes our economic activity meaningful.

This interdependency is not just a theoretical assessment of economic life, but defines one of our most basic activities: what Adam Smith identified as our "propensity to truck, barter, and exchange one thing for another" (*Wealth of Nations*, Book I, ch. 2). Smith writes further,

Whether this propensity be one of those original principles in human nature of which no further account can be given; or whether, as seems more probably, it be the necessary consequence of the faculties of reason and speech, it belongs not to our present subject to inquire. It is common to all men, and to be found in no other race of animals, which seem to know neither this nor any other species of contracts.

Participating in exchange—the basic experience of economic interdependence—is definitive of our human condition and, as Smith suggests, this is not arbitrarily so, but is of a piece with our being, as Aristotle says, "animals with *logos*": beings who realize their nature by participating in social practices of "taking account," by cooperatively communicating about how we will evaluate and measure things with each other and ourselves with other things. Because of the division of labor—because of the fact that we each perform specialized tasks—we must exchange the fruits of our labor for the fruits of others' labor, where I receive your support of my needs in exchange for my support of yours. Though we often think of exchange as the buying and selling of goods in the market, this is in fact a rather specialized form of the more basic and universal experience of the sharing of enterprise, an activity of economic co-dependence that we cannot realistically live without.

Though in fact the capacities for economic accomplishment are thus socially organized, it is individuals who must consume, and individuals thus find themselves in the situation of having to "make a living" by personally taking up the economic opportunities afforded by their situations, and negotiating and thus actualizing the relationships of interdependence that define them through actual processes of labor and exchange. In other words, the basic resources individuals have for economic achievement are the resources that can be commanded through their labor and the capacities those resources give them for exchange with others. Let us consider these two processes of labor and exchange.

Labor

The essence of our economic condition is that we must work in order to exist, and this is true with regard to satisfying the minimal needs of our organic existence, but also with regard to satisfying deeper needs of our subjectivity. Through work, we come to feel at home in our bodies, learning to live from our hands, shoulders, and back and, simultaneously, we learn to live in the material world, cultivating an intimacy with wood, metal, and soil. Through work, we come to feel at home with others as we learn the joy, the frustration, and the power of cooperation. Work, far from simply being the burden that many experience it as being, is in principle an inherently fulfilling human practice, a practice through which we come to be meaningfully at home in our natural, bodily, and interhuman world. Beyond these relatively immediate rewards of work, our work as adults also becomes a vocation or a career: it is "what I do," shaping my fundamental sense of identity as a meaningful contributor to my community, my society, and the world. In addition to these inherently rewarding dimensions of work, work is also instrumentally rewarding, that is, it is valuable because of its products.

It is our work that provides for us the resources we need to consume—to use—in order to live. Most minimally, our effort at harvesting brings us the fruits that nature spontaneously offers. More substantially, our labors at cultivating a crop, through ploughing, planting, irrigating, weeding, and harvesting, supply us with the wheat that will support the whole family through the winter. Further labor of grinding, sifting, blending, kneading, and baking produces bread. Again, the cultivation of flax or cotton supplies the resources that, through subsequent labor of threshing, retting, ginning, crushing, dressing, spinning, and weaving will ultimately produce the cloth that, through further labor of designing, cutting, and sewing will produce clothing to keep us warm and to support our desire to navigate our relationships with others through shaping our appearance. Yet again, the cultivation of trees or papyrus reeds provides the materials that, once again through the transformative application of human labor, produces the paper upon which the ink (refined, by labor, from soot) can be applied with the stylus or pen (shaped, by labor, from a reed or a quill or from copper), these resources thus providing the medium within which the work of creative thinking can find expression in written documents that can then be read by others, who will respond to them by laughing, by learning, or by any of the myriad other ways of appreciating the values offered by language. Beyond the intrinsic rewards of the process of labor, then, labor transforms the fruits of nature into valuable resources for our consumption: it is through labor that we have the "goods" that supply the needs of our lives.

It is important when we consider our consumption to remember that we do not always consume the products of our labor immediately.

It is typically important to supply for future needs, whether by making and packing a sandwich for lunch, preserving summer vegetables for use in the winter, or preparing an extra large quantity of soup or sauce and freezing it for use later. In this last case, one stores up one's labor, doing extra work now so that one does not have to do the work later. Indeed, even in tilling the soil, the farmer invests labor now into the earth in order to make it a more powerful resource for the subsequent growing of crops. These different examples point to the way that, through our labor, we can care for our future: the deployment of labor now stores up its power for use later. This futurity to the value of labor is especially relevant to the other economic process we engage in: exchange.

Exchange

As we have seen, the specialization of our economic lives entails that the products of our own labor do not precisely and uniquely match the needs of our lives, and so the value of these "goods" is not precisely their value for the producer, but their value for another, their value for "someone." In intimate settings, we share the work and share the products, my work supplying your needs and your work supplying mine (a structure that has its more elaborate development in the systems of redistribution and gift giving that, as Marcel Mauss originally documented in *The Gift*, characterize respectively the internal and external economic relationships in many traditional societies). In less intimate settings, we exchange goods in the more familiar meaning of that word: we trade, determining an appropriate equivalence between the products of my work and the products of yours. In this latter situation, the product of my work, by providing a product for your possible consumption, provides me with something with which I can "buy" a product you have produced that, analogously, is a possible object for my consumption. In such a context, then, the value of my product is not just its value as something con-sumable (which is the value it has for you) but its value as something exchangeable, something that can get for me something I did not make but that I desire to consume.

If I work for the sake of producing an object of exchange, I am fundamentally investing my labor in the future. As something exchangeable, a product has no immediate (consumable) value for me: it is valuable only for what it might allow me to acquire, and its value-for-me is thus not dischargeable until such time as another in fact finds it sufficiently valuable to her-, him-, or themself to carry out a trade with me. In making a product for exchange, then, I invest in my own future, but I also make my own future contingent upon another: the product does not realize its value-for-me until another actually exchanges with me.

The exchangeable product is my resource for negotiating with others to acquire necessary or desirable objects of consumption into which I have not invested my own labor: they allow me to benefit from the labor of others. In this sense, the products of my labor are a crucial development of the "I can" that defines my practical engagement with the world. My exchangeable goods are my power for living through the labor of others. Precisely because they are a means for engaging with others, though, the value of such exchangeable goods, like the value (as we have seen) of anything shaped intersubjectively, is shaped by the perspective of the other(s): the value of my exchangeable goods is the value that others place upon them, for such goods can only command the will of the others to the extent that those others allow themselves to be commanded. In exchange, then, the value of (the products of) my labor—and, therefore, of *our* labor, since the situation is the same for each of us—is made subject to intersubjective estimation: the value of my work is publicly determined, rather than being something specified by me. And, inasmuch as the value-for-me of my exchangeable goods is their ability to secure my future needs, exchange makes the ability of my labor to secure my own future—my economic "I can"—subject to public/intersubjective determination.

In exchange, then, we see again that our most intimate needs are inherently mediated by what Hegel described as the "dialectic of recognition," by that intersubjective negotiation of value that establishes the shared terms for our shared involvement (*Phenomenology of Spirit*, para. 184). This is another way of recognizing what we noted above, namely, that the division of labor makes human economic activity an essentially shared, social endeavor. By looking a little further into this issue of economic intersubjectivity, we can now understand why it is that the invention of money is a natural development of our economic life.

Money

Precisely because of the inherently futural value of goods we commit to exchange and because of the risk of our dependence upon others to exchange with us, the goals of exchange are best fulfilled when our goods maintain the maximum of futurity and the minimum of risk. This norm, furthermore, is not true distinctly for me, or for any individual, but is true in principle for all who are committed to exchange. For that reason, it is in the interest of those who exchange to find something that can maintain its exchangeable value without deterioration (so that it can hold maximally open its future deployment) and that is universally valuable (so that its exchangeability is always guaranteed). Historically, such products as beaver pelts in North America at the time of European colonization, salt in premodern Ethiopia or ancient Rome, or grain in ancient Mesopotamia appear thus to have approximated universal articles of exchange: by exchanging one's specific goods for one of these relatively long-term, relatively universal goods, one preserved the "exchange value" of one's initial goods in a way that could be deployed almost anytime, almost anywhere; "for example, tallies of debts for beer consumed would be kept, with the tally settled at harvest by delivery of barley at the official price" (Tymoigne and Wray, "Money," 6). In such circumstances, these commodities have become a kind of "money," that is, goods taken up collectively as repositories of generic exchangeable value, rather than simply as distinctive, consumable goods. Such "money," the embodiment of "exchangeable value as such," functions as a means of exchange, by which one makes payment for goods and services and as a store of value, allowing one to hold on to the value of one's goods until a later time. When such standard units of value are broadly recognized and trusted, they become the standard unit of account, by which debts, payments, and so on are measured and, as we will see in more detail below, when legally recognized by a government, can function as an official means of payment of taxes or fines. The development of money thus answers to the inherent norms of the situation of exchange, itself the natural result of the development of the division of labor which is definitive of our interhuman situation. This is why, as Sitta von Reden writes in *Money in Classical Antiquity*, (3): "Money, in contrast to coinage, has never been deliberately invented (either by traders, citizens or states), but comes into being as regular transactions are made by means of the same medium." Money comes into being in response to the needs and possibilities that emerge in our economic relationships. The historical development of money allows the liberation of our economic "I can," freeing us of the limitations put upon us by the inherently specific and local economic practices we engage in personally.

On the face of it, money seems like a simple reality, and one that primarily functions as a convenience that eases exchange. In fact, however, its reality is far more complex, and its role in our experience is quite a bit less neutral than being a mere "convenience." To understand this reality, we will need to look more precisely at what is involved in the functioning of money, and especially see how this is related to government and to the history of banking. In investigating the nature of money in its contemporary form, we will see, in fact, that the consequences of its development have not all been liberatory.

Money, this distinctive institution of human social life, has itself gone through substantial and significant developments in human history, and the particular forms in which this institution has been realized have had distinctive and important political and social effects. Grain has often been used as a means of payment of rent or tax, gold or silver for the storage of value, animal hides for transactions. All of these materials—grain, pelts, silver—are themselves valuable *commodities*, but they become *money* when they come to be experienced not as valuable in themselves but as bearers of (exchangeable) "value as such": they become, that is, avatars of a kind of infinity that, like space or time, is never experienceable as such, but that is definitive of the reality of all the finite "valuables" we do experience. But this transformation of function from commodity to money—from immediately present value to a sign of absent value—is not a "natural" occurrence: gold, silver, or electrum, for example, does not become money simply by being coined and stamped with the sign of the issuing authority. For these coins to function as money, they must be accepted as carrying a value that is not reducible to their value as a commodity. Money exists precisely in that moment when some network of economic agents collectively trusts in the capacity of these tokens to accomplish the exchange of value. Once the system of exchange becomes based upon trust, new possibilities open up.

In a context of trust, the individual parties to an exchange no longer need to use, as their medium of exchange, goods that are themselves equivalent in worth to the commodities they exchange; instead a simple representation of the exchangeable worth of their goods is sufficient. Thus, coins, for example, in order to function as tokens of exchange, need not be (and typically are not) intrinsically worth the value they represent, provided the recipient of the coins believes that those coins will continue to be accepted as representations of their specified worth. In such contexts, one accepts the endorsement—the promise—by an overseeing, third party (namely, the authority issuing the coins), that the convertibility of the media of exchange into goods of their specified worth is guaranteed; hence, the former practice in the United States (until 1963) of printing on government-issued dollar bills the statement, "will pay to the bearer on demand," indicating that the bill could be "cashed out" for a standard *commodity*—gold—of the specified value. In these contexts, the coin or the bill is not itself a commodity of much worth, but it is a document attesting to the fact that the exchanger had materials of such and such worth and that that worth has now been transferred to the new bearer of the coin or bill. These coins and bills will maintain their value exactly as long as others continue to consent to recognize their worth.

Any number of different groups or individuals can assume the role of the third party overseeing and guaranteeing exchanges. In Canada, for example, since 1958, the Canadian Tire Corporation has offered its customers "Canadian Tire Money" as a rebate on cash purchases, a system like the "reward points" now offered by many other retail organizations. Canadian Tire Money can be used, just like government-issued currency, to buy products in Canadian Tire stores. Because it has this (limited) purchasing power, Canadian Tire Money could, for example, be used as a medium of exchange outside of the Canadian Tire system if some individual were prepared to receive it as payment, presumably because that person imagined that they would subsequently spend it in the Canadian Tire system. Because the value of Canadian Tire Money is only guaranteed by the Canadian Tire Corporation, however, if that corporation were to go out of business, those bills would no longer have the value they had when their exchangeable worth was guaranteed by the corporation. Indeed, precisely for this reason, someone outside the Canadian Tire system might accept these bills as payment, but at a discounted rate, because of the risk of their losing value, an "exchange-rate" you might accept if, for example, it allowed you to use Canadian Tire Money that would otherwise go to waste; thus, I might accept your Canadian Tire money at, for example, fifty percent of its face value, allowing you to purchase a product from me that is not available in a Canadian Tire store and that you could not otherwise afford, or I might have an ongoing practice of purchasing Canadian Tire Money at this discounted rate from foreign visitors for whom the bills would otherwise be useless once they left the country. The bills in this context have no "intrinsic" value as a commodity, but as a currency they have a value; since that value as currency is dependent upon the nonnecessitated, continuing endorsement of it by the Canadian Tire Corporation, however, this currency becomes a kind of commodity, and a commodity of negotiable value according to the degree of trust one has in the guaranteeing source, which determines the level of risk in either keeping or receiving it as payment. The exact nature of the authoritative entity overseeing the value of the currency, then, has a decisive role in shaping both the viability of the currency as a medium of exchange and, consequently, the volatility of that currency as itself an exchangeable commodity. Before now looking more closely at the two particular authoritative entities that have been decisive for the history of money—banks and government—let us first look briefly at a different example of an economic enterprise acting as an overseeing authority.

Canadian Tire Money is portrayed as a bonus to customers: it is not a straightforward lowering of prices, but, in place of that, it gives customers a currency that is equivalent to government-issued, legal tender provided it is used to purchase goods within this retail chain. If employees were paid in Canadian Tire Money, though, the implications of this system would be somewhat different and, indeed, that would be exactly the situation of "company scrip," famously associated with exploitative coal mining companies in the United States (and with Wal-Mart in Mexico until it was outlawed by the Mexican Supreme Court of Justice in 2008). In the nineteenth century, coal mining companies operating in remote areas would pay their employees in scrip, which was presented as a statement of the debt in wages that the company owed the employees, because of a shortage of cash resources. This scrip currency could be exchanged for cash at a discounted rate, but would be honored as cash in the company-run stores. Because the currency in which employees were paid was thus usable only in these stores, however, the company could charge exorbitant prices for goods and the employees would have no choice but to purchase them. This case of scrip reveals again the crucial role of authority in allowing some medium to function as money, but it demonstrates the coercive side of this authority. In otherwise economically challenged areas, the local men had no real option except to work for the coal mining company, which could then use its power to force them to accept a form of money the functionality of which was itself controlled by that same company. Initially, this obviously exploitative behavior of the coal mining companies in coercively establishing their own system of money seems like a perversion of money made possible only because

of their isolated and unregulated situation, a situation we imagine to
be corrected in the normal functioning of money that is overseen by
the government (a correction exemplified in this particular case in the
outlawing of payment in company scrip in the United States by the
"Fair Labor Standards Act" of 1938). In fact, however, the guaranteeing
of currency by the state has a coercive structure highly analogous to the
coal mining companies' use of scrip.

Government Currency and Taxation

Government has a unique reality with respect both to law and to economics. A government, because it makes the laws, is not a "legal" entity
like those it regulates. Thus, even when the government makes laws that
pertain to itself (such as determining the number of elected representatives
for the nation or determining the procedural rules for passing legislation), it has the capacity to change those laws: it is the governing, not
the governed. (For this reason, then, subordinate "governments," such as
state and provincial governments in the United States and Canada, or
municipal governments, are only "government" in a secondary sense, for
they are not legally autonomous—not sovereign—but are legally subject
to the national authority, a point that also has considerable economic
significance.) There is a fundamental and ultimate sense, then, in which
the government cannot be said unambiguously to "break the law," since
the law is what the government stipulates. Of course, there can be errors
of daily functioning, such that practitioners abuse their powers and break
the laws, and the government can be criticized from the point of view
of justice—of "natural law," so to speak—but in terms of the simple
functioning of it as a self-governing authority, government is the standard
for determining what is and is not legal, and, consequently, its actions
are legal simply because it stipulates them to be. This same situation is
true of government as an economic entity as long as government has the
role—which national governments virtually universally do have in our
society—of establishing the national currency. Just as the government is
not a "legal" entity, like those are for whom it legislates, so is it not an
"economic" entity like other economic entities. Those whom it regulates
buy, sell, profit, and save, but these words cannot properly be applied
to governmental activities, at least not in the same sense in which they
apply within the economic domain regulated by the government. We
fundamentally misunderstand the nature of government and the nature

of money when we apply the terms that apply within the "space" of a national currency to the source of that economic space or, in the terms that Georges Bataille uses in a different context, when we confuse a restricted economy with a general economy (*The Accursed Share*, Volume I, 19–26). Let us consider the source of currency.

The functions of government exist only if individuals carry out those functions, and, accordingly, the government hires members of the society to build roads, fight in military campaigns, staff administrative offices, and so on. It pays these individuals with its currency—with the currency (dollars, yen, rupees, etc.) that it *makes* (in printing presses, mints, and account books). Indeed, this payment for service seems to be the very origin of coins, which were produced by the Lydian king apparently to pay mercenary soldiers (Seaford, *Money and the Early Greek Mind*, 127–28; Kraay, "Hoards, Small Change and the Origin of Coinage"). What it is crucial to notice, though, is that no one has "paid" this money to the government: necessarily, this money can start nowhere other than with the government. But because "the buck starts here," so to speak, the currency effectively means nothing other than "you have now been paid by the government": the money is just the piece of paper (or other form of currency) that documents that attestation. Consequently, this should seem like a rather useless wage, and indeed it would be completely useless economically unless someone else were prepared to accept it as a bearer of value. In fact, however, others are willing to accept these notes. Because others accept these notes as bearing value, the wages of those who work for the government can be spent on the purchase of other goods and services, and those who take those notes in payment can, in turn, purchase further goods and services from any others who accept those notes as bearing value. What is the value that is stored in those notes? When the bills are accepted in exchange, the exchangeable worth of those bills is the labor those individuals invested in work for the government—and hence for the society: this is the value that those who work for the government have "stored" in the bill, which subsequently becomes the basis of the various further exchanges. The bills allow the government employees to pay for goods and services with their labor to the society. Why, though, do other merchants accept these bills?

Initially, accepting government bills as payment would seem an unlikely occurrence because the other who would accept them, like the initial government employees, would be getting only the bills in payment, that is, since the value they reflect is only the labor that the government employees have already done for someone else, the bills do not reflect some other commodity for which the merchant can "cash them in." The crucial issue, then, is what those bills could ever successfully "pay" for. Here, we see the second half of the economic meaning of the government's "minting" of currency: others accept this currency because the government requires them to do so as a condition of economic functioning, a requirement that has a weaker and a stronger form. Thus, on U.S. dollar bills, for example, the words are written, "This note is legal tender for all debts, private and public." This is, first, the government's attestation that all of its citizens are required—the weaker requirement—to recognize these notes as bearers of exchangeable value; in other words, if you are offered U.S. dollars as final payment in a private exchange and you do not accept that form of payment, you have no legal recourse for securing payment within the United States of America. This is the weaker requirement because, as we will discuss further below, an individual or an organization can still choose to ignore this system of currency if it feels itself sufficiently beyond the government's effective reach; and, given the apparent absence of value in government bills, we can easily see why this would be likely. Second and more importantly, though, these words are the government's attestation that it will accept these bills—and, typically, only these bills—for the payment of public debts, that is, taxes. Anyone who has to pay taxes will have need of whatever form of payment that debt requires—in this case, government currency. By its ability to enforce taxation, therefore, the government makes its currency valuable (Innes, "What is Money?" 398; Mitchell, Wray, and Watts, *Macroeconomics*, 137). By its own authority, then, which most especially means its ability to require the payment of taxes, the government establishes that its currency will be the legally required means for taking account of one's economic value, and, for this reason, its money is recognized as "good" by all who operate economically within the United States. Let us explore further this side of government-issued currency.

     The state can command taxes—it, by fiat, can legislate that its member-citizens have a debt to it—and can then legislate what will be acceptable as payment of that debt. Because of the primary place of this relationship of citizen or subject to the state (the relationship we will study in the next section), this economic transaction has a powerful normative force for other transactions and thus the currency of debt repayment comes to be normative for other exchanges, that is, the repaying of tax debt becomes the dominant economic value that thus defines the value of other goods, services, and currencies. If, for example, grain is the required currency for tax payment, then those who have to answer to the threat of punishment by the state will tend to think of their other exchanges in terms of the resources those exchanges offer for securing the required grain payment. If grain is comparatively easy to come by and if tax rates are low, than grain will have a comparatively low value as currency; if, however, grain is comparatively hard to come by and if tax rates are high, then grain will command a high price for individuals who will be in need of it to pay taxes and will have difficulty acquiring it. Similarly, if dollar bills are required to pay taxes, then economic agents will be prepared to exchange as much of their goods and services as is necessary to acquire the sufficient quantity of dollar bills needed to pay their taxes—a smaller quantity if dollars are easier to come by and taxes are low, a larger quantity if they are harder to come by and taxes are high. Thus is initially established one aspect of the price in dollars of goods and services: higher prices when currency is more plentiful, lower prices when it is more scarce. And, once the relative value of the dollar bill has been thus established, it can be used for any and all economic purposes other than payment of taxes: it has now become the currency of economic life within that society, by which we finance our enterprises, store our savings, and so on.

The government, then, does not use its currency to buy and sell some product; on the contrary, through its employment of labor and its requiring of taxes, it establishes the currency through which those whom it governs can buy and sell products. For anyone else—anyone among the governed—currency for purchases must first be acquired through selling something of independent value. For the government, its initial "purchase" is the invention of that currency: the currency with which it "buys" the goods and services that constitute that infrastructural functioning of the society was not acquired through exchange and had no existence before being payment for those goods and services. Those services are paid for only with the promise that that currency will be worth something in future exchanges with others in the economic system. This promise is fulfilled if and only if others recognize that value, which they do primarily because they will themselves be required to use that currency to pay taxes.

Governments thus "spend" freely, without exchange, (which is how Bataille defines a "general economy"). Whatever they thus "buy" has been fully paid for solely by the issuing of currency, a token that will be useless if the economic system becomes no longer authoritatively governed by the government, but that carries a unique value within that system

(Bataille's "restricted economy") as long as it functions. This government "spending" (equivocally so called) has come to be misleadingly referred to economically as the "deficit"; in reality, this "spending," which is the government's practice of introducing currency to its economic system, effectively means the employment generated by the government, and thus what to the government is "deficit" or "spending" is, to the governed, "dollars in the bank." Because most of us commonly use the (limited) terms of our everyday interactions as our frame of reference for understanding economics and government, we commonly imagine (wrongly) that government "spending" is like our spending, and, consequently, that the so-called deficit of government "spending" is a debt waiting to be repaid, like the debt we might incur through the use of a credit card. In turn, we wrongly imagine that the taxes we pay are getting money to the government by which it will "pay off" this debt. This, however, is a complete inversion of the situation: it is a fundamental misunderstanding of the nature of currency and of the nature of taxation (and, indeed, a misunderstanding that is powerfully encouraged by the contemporary banking industry, which benefits economically through cultivating this misconception). Taxation does not "pay for" government activities: any goods and services the government requires have already been paid for by the initial generation of currency. Taxation simply returns to the government its own notes, which, because their value is not defined in reference to any authority beyond the government, are in fact economically useless to the government (which prints up notes for its own purpose whenever it needs goods or services). The government does not "profit" from taxes, or from anything else—it is not, in that sense, an economic agent at all; taxation serves, on the contrary, only to remove currency from circulation. In the modern world, then, taxes do not fund government spending; they do, however, have an important role in responsible governance, which we will investigate shortly.

There is thus a radical change in the character of economic life when the government and the economic system it regulates switch from operating with "commodity money" to operating with government-backed "fiat money." When an intrinsically valuable commodity such as grain serves as money, your tax payment of grain is what you contribute to the government. With government-backed coins and notes, however, the fundamental contribution you make to the government is either (1) the work you did for the government to acquire currency in the first place, or (2) your establishing and maintaining of the public value of this currency—your recognition of the founding value of the labor already contributed to the society—through using it. This change moves the government from being a recipient of goods to being the very foundation of the economic system, a position of unprecedented power. With this in mind, let us now return to the issue of authority, and especially its coercive side, that we introduced in our discussion of "scrip" (though our fuller study of the use and abuse of government power will be reserved for the next section of this chapter).

Currency and Coercion

The state grants to itself, by its legislative authority, the defining role in determining the currency that represents the monetary standard of value; and, inasmuch as this primary monetary relation is taxation, the government also exercises a fundamental and structuring economic force in its society through its decision about whom and how much to tax: effectively, the rate at which a tax is levied defines the extent to which the value of some transaction is "discounted" compared to its face value and reflects a fundamental decision by the government about how economic power within the society will be distributed; if, for example, the relatively poor are taxed at a rate of 30 percent and the relatively wealthy are taxed at a rate of 5 percent, then the gross sums earned by each group have a different functional value, the earned dollars of the poor being worth only seventy ninety-fifths or seventy-four cents compared to the earned dollars of the rich, and, correspondingly, the poor are hindered in their efforts to improve their economic situation while the rich are accelerated in their economic advancement relative to the poor; if, on the other hand, the relatively rich were taxed at 30 percent and the relatively poor at 5 percent, the relationship would be inverted such that the poor would be supported in their efforts to improve their economic standing while the rich would face a greater challenge in increasing the gap between their economic power and that of the poor. Through its establishment of an official currency, then, the state, like the company store, coercively establishes a kind of "scrip" that, because of the "universal" authority of the state (within its domain of effective power), can dominate the larger market just as the company store and its system of currency can control its local, remote domain. The responsible decision about how to deploy taxation to control the disparity between rich and poor is one of the most important uses of government power.

That the establishing of currency is a matter of power becomes intuitively clear if we reconsider the relationship between government-backed
currency and scrip in the context of the mining town. As we noted above,
coal mining companies would offer to substitute "cash" for scrip at a
discounted rate, and, others outside the company, similarly, could offer
to accept scrip as currency at a discounted rate. We can also imagine,
though, that, even though the government can specify that "this note is
legal tender for all debts, public and private," the company store, in its
isolated location, could very well specify either that it would not accept
government-backed currency or that it would accept it only at a discounted
rate. From the point of view of the government, this would make the
company's actions illegal, but the company could nonetheless choose to
act in this way, either in the belief that it could successfully resist the
authority of the government or in the belief that it would never be found
out. At this point, it is clear that the value of either currency—scrip or
government-backed bills—goes hand in hand with how one participates
in the domains organized by those two authoritative forces: accepting the
government-backed currency is a matter of operating within the limited
terms the government can enforce, both in terms of its permissions and
its punishments, while accepting the scrip is a matter of operating within
the limited terms the company can enforce. In the isolated mining town,
the power of the government (both protective and coercive) might be
stretched too thin to support the worker effectively or to restrain the
company effectively; or, again, the power of the company might be,
though intimidating, a force that can be resisted if enough workers and
other town residents unite in an effort to preserve state authority. This
"internal" conflict between company and state is in turn paralleled in
"external" conflicts between states (and, indeed, between companies), as,
for example, in the case of international recognition (or lack thereof) of
currency from the Confederate States at the time of the American Civil
War, or of Germany after it was defeated in World War I; it is also, in
general, the situation that has been created in our contemporary world
by decades of governments handing power to banks, which now have
the strength to oppose and resist attempts by national governments to
regulate their fiscal policy responsibly. What all of these cases make clear is
that the establishing of a currency is equally the establishing of a regime,
and that participating in a money economy is always a participation in
a contested domain: a domain of competing authorities that, like any

other political powers, can run the range from despotic to democratic, a point to which we will return shortly.

The use of money depends upon a trust in the reliability of the value of the currency, but the overseeing authority that guarantees the currency is by no means a neutral party: the "trust" required for money to function, that is, is fundamentally rooted in a coercive power that can command compliance. An analogous but importantly different structure applies when it is banks that guarantee currency. For the history of money, the emergence of the state is the decisive and founding moment; the emergence of credit banking in the Early Modern period is a second decisive moment, representing a fundamental revolution in the world of money.

Banks and Credit

There is a simple sense of "bank"—one that many "adults" naively accept—that imagines a bank simply to be a storing-house for wealth. One imagines, that is, that the economic work of production and exchange happens elsewhere, and that the bank exists only as a convenient location for the coordinated and secure preservation of the wealth a number of people have thus acquired. This is, to be sure, an important dimension of banking. In fact, however, banks are not simply such derivative supplements to the economic system; on the contrary, banking, especially in the context of the emergence of capitalism in the early Renaissance, is an autonomous and transformative economic force, primarily through its role of offering credit.

Just as the coal mining company guarantees the value of scrip and the government guarantees the value of its coins or bills, banks guarantee the value of personal or corporate debts. A bank offers a loan to an individual, and thus "credits" that individual with an amount of money that that individual now owes the bank. That "credit" is now a reliable value that the individual can trade with others. Thus, when a contemporary shopper uses a credit card to make a purchase, the vendor receives from the purchaser only the "marker" of that individual's debt, with the assurance of the credit card company that the debt will be honored. That transferred debt enters the accounting books of the vendor, and becomes the basis in turn of the payment for some debt that that vendor has incurred. The circulating currency that allows these exchanges is simply the original client's "promise to pay (the debt)" backed by the bank's "promise to pay (the credit)." Borrowing the credit—incurring the debt—allows the original client to finance a profitable enterprise they could not otherwise undertake, the earnings from which allow the individual to pay off the debt to the bank along with whatever sum of interest the bank charges for guaranteeing these exchanges, and, in this circumstance of success, the individual has made a profit, the bank has been enriched through interest payments and the various other vendors involved along the way have carried out a range of other successful exchanges. What is striking about this situation, though, is that the "money" that made this possible was only ever a promise, only ever a debt: all of the exchanges and their subsequent economic consequences took place only on the basis of the exchange of the bank's guarantee of the promise to pay. We thus see a comparable situation to the earlier examples of an authority who secures trust: as long as the various exchanging agents believe the bank's promise, they can confidently and successfully engage in exchange. And notice that all that the bank offered was its own "trust": "We believe that you will repay the loan." There is nothing involved in any of these transactions beyond the mutual statements of belief. Now, of course, things can go awry, and in a few different ways. Most obviously, the original client can fail economically and not acquire the resources to repay the debt; this is the risk the bank takes. Equally, any vendor along the way can seek to "cash in" the bank's promise and exchange it for, for example, government-issued currency (or, perhaps, some other commodity such as gold or grain) and here it is possible for the bank to default if it does not in fact have the liquid resources to pay as it promised—this is the risk the one "holding" the bank's "note" takes. For the bank ongoingly to operate successfully (and to earn its interest), then, what is required is that these risks—the risk of the borrower defaulting and the risk of its own defaulting on its promise to pay—not be too great. Consequently, the security of "bank money" basically rests upon the bank's judging the reliability of the borrower—which generally means the reliability of the economic enterprise for the support of which the money is being borrowed—and maintaining for itself sufficient reserves (presumably drawn from the interest received in various debt repayments) to be able to make a payout in those cases in which someone does want to "cash in" the bank's promissory note. It is in these two areas—debt assessment and cash reserves—that the distinctive coercive power of the banking authority becomes apparent.

The loaning—the creating—of money by the bank establishes economic power for the borrower and it "earns" interest for the lender (the bank). By having this authority to extend credit, banks thus have, first, the leverage to determine which enterprises do and do not get financed. In other words, in the context of banking, money is not a "thing" in the world, but is a relation of power between creditor and debtor, and it is the relationship that establishes which further economic activities will be financed. Such decisions can be a matter of fiat, but in the actual history of banking these decisions are actually reflected in a "credit rating," that is, in an assessment of the reliability of the borrower. The credit rating is initially used to determine whether or not one can borrow, but, even more importantly, it determines the rate of interest the borrower will be required to pay on the loan, with lower-rated clients—the one's deemed less reliable, or of greater risk to the bank's interest—having to pay higher interest. (And, it should be noted, such loans thus themselves become commodities that can be traded, with higher-risk loans being purchased at a discounted rate by those who will exchange a short-term profit for a long-term risk, and so on.) Now notice that there is an essential economic exchange happening here, that is, the practice of the bank that lets there be money is not the neutral facilitation of economic activity (exchange) that happens elsewhere, but is itself a founding "exchange" in which there is a price (interest) being paid for a service (access to money, the power to engage in economic activity)—and this price is different for different borrowers. Through their (self-determined) authority to dictate how the reliability of borrowers is evaluated, then, banks, in their role in "guaranteeing" money, are able to employ significant coercive power to actually determine who is able to participate in economic life and at what level. This power is further enhanced through the complementary practices of negotiating their own reliability as institutions able to "cash out" claims made against them.

Money guaranteed by the bank is essentially the bank's promise to pay upon demand the loan it has offered. Generally, making good on this promise is not important: the sums loaned are indicated in a promissory "note" from the bank, and it is this note that is traded at each stage of purchasing without ever being cashed in. Indeed, in the modern day this "note" is not a separate article at all, but is simply the number printed in an account book or indicated in an electronic file: whether it is a document that moves from borrower to contractor to supplier or whether it is simply numbers that change in the banking accounts of each, there is generally no point at which the bank need translate its promise of funding into the presentation of some other form of cash, whether government-backed coins, gold, or grain. Of course, such demands to "cash in" can happen at some points, and for this reason banks generally do keep some form of cash "in reserve." But banks can effectively lend out sums much higher than their cash reserves precisely because most of the time they will not be called upon to pay out cash. Simply by their power to lend, then, banks can create money—the power for others to engage in economic enterprises—while keeping only a fraction of that total amount in reserve in case they are called upon to make good their promise to pay. The second great power of the bank is this, its ability to "spend" well beyond its means, that is, to lend on the basis of its (self-determined) level of financial reliability. Banks are powerful precisely by maximizing the demands they (can) make on others to "be reliable" while minimizing the extent to which they hold themselves accountable.

Government and Banking

In fact, the two fundamental monetary powers that we have now identi-fied—government taxation and bank credit—are intimately connected to each other. This is primarily because the government currency, the value of which is secured by its power to require taxation, is almost by defini-tion the most secure and definitive economic anchor in a given society and it is the reliability of this currency that, in contemporary capitalist societies at least, plays the primary role in establishing the banks' ability to guarantee their own loans. Basically, governments typically require that "commercial" banks regularly demonstrate that they have maintained a sufficient "reserve" of government currency to "back" their promises to pay; the government's own "central" bank then guarantees that it, as the so-called lender of last resort, will loan its own currency to banks at a low interest rate to allow them to reach the reserve level in case they are lacking funds or that it will allow banks to get rid of excess reserves (that do not earn the banks interest) by using those funds to buy interest-bearing government bonds. This governmental process is itself the ultimate "guarantee" that underlies the loans made by commercial banks to entrepreneurs and households. This governmental backing of bank credit in turn allows the government to recognize bank money on par with government money as payment in taxes: in other words, you can pay your taxes with a check written on your bank account because the banking system is integrated with the system of federal currency such that the government ultimately guarantees the value of bank money. Bank credit money and government tax money are thus intimately linked, and this is the key to the operation of our money system.

By establishing a national currency the need for which is secured through taxation, the government is able to establish an economic base for the credit process that allows banks to support productive economic enterprises: this government money allows the work of individuals done in the service of the nation (that is, whatever the government "buys" with the money it produces, whether the direct labor of individuals or products made through individual labor) to function as the primary exchangeable wealth within the national economy. Because bank money is rooted in credit, its worth, on the contrary, comes from the wealth that will be generated by the system of individual economic enterprises (themselves ultimately enacted in and by the work of individual economic agents). This integration of government money and bank money that has come to define contemporary capitalist societies is thus the integration of two sources of value—past labor and future labor—that provides the crucial "mechanism" for funding the growth of present economic life by its own future. Now, we have already seen the coercive power inherent to bank credit money, located in the banks' defining role of assessing credit worthiness and minimizing its own reserves, and it is important to recognize that, in their carrying out of this role, banks function as economic agents that (unlike government) are primarily oriented by the pursuit of their own profits. The integration of this profit-making enterprise with government is definitive of the structure of contemporary capitalist society, and that fact has significant implications.

The government money that is the foundation for the society's economic life is anchored in the need to acquire resources to pay taxes. By making its decision about whom and how much to tax, the government decides how economic power will be distributed in society and its further legislation surrounding economic practices in general and banking practices in particular determines who will benefit or suffer from these practices and how much. These powers to command tax and to regulate economic practices are the fundamental coercive powers that distinctly attach to the government as the authority overseeing the value of its currency, and the precise way that this coercive economic power of the government is deployed—the justice or injustice of its organizational structure and its treatment of the primary economic agents through the system of taxation, and its system of regulation of banking practices—is implied and reinforced in every monetary transaction. In fact, the government-banking coalition that defines contemporary capitalist society uses the prerogatives of its authority—exercised primarily through the government's power to set tax rates and the banks' power to set risk rates—to direct the society's economic resources disproportionately into profits for the banking industry.

With scrip, government-backed currency, or bank money, one is in each case dealing with what is effectively a "license" to enter into economic activity: each of these currencies is an expression of one's authorization, by the guaranteeing authority, to engage in trade to a specified degree. In each case, the overseeing authority (1) charges something (whether a fee in the case of banks or legal obligations including paying tax in the case of government) for guaranteeing this privilege, (2) exercises control over who does and who does not receive this license, and (3) preferentially empowers some agents by the social and material means it employs for defining its currency and its system of functioning. In contemporary capitalist society, national currencies interweave the guaranteeing authority of the state with the authority of banks to guarantee loans such that the (necessary) use of the national currency is at one and the same time an embrace of the government and of the commercial banking system. Because the commitment of the government to "bail out" banks that are called to make good on their promises to pay is not attached to a requirement that those banks be organized and operate in the public interest, the profit making of the banking industry is preferentially empowered by the state's authoritative decision about what functions as currency. By establishing that taxes will disproportionately be paid by those in the lowest economic tiers of society—those who take "off the rack" jobs, working for a wage for a larger industry—and not by the wealthiest "captains of industry" who control large industries, while simultaneously allowing banks to use their (self-interested) systems of risk assessment to determine which economic activities will receive financial support, this system structurally establishes and, indeed, magnifies a radical and exploitative division between a relatively poor class of paid workers and an extremely wealthy class of industrialists and bankers. In short, in contemporary capitalist society, money itself—the state-guaranteed lending by banks—far from being a neutral mechanism that simply facilitates exchange, is a means for distributing wealth and distributing it disproportionately toward what Marx called "the aristocracy of finance" and "the industrial bourgeoisie" (*The Eighteenth Brumaire*, 334); indeed, as we shall see in the final section of this chapter, this economic coalition of government and banking amounts to a fundamental compromising of the role and authority of government.

Money—in whatever its form—amounts to a collective commitment to see all goods as belonging to a system of value, such that the worth of each is simply a specific quantity of some specified unit of exchangeable value. Simply to participate in a money economy, then, is to embrace the relativity of one's worth and the worth of one's enterprise to the worth of all other participants in that system: it is the embrace of the authority of that system to determine the relative worth of all things. Now, inasmuch as we must interact with others, we must always already have accepted the authority of others to determine our worth—this is the basic reality of interpersonal life in general and economic life in particular. With a money economy, however, we alienate ourselves from determining those relative evaluations, and instead subject ourselves to the determining power of the defining authority of the money system, a system that, in fact, is fundamentally oriented to establishing economic inequality and subordinating a large and relatively poor working class to economic control by a small, wealthy elite.

Economic Agency

We saw above that engaging in productive work is one of our fundamental needs: it allows us to "earn" an individual sense of belonging to the world and it is the essential adult experience of providing for oneself and one's dependents. And by participating in an economic world structured by a division of labor, one does not simply "fend for oneself" against nature: instead, working is a form of engaging with others in a collective action of establishing for ourselves a human world. The world in which we earn a place through work is thus simultaneously natural and social. This economic system that buffers the individual from answering to the full, unmediated force of nature, however, is also a force in its own right and must be contended with on its own terms. In chapter 2, we studied the ways in which negotiating the psychological domain confronts us with a significantly different range of challenges, problems, and resources than does negotiating with nature, and analogously we are now recognizing the novel terms of economic life to which our adult "objectivity" must answer. A money economy in particular requires of us a significant reinterpretation of our normal sense of (economic) agency.

We typically think of our economic life as beginning from our work in the world, and we imagine exchange as a derivative practice—a practice in which you and I come to some agreement about the relative worth of the products of our labor that each of us has to offer the other. In a money economy, however, this situation is entirely inverted: first, our fundamental "work" is exchange and, second, in individual relationships of exchange it is not you and I who define the value of our exchange, but the money system. The very meaning of our economic activity, in other words, whether in producing or in exchanging, is determined for us by the system that has already established its "price": one's productive activity is not a matter of making something for oneself, but is one's entering into a role in the much larger economic enterprise that defines our society, and that productive activity in fact "provides for" oneself and one's dependents only insofar as it is recognized as a quantity of exchangeable value within the terms of exchange that are dictated by the government-banking coalition. In a money economy, the very meaning of our agency is specified from without, and there is thus a fundamental alienation that defines our participation in economic life: we do not understand what we are doing or why it is worth what it is worth.

It is certainly possible to have a manifest experience of this fundamental self-alienation. A young Asian woman working for the multinational computer technology corporation IBM who wears a sealed body suit and has one arm affixed by a cord to her desk while performing quality checks on integrated-circuit chips with a microscope, for example, can certainly recognize that she has no sense at all of what the function of those microprocessors is and has no sense at all of how her actions fit into the world of IBM's business enterprise. By and large, though, this alienation that defines our economic agency is concealed from us. Eager college students, for example, can enthusiastically take up work raising money for some prominent "charitable" organization, proud of themselves for using their productive labor to contribute to a good cause, completely ignorant of the actual structure of the corporation for which they work and especially ignorant of the fact that the money they are raising is primarily divided between paying the huge salaries of the corporation's administrators and being invested in other economic activities that are largely responsible for creating the problematic situations the "charity" purports to address. Similarly, a university professor can imagine herself to be "teaching students," which, no doubt, she is doing; in carrying out that practice through the university, however (which, of course, is the only realistically available avenue for carrying out this activity), she is also providing the service for which the university charges huge fees, generating for the university a huge budget, very little of which is used to fund education; on the contrary, as with the "charity," the bulk of the massive income generated by the "sale" of teaching is divided between paying the large salaries of the university's administrators and being invested in other economic activities that typically run counter to the very goals and values that the teachers are trying to instill in their students. This phenomenon of the "charity" or the "school" that is a kind of deceptive façade for a deeper economic reality is in fact pervasive in the contemporary capitalist world. In particular, it is with "joint stock" companies and the "stock market" in general that the apparently primary economic activities that define businesses have become the occasion for a more fundamental economic activity: the activity of trading businesses for a profit.

Though there are smaller examples from earlier times in history, it is the British East India Company that is usually thought of as the first great "joint stock company," and it is shortly after its founding around 1600 AD that the "stock market" began in Amsterdam. The basic idea of the joint stock company is simple: a number of different individuals provide the money to launch an enterprise—they "buy stock" in it and determine its "board of directors"—and that company then "does business," either paying back the investors out of its profits or paying them dividends on their stocks; if the company fails, however, the stockholders get nothing back. The basic idea of the stock market is also simple: one can sell one's stock in a company to another so that that other can take the risk and receive the dividends. Stock in a company that seems successful may well sell for a higher price than one initially paid for it or for a lower price if the company appears to be failing.

The British East India Company, the first great joint stock venture, established its operations in India with the sanction of the British government and with the compliance of various local rulers in what is now northeast India. The wealth that was returned to the stockholders (and to those carrying out the enterprise in India) came from the goods produced by Indian labor that the company was able to sell in Britain for a much higher price than they paid in India. Those buying and selling stock in the company back in Europe did not really need to know much about India (though their insight into whether or not the company was likely to succeed would surely vary with their level of insight into the workings of the company). To make (or lose) money, all they had to do was exchange some money for a slip of paper identifying them as shareholders.

Furthermore, the wealth these stockholders used to buy the shares was itself the product of the labor of workers in England: if someone traded grain for shares, for example, that grain was the result of many hours of human laboring to plant, cultivate, harvest, and transport the grain, and similarly for any other kind of wealth. In order to spend that wealth, a wealthy English landowner who owned large farms and received rent payments in grain from many tenant farmers did not need to know anything of the ways of farming. The wealthy buyers and sellers of stock in this situation thus have a very particular experience: they are exchanging the wealth produced by Indian laborers for the wealth produced by English laborers without ever necessarily coming into contact with either domain of wealth production; their experience, on the contrary, is limited to an exchange of one piece of paper identifying ownership of grain for one piece of paper identifying ownership of stock.

In fact, the decisions of such wealthy men of commerce to fund or not to fund an enterprise have substantial economic (and, ultimately, social) consequences. Indeed, had various such men not subscribed to the British East India Company, the sea trade with India would not have developed and, without the development of that sea trade, we would not have the other world-transforming economic and technological developments of the nineteenth and twentieth centuries that we now take for granted, or the contemporary global consciousness and multicultural society that that encounter between Europe and Asia ultimately made possible. In this sense, it is surely true that the wise deployment of wealth is essential to the development of productive enterprise and lack of financing can be what precludes the development of important businesses.

At the same time, the greed and violence of the company's policies and practices—policies and practices that were backed by the British government—resulted in various awful circumstances for the Indian population, including repressions, famines, and wars. Further, the company's monopolizing of the Indian trade resulted in the destruction of various already existing practices of trade for Asian goods, and the established world of social and economic relationships with which they were interwoven. And the political landscape in India was redrawn through the power that the company deployed to install local leaders who would facilitate their plundering. European colonialism in India—and in Asia more broadly—so decisively and devastatingly transformed the existing social order, and did it for so long, that its effects continue to haunt that world today. Thus, while the investors who sponsored the company may well be indirectly responsible for some positive dimensions of global development, they are most immediately responsible for some of the worst and most destructive crimes ever committed by one society against another.

In our English idiom, the experience of the businessman who buys stock that he can subsequently sell for a higher price is that, by his wise trading, he "made money." This idiom, though, is highly misleading. The trader now has legal control of greater wealth than he had before; in fact, though, he *made* nothing, in the normal sense of that word. The Indian and English workers made the wealth he now controls. The role of the financiers "making money" while facilitating or hindering productive enterprise by buying and selling stock is, to be sure, economically productive: the organizing and directing of different but complementary resources—here the coordinating of the work and the desires of the English population with the work and desires of the Indian population—can produce mutually beneficial results for otherwise isolated communities that, when brought together, produce a richer world for both. Such organizing and directing—the management that is typically carried out by the board of directors, who act as representatives of the stockholders—is a task and a skill that is not simply reducible to the production of the resources exchanged: it is therefore a kind of labor that does contribute value to the economic "product" thus achieved, and it makes sense, therefore, that those who have excellent abilities at carrying out this organizing for the betterment of all involved be respected for their talents and rewarded for their efforts. This, however, is not typically what "making money" means in the context of trading stock.

Once businesses can be traded on the stock market, they have themselves become commodities. In other words, whereas, for example, the making and selling of clothes may seem like the definitive economic relevance of a clothing business, if that company is publicly traded then it as a whole is being evaluated by traders for its "future"—its capacity to bring in income—and will be bought and sold according to how potential owners view their willingness to accept the rate of its success and the risk of its failure. Now, the business itself, which brings in income from its ongoing sale of clothing, must use that income both to maintain its continued functioning (which includes purchasing raw materials, maintaining premises and equipment, paying wages for its employees, and so on) and to generate whatever profit its owners will appropriate for themselves. When the business is traded as a commodity, the potential owners who are evaluating its rate of success or the risk of its failure are evaluating it as a source for their own profit. In other words, whereas, "internally," the economic norm that defines the business is its flourishing as a clothing manufacturer, the economic norm that defines the business for the traders is its potential to bring them a profit. Publicly traded companies, in other words, are managed by their owners for the sake of their profit, and not for the sake of the manifest economic enterprise that defines the business. Thus, a well-functioning business that makes an important contribution to the ongoing life of its community may well be "liquidated" by its owners, who see more personal benefit in taking the whole of its accumulated wealth as their own short-term gain than in accepting an ongoing lower rate of profit that allows for the continued self-sufficient functioning of this communally valuable enterprise that also supplies an economic livelihood to its employees. In this way, "making money" through trading stock does not primarily mean earning a warranted reward through the excellent organization of an economic enterprise, but typically means, on the contrary, exploiting one's control of an enterprise to extract from it the maximum wealth one can secure for oneself.

The stock market, then, radically transforms our sense of what the primary economic activity is—indeed, it veritably inverts it. In the context of publicly traded companies, the real "business" associated with the clothing manufacturer in our example is not manufacturing clothing, but is "investing." The owners buy, sell, and manage the company not in the interest of its practice of manufacturing clothing but in the interest of returning them the highest rate of "interest" on their investment. The putatively derivative, "meta-economic" activity—an activity built upon the putatively primary economic activity—thus becomes, in the world of the stock market, the primary economic activity, that is, it is this activity of buying, selling, and managing businesses for profit that governs which of the otherwise "primary" economic activities are actually carried out and how. In what we would normally think of as the primary economic activity, management is a means for working toward the end of the flourishing of the company, but it has here become the end toward which the company's functioning is now a means. This inversion redefines the very meaning of our economic agency, as we saw above, and something closely analogous characterizes banking and the capitalist money economy more broadly.

This buying, selling, and managing of companies for the profit of stockholders is analogous to the way in which debt (which, we have seen, is itself the fundamental meaning of "money" in the context of the world of contemporary banking) is handled in our contemporary economy. Debts, like joint stock companies, are themselves commodities, that is, they are themselves entities that can be bought and sold. We already noted above that different currencies (such as company scrip versus government-backed bills) develop values as commodities when, in specific social situations, individuals establish different ("discounted") rates of exchange between them depending on the perceived authority of the agency that "guarantees" the currency to exercise its coercive force in controlling the value and functionality of its currency, and something similar characterizes the contemporary economics of debts in general. Once you owe me money, and especially if you also must pay me interest, you are now both a source of income for me and a risk (for you might not pay me back). Like the clothing manufacturer in our example above, this debt is a kind of "investment," and it may be one I am content to maintain long enough for you to pay it back or it may be something I "liquidate" for short-term profit: if, for example, you owe me one thousand dollars which you will pay back in ten monthly installments of one hundred dollars along with monthly payment of 10 percent "interest" on the outstanding balance at the time of payment, I may choose to wait out the ten months and receive back from you a total of fourteen hundred and fifty dollars, or I may choose to sell your debt for, say, twelve hundred dollars to someone else who can better afford to wait out the year and can more easily enforce repayment than I can. In that latter case, I have still "made" two hundred dollars (which I now securely possess) and the one to whom I sell will also "make" two hundred and fifty dollars, provided the payments are all made (or will have lost some or all of the twelve hundred dollars if the debtor cannot be made to pay). Once the debt is in place, it can be traded just as a company can be traded. (And, indeed, a further contemporary economic enterprise—the selling of "insurance"—arises within this context, for the buying and selling of debts also makes possible the buying and selling of the promise to secure one against possible losses in such exchanges.) As with management of a company by a board of directors, "financing" would normally seem to be a derivative (though powerful) economic function in service of the more primary or primitive economic activity of production, but, as with joint stock companies, the primary economic reality for those involved in the financing of debts is in fact this use of debts as profit-bearing investments rather than as ways of facilitating whatever more "primitive" economic enterprise the debt is funding.

From both the side of the financing and the side of the management of the "primary" economic enterprises in a society, then (and there is often a very close tie between the financiers and the managers), we can see that our primitive economic activity—our economic agency—is generally not what it appears to be. That our work is already inscribed in an economic system that defines its significance is the very notion of the division of labor, which, in itself, represents a major enhancement of our economic agency in comparison with the situation of one's individually working on the natural world. It is precisely the duty of the economic system to "employ" our labor well for the collective benefit of all in the economic system. In fact, however, since the alliance of government and banks in the formation of the capitalist money economy, the economic system in which we participate—to which we belong—has inverted this relationship of means and end, and has produced a situation in which collective work serves the economic authorities who define that money economy; indeed, in contemporary capitalist society, by and large we work in the service of generating profits for financiers.

We reflected above on the distinction between getting a job "off the rack" and developing one's own economic enterprise. It is certainly true that that latter option does in some ways seem more fully to "own up" to—to be "adult" in relation to—the economic reality of our existence. In fact, however, owning up to our economic reality more fundamentally requires that we recognize our need to participate in a social division of labor: it requires us to recognize that we are not economic "individuals." For that reason, in contemporary society, "entrepreneurs," who are often celebrated within the familiar rhetoric of our capitalist system, are, first, really doing nothing fundamentally different from those people who get their jobs "off the rack" in that they are simply taking a different route into adopting a predefined role within the economic system. And, in fact, such entrepreneurship is often ultimately less self-responsible inasmuch as it relies upon taking advantage of the forms of exploitation this capitalist system allows while perpetuating the anticommunal myth of individual economic agency that is the deceptive veneer of this system. We will have reason to return both to this issue of the determinate character of the division of labor in (capitalist) society and to the issues of finance and the money economy when we study the nature of government in the final section of this chapter.

The Conflict of Economics and Intimacy

Economic activity is an essential dimension of adult life. Through our economic activity, we both provide for ourselves and establish for ourselves a distinctive sense of belonging in the world: through working, each of us individually establishes a kind of "earned" (and, in that sense, conditional) belonging alongside the collective, "inherited" (and, in that sense, unconditional) belonging that defines intimacy and family life. Economic activity, therefore, is not simply a matter of instrumentality: the need to work is as much an existential need as it is a material need. Consequently, there is an issue whether one "does what one wants" when one works, satisfying a fundamental sense of human desire and aspiration, or whether one is constrained to work in a fundamentally dehumanizing context. On its own terms, work is defined by an existential norm that allows us to distinguish between its better and worse realizations. But even as an existential domain, whether taken up in a fulfilling or an unfulfilling way, work stands in tension with the existential domain of intimacy.

Work situations can indeed be social but, outside of traditional societies, those with whom we work are typically not our intimate others. Consequently, in relation to the family, "work" is an individual matter, that is, one leaves the family context to participate in the work context, and one's work is how one as an individual deals with one's existential satisfactions; thus, for example, "making one's way" in the economic world can be for a teenager or young adult a way to establish independence from the family. And this tension in principle between intimacy and economics—this tension in how one is construing one's very reality—can quite naturally lead to a tension in practice: in my work, do I seek the satisfaction of my own passions against the desires and values of my family, or do I take a job I do not like for the sake of answering to the perspective of my family? One's personal, psychological health depends on one's work satisfaction, and so to choose the family over work can be damaging to one and, indeed, it can sufficiently undermine one's experience that, depressed or angry, one cannot function well as a relationship partner or parent, thus resulting in the degeneration of the relationship itself; on the other hand, of course, sacrificing familial and other intimate relationships for the sake of one's job can be just as undermining, removing from the individual her or his or their basis in meaningful life and stripping those intimate relationships of the nurturing commitment they need to survive. Thus, the economic sense of agency may well complement one's sense of family membership, but it needs to be recognized, nonetheless, as a fundamental challenge to the primacy of family life. In economic life, one defines oneself through one's individual efforts in the impersonal world of public life, and this is an alternative to the definition one receives in the family. And in addition to offering this route to existential redefinition of oneself, the economic realm itself is a challenge culturally to the place of the family: the market makes (and makes very effectively) a claim to be "what is really happening" in human life, taking the world of the family simply as its own resource (for employment and as a market).

Both intimacy and economics define essential existential domains of human life, and adult life requires deciding both how to fulfill each and how to situate the fulfillment of each with respect to the other. Indeed, in general, these domains of intimacy and economics are the two most fundamental contenders for the authority to say "who we are." And these issues are also not just personal: as we will now see, negotiating the conflicting demands of intimate and economic life is also integral to the meaning of the third essential domain of human life: politics.

Politics: The State

The Political

The third essential domain of adult life is the domain of politics—the domain of "rule." Now, historically, human beings have, of course, lived under all sorts of rule, including subjection to an emperor who is construed as semidivine, participation in a "clan" group with traditional leadership, subordination to an occupying military force, and so on. At some level, adulthood, in any such situation, will require recognizing and responding to the "reality" of that situation. My concern here, though, is the particular sort of rule that is "government," the reality with which we must negotiate in the contemporary world.

Just as we grow up into a world in which money is already a reality, so do we grow up into a world in which government is already a reality.

We do not independently face a "raw" world as detached individuals, but instead find our way within the terms of a social world in which various paths of action are already prescribed and proscribed under the authority and power of a ruling body. On its own, that description could also fit the experience of the family and the market, and so to establish more exactly the distinctive nature of the government, we must point to a body that is precisely not family or market, but is a body that has the governance of social life as its explicit, self-conscious definition—a body, indeed, that, among other things, specifically determines the terms for legitimate family and market life.

Analogously to the way in which we automatically expect the bills in our pockets to have purchasing power, we are accustomed to expect a world that is well run, counting on there being an authority to which we can appeal for endorsement and enforcement of the right when we are wronged, and a caretaking agency that will ensure that the "infra-structural" scaffolding of social life is maintained in good order. "They should fix that road!" or "Where are the police when you need them?" are familiar sorts of remarks that express this attitude, for these remarks presume the existence of an overseeing agency that is taking responsibility for our social needs.

Government is this agency by which a society takes responsibility for its own needs as a society. Like the division of labor, government is the way that individuals renounce the ultimacy of their own authority in order to participate in a community that collectively governs itself. Government—unlike subordination to patriarchal authority in a family or clan, subjection to an emperor, or enslavement by force—is a feature of a social system: it is a matter of social self-governance, rather than rule by another.

Government, in this distinctive meaning as the way a group makes decisions for itself about the end and means of its collective life, has its origins in ancient Greece. It was the Greeks who developed the idea and the reality of the self-governing *polis*—the "city-state" or, more exactly, the "citizen-state"—that came to be called "democracy," and became the model for our modern conception of political life. The self-governing *polis* emerged in Greece in opposition to a variety of different forms of rule, which included the contemporaneous empire of the Persian "Great King," the historical rule by Bronze Age "chieftains" in its own cultural past, and the ongoing efforts by the traditional aristocracy within its own society to establish rule. Though different in their specific features, these three contending forms of rule all present some form of monarchy or oligarchy rooted in the social reality of the *oikos,* the "household"; in other words, these are forms of social life that operate within the horizons of *family* life. The aristocratic families that posed an ongoing challenge to the democratic tendency of the ancient Greek cities, in their extended clan structure, resonated with the social reality of the Bronze Age chieftains (*basileis*) poetically remembered in the Homeric epics, who were the heads of their own "royal" households and of the loose-knit community of households they controlled. The Persian empire was much larger than those dynastic Bronze Age "kingdoms" of Mycenae or Troy, and it had a more complex infrastructure and comprised a more varied social world, but it was nonetheless a society ultimately premised on the family as its primary unit, whether the households of its subjects or the royal household. What is truly unique and original about the Greek *polis* is that, in contrast to all these contending models of social rule, it introduced to the world a form of social (self-)organization that defined itself above and beyond the reality of the family.

What is distinctive of the *polis* is that its members come together to make decisions collectively about the governance of the city. In other words, in their assembly (*ekklēsia*), the citizens discuss and debate as representatives of the city, and not as representatives of their families, about "the just and the unjust, the expedient and the inexpedient," as Aristotle puts it in his *Politics* [I.2.1253a10–15]. The distinctly political community is thus the one in which the members of that community experience themselves as members of that community, and act on the basis of that self-identification, in contrast to acting on the basis of an identification of themselves either as family members or, indeed, as discrete individuals. Membership in the city is thus not simply a matter of being spatially present within the city walls: it is a matter of personal and social self-interpretation, such that one recognizes the collectively constituted reality of the city as one's own reality. The members of the city are thus *polites,* "citizens."

Unlike the ancient Greeks, we no longer live in such small city-states but, even in our age of nation-states and globalization, the fundamental norm of distinctively "political" life remains unchanged to the extent that we understand the basic meaning of human political life to be the way in which a community is organized to govern itself. Unlike the "participatory" democracy of the Greek cities, however, in which in principle every citizen could—and should—participate in the assembly, we empower a small body of our "representatives" to make the decisions of community governance for us. It is this structure that produces the distinctive challenge of contemporary politics.

Modern Government

In principle, our system of "representative" government enables a kind of community self-governance, but in fact it introduces significant obstructions to realizing this goal. First, this is because it establishes a small body to which we alienate our individual powers of reflection, judgment, and decision making, thus removing ourselves from direct, active participation in governance. While one can imagine a situation in which such a structure would facilitate an effective mechanism for enacting a "democratic" community, it is also easy to recognize fundamental ways that it can actually work against this goal. Because government is established as a separate body, it has a tendency to develop a "life" of its own, while those whom it is supposed to represent become themselves detached from its reality. In other words, though its reason for existing is to facilitate the self-governance of the community, the government can in fact operate in its own interest as a separate body, against the interest of the larger community while, simultaneously, the members of the political community can lose the sense of their own distinctive role as citizens. While this is true in any society in which the government is a separate body of individuals—this is the "problem of the guardians" that is the central theme of Plato's *Republic* (see *Republic*, Book II, 375a-d)—there is a distinctive way in which this applies in contemporary society, and we can see how this is so if we reflect on what everyday life is normally like in the context of modern government.

Just as we are inclined to get our jobs "off the rack," on the expectation that the economic world will provide us with a ready means of "making a living," so do we expect government to provide us with a well-functioning general context without the need for us to attend to it explicitly. Typically, we live our lives with the desire to be oriented toward the demands of our intimate life, and we want to devote our energies to cultivating our personal and interpersonal relationships—our happiness—rather than focusing on the demands of establishing a world in which this is possible. While those of us who have careers that are personally fulfilling may well include their "work" in the domain of what is desirable to pursue, for most people work is a means to the end of intimate life and thus something to be endured and then forgotten as quickly as possible. Perhaps even more so, this forgetting is true of government, since, unlike a job, modern government generally does not even require us to attend to it at all, beyond requiring that we pay taxes and obey laws. Our modern governments have developed a strong institutional character, that is, they function through vast, impersonal networks of rules, agencies, and civil servants. This system has the effect of maintaining its coherence through changes in leadership, and it thus inhibits single, powerful individuals from unilaterally "ruling" us, but it also encourages us to imagine that the functions of government are automatically taken care of, as if by a machine. Modern government, in other words, actually encourages us to ignore it, to rely on it to take care of itself. This institutional character, however, is not a politically neutral reality.

On the one hand, this vast "machine" of state becomes a political force in its own right. Establishing any specific body in the role of governor brings with it the possibility that that body will work in its own interests rather than in the interests of the governed, and this is no less true of the institutional machine of contemporary politics, the form of government often critically characterized as a "bureaucracy" or "rule by the office." In contemporary society, it is common to experience dealing with government as a matter of "red tape," that is, a system of rules and procedures that unnecessarily complicate and hinder one's efforts to deal with simple matters, a reality pointedly portrayed in Kafka's novel *The Castle* (1926), in which the protagonist K struggles with an unending stream of officials, procedures, and documents in an ultimately unsuccessful effort to make contact with the governing authorities. Rather than being a neutral mechanism, contemporary bureaucracy has a logic of its own: even without any self-conscious intention to act in its own interest, bureaucracy has its own set of norms, structures, and expectations to which one must answer in dealing with it, and which generates its own internal hierarchy and power structure. To set up a bureaucracy is to establish a specific regime of power that shapes the lives of those who must live under its rule. In addition to thus establishing a very particular kind of environment for the governed—an environment that encourages (or requires) orderliness, record keeping, rule following, and all the other behavioral and character traits that are conducive to being able to define one's life by the requirements of smooth institutional functioning—it does also establish an environment that is susceptible to being taken over by particular kinds of individuals. Just as other forms of government are open to being seized and exploited by, for example, powerful and ambitious generals or charismatic orators, so are bureaucracies particular domains that can be mastered by particular individuals or groups who grasp and can exploit their distinctive functioning as systems of rules and records—the same individuals who make good bankers and spies—as is demonstrated powerfully by the case of J. Edgar Hoover, and his development of the Federal Bureau of Investigation in the United States into one of the most powerful forces in contemporary American politics. Hoover was a former library clerk, and his distinctive contribution to contemporary political reality was to apply the systems of cataloguing used in libraries to the intimate lives of U.S. citizens, which resulted in the FBI becoming an institution that rivalled Congress for its ability to control the United States and in general changed the shape of contemporary government. Our contemporary form of government, then, does not solve the "problem of the guardians" by putting an impersonal machine in the position of rule; it simply establishes new terms in which that problem emerges.

On the other hand, in encouraging us to ignore its functioning, this form of political life actually discourages our becoming political, that is, it discourages us from experiencing ourselves meaningfully as citizens, and thus undermines the very meaning of democracy. The very premise of the "machinic" character of contemporary, bureaucratic government is that it can be trusted to function on its own. In this way, government has come to be conceived analogously to the "labor-saving devices" of modern, technological industry.

We commonly think of the dishwasher, for example, as an improvement in modern living that frees one from the undesirable drudgery of cleaning up after oneself. The dishwasher, the washing machine, and the vacuum cleaner all allow us to ignore our otherwise challenging responsibilities by trusting a machine to perform the process for us, leaving us the leisure to focus on what we truly care about. Modern government similarly encourages us to trust in the "system" that will take care of paving roads, policing neighborhoods, and generally ensuring that the overall conduct of social life is carried out in a way that is just and fair. In fact, "labor-saving devices" are deceptively so called, for they emerged as the defining products of the Industrial Revolution—most famously, the sewing machine, the cotton "gin" (engine), and the steam engine—not primarily to reduce the household labor of private individuals but to save industrialists from paying labour costs. Consequently, the introduction of labor-saving devices actually dramatically reduced the "leisure time" of most individuals by eliminating jobs and thus making life an ever-greater struggle, while simultaneously producing a more alienating situation for laborers in general by reducing their function from meaningfully fashioning products from simpler materials to repetitively operating machines the workings of which they did not understand.

The technology of modern governmental process functions analogously: First, the inherently meaningful and fulfilling activity of participating in our self-governance is rhetorically construed as "drudgery." Second, we are encouraged to trust in the reliability and transparency of the impersonal procedures into which all of our political relations are translated. Third, we are ultimately both subjected to a life governed by limiting and oppressive rules and simultaneously alienated from the experience of meaningfully controlling the shape of our personal and social lives. Thus, modern government challenges its own justification as a realization of self-governance by fundamentally alienating us for the experience of citizenship, which is in fact precisely what it means for us to be self-governing.

Collective Decision Making

The reality and significance of this alienation from the experience of citizenship is especially clear in the phenomenon of voting. Voting is very clearly a mechanism a group can adopt for decision making. There are in fact, many different ways a group can make a decision, and to grasp the significance of voting, both in general and in its specific relation to democracy, it is important to compare it to other forms of decision making. We can then grasp both when such a mechanism of decision making can be valuable and what its limitations are.

Without a doubt, the most effective and meaningful method for making a decision is discussion, through which the members of a group share their perspectives with each other in a process of mutual education and mutual persuasion. The process of putting one's own views into words is already inherently valuable and, indeed, transformative, for rendering one's otherwise inchoate thoughts into determinate form typically reveals to oneself aspects of those thoughts—both positive and negative—of which one was otherwise unaware, and it is precisely through this process of self-articulation that one gradually "takes possession" of oneself and one's views. Further, in thus putting our views on public display, we not only allow others the benefit of seeing a situation from a new and possibly transformative perspective: we also open ourselves up to the critical perspectives of others—at times a challenging process, to be sure, but a process in which the true weight of our words can become manifest in ways that, on our own, we would never recognize. By being open to each other's perspective and by thus sharing our views in a collaborative process of mutually transformative communication, we have the possibility of developing a genuinely shared perspective—a perspective none of the participants could have come to in advance on their own. One of the features that is most striking and most important about this method of collective decision making is that it leaves each participant with a sense of ownership—both in the process of decision making and in the decision that results. In other words, the different parties to the decision-making process can each affirm that that is "my" decision, or, more exactly, it is "our" decision. Consequently, each feels themself to be part of the world that results from the decision.

Of course, sometimes discussion does not result in a shared decision. This can be due to one or more of quite a few reasons. Those with compelling views, for example, may be ineffective at articulating the rationale for those views. Or, again, those listening may be resistant, and unwilling to let go of their firmly held prejudices. Or, again, there may be a range of different, equally reasonable perspectives, and the discussion may leave different individuals holding different views. Sometimes, when interactions end with such inconclusive discussions, the different parties are content to separate and carry on their affairs independently. Sometimes, however, a decision must be made, whether in the simple social environment of a group deciding where it will hold its celebration or in the more politically charged situation of a threatened group needing to flee a dangerous situation. It is in such situations that groups must turn to fixed decision-making procedures.

One such procedure for coming to a decision is turning to a single individual to make a decision on behalf of the group. This, like discussion in general, is a particularly powerful method, for a single individual can reflect upon and weigh the competing perspectives and interests within the group and make a wise decision regarding the best interests of the group overall. What this method does not accomplish, however, is stepping beyond individual perspective; in other words, the initial challenge is the conflict between individual perspectives, and this method allows one individual's perspective to become authoritative. This method will therefore produce an analogous sense of "ownership" and belonging to that produced by successful discussion only if the different participants in the group who cannot agree on the decision in question do agree on the propriety of investing authority in the single perspective of the one empowered to make the ultimate decision. This method, too, will produce good group decisions only if the authoritative individual is relatively good at appreciating the differing perspectives of the others and relatively wise in adjudicating the issues around which there is conflict. When there is a lack of trust in such an individual, another procedure is necessary.

A closely related method is to turn to a subgroup of the original group to perform the same function as would be performed by a single judge. A large group especially may deem collective discussion to be too unwieldy a practice for it to handle effectively, while nonetheless desiring a substantial process of discussion to provide the context for decision making. In such a case, a representative committee may be struck to carry out the discussion on behalf of the group. Once again, this can be a very effective procedure in situations of trust and good judgment, but will produce poor decisions and an insufficient sense of group "ownership" if the members of the committee cannot themselves do a good job of handling their paired tasks of representing the perspectives of the larger membership and discussing well with each other. Thus, like both collective discussion by the group as a whole and authoritative decision making by an individual, decision by committee is a method inherently dependent upon trust, wisdom, and judgment to be effective.

Indeed, trust, wisdom, and judgment define the essential and irreducible terrain of human decision making in general. Together, the capacity to trust, the capacity to judge, and the possibility of wisdom in these contexts both constitute the unique power and possibility of our humanity and define the unique necessity we face if we are to flourish: these are the powers that make a meaningful and worthwhile world possible for us. Precisely in making our decision making meaningful and worthwhile, however, they also make it a dangerous and vulnerable domain, for trusting in the wise judgment of another means making oneself dependent upon the another's good will and on the insight of that other's limited perspectives. Voting evades the challenges presented by these dangers and vulnerabilities, for it allows us to get decisions made without going through the medium of human interaction and discussion. As such a "machine" for decision making, it can be a useful tool for solving specific problems but it is in principle the weakest method for decision making and, in general, it strips the human decision-making process of meaning and value.

Voting is effective when it is a method of last resort: when discussion has failed and there is no apparent possibility of overcoming differences of perspective but it is nonetheless imperative that a decision be made, voting is a way of resorting to "might"—simple quantitative superiority of numbers—to determine the result. Such situations do arise, and, consequently, voting is an important method to have at one's disposal. It too, of course, is much more meaningful a method within a context in which the participants in the process are in agreement with its use, that is, this method, like all the others discussed above, remains dependent upon a more basic context of trust and agreement if it is to produce decisions that the participants (the "voters") will feel to be their "own." For this reason, voting still does not avoid the requirement of trust, and it is, consequently, answerable to it when it comes to determining the integrity of its use and the quality of its results. Nonetheless, voting is, as far as possible, a method that strips human decision making of its humanity, turning the process into an anonymous calculation of "inputs" from "participants" who are essentially alienated from each other. This mutual alienation is evident at a number of levels.

The most immediate and obvious form of alienation involved in voting is the fact that it requires of each participant that that participant have a settled and resolved perspective on the issue in question (and in the terms in which the issue is presented). In other words, it requires that the participants, as individuals, have "made their decision" prior to the decision by voting. Voting, in other words, puts pressure upon each of us to function as a discrete individual, rather than as a member of a collectivity: it pressures us, that is, to house our decision-making process within the limits of our own, isolated perspective. This pressure upon individual, behavioral self-interpretation has a complementary consequence for our behavioral interpretation of group identity, namely, it encourages us to interpret the group, not as a shared reality in and through which our perspectives are formed—a "we"—but as an aggregate of already fully formed individuals whose perspectives are insulated from each other. It also pressures us to interpret decisions as matters that should be addressed and settled independently, rather than encouraging within us an openness to learning from each other. Voting, in other words, is fundamentally based on a competitive rather than a cooperative mentality, and to embrace it is to embrace an attitude toward one's fellow participants of "me against them." Further, in addition to thus closing us off from each other, the embrace of voting as a method also closes us off from a meaningful engagement with our own responsibilities, for it encourages us to believe about ourselves that all that is required of us is to "make up our own minds," and then to rely on the mechanical process to settle matters. In other words, it does not just pressure us to make decisions on our own, but encourages us to limit our engagement with the relevant issues to this, since "there is nothing else for me to do." It encourages, in other words, both an insular attitude of individual self-satisfaction and an attitude of comfortable detachment from the larger process.

As a means of last resort, voting is an effective and important tool; to mistake it for an end, however—to take it, that is, as the inherently desirable means of decision making—is to adopt a particularly barren and, ultimately, destructive view of human relationships. To hold voting as an ideal is precisely to desire the elimination of what is distinctive and definitive of our humanity. As a political structure in particular, it is the ultimate abrogation of political consciousness as such, and hence the opposite of political participation, for it precisely encourages us to disregard the larger context of collective decision making in favor of adopting a self-satisfied perspective of isolated individuality. In our culture, we have come (naively) to equate "democracy" with "voting," when in fact voting, as the primary means of political participation, fundamentally undermines the very meaning of "democracy": culturally, reliance on voting encourages us to deny, rather than embrace, the sharedness of our endeavor of living together and, politically, it produces a situation in which the larger mass of voters have almost no role in political decision making and, hence, almost no sense of "ownership" of the decisions putatively made "on their behalf" by their putative "representatives." The culture that installs voting as the primary means of political participation thus cultivates precisely the opposite of citizenship.

The Distinctive Role of Government

Because of its bureaucratic, machinic character, the very form of modern government presents us with political problems, namely, the substitution of machinic relations for human judgment and the active discouraging of our adopting our roles as citizens. The actual "content," so to speak, of modern government presents us with further political problems, both with respect to its own functioning and in its relationship to the other crucial domains of adult life: the family and the market. Let us consider first the relation to family and market.

The family and the market each operate with a distinctive and different interpretation of the fundamental nature of the person. Within the domain of intimate life it is the unique human relationship that is the primary "unit," and the individual takes her, his, or their definition from this relationship, from her, his, or their "role." Here, our roles are qualitatively distinct one from another (father from mother, wife from son, friend from lover, and so on). Within the domain of economic life, it is the generic, quantitative relations of exchange that constitute the primary reality, and the individual takes her, his, or their definition from her, his, or their position in this monetary system. Here, our identities are quantitatively distinguished, that is, we each have a specifiable "value," which is the measure of our ability to participate in economic life. These different interpretations of the person run fundamentally counter to each other and, indeed, as we have seen, they compete with each other for primacy in determining the basic character of human affairs.

In all situations, individuals and social groups are called upon to decide between these two interpretations of ourselves. When I am out with my friends, for example, my feelings of intimate companionship naturally impel me to buy drinks for them, whereas it would be wiser, given my general state of financial impoverishment, to adopt a more frugal attitude and insist on dividing up the bill. Analogously, your family will have to shape itself around the conditions of your employment, either consenting to allow family life to have its terms dictated by the requirement of your job that you move to a new city or subordinating economic life to the priorities of the family by requiring you to change your job. Businesses, analogously, must decide whether they will hold their functioning answerable to the demands of accommodating family life through flexibility in scheduling, limiting hours of operation, and embracing the cost of extending healthcare benefits to employees' family members, or whether they will operate exclusively in pursuit of maximizing profit through disregarding the emotional and interpersonal needs of their employees. And, at the highest level, a society as a whole will be defined by how it determines the relative priority of family and market in defining the functioning of that society. It is this last issue that brings us to the issue of the first aspect of the distinctive "content" of modern government.

Government is charged with the responsibility of deciding the end and means for the society as such. We are most familiar with thinking of this in terms of decisions about war, and it is generally as militarily defined units—which in turn we generally interpret in terms of geographical boundaries—that the history of societies is told. It is this notion that we rely on, for example, when we look at the distribution of "countries" on a world map. While this externally directed matter of the state in relation to other states is undoubtedly important, a government is defined more fundamentally by the internally directed matter of determining what it is, or, perhaps more accurately, who we are. At its most basic level, this "who" is a matter of culture—the "spirit" of a people—and there is no guarantee that there is a single "we" that corresponds to any given nation-state, any "country": in addition to the "subcultural" divisions between, for example, affluent, urban youth and poor, rural individuals or, again, between militant working-class activists for racial equality and conservative working-class individuals who fear the loss of their cultural homogeneity and privilege, politically defined "countries" can also house massively different religious communities, such as the Muslim and Hindu populations simultaneously differentiated and fused together in the forced partition that defined India and Pakistan in 1947. Government—the state—is the institutional interpretation of this identity, an interpretation that can overlap more or less with the lived reality of cultural unity—the "spirit"—that defines the society it represents. This interpretation is enacted through myriad policies addressing all matter of internal affairs, from educational requirements for high school courses to budgets and guidelines for the maintenance of highways. Most fundamentally, though, this interpretation is an interpretation of the relative importance of those other fundamental interpretations of our identity, the family and the market.

By itself, each of the self-interpretations of the family or the market is, in addition to being a challenge to the other, a denial of the necessity and the authority of the state. The family holds itself responsible only to the sphere of intimacy, not acknowledging its own answerability to the impersonal realm that contextualizes it and to whose authority it is subordinated; the market defines itself by profit, without holding itself answerable to the needs of the human world from which and within which that profit is generated. Family and market are simultaneously interpretations of the nature of the self and of the nature of value, and, in and of itself, neither intimacy nor profit—the relevant conception of value in family and market, respectively—involves the notion of subordination to the authority of the larger community to determine the proper terms of "worth." Government, however, is precisely an interpretation of the nature of society—and correspondingly, the nature of its members (as "citizens")—and an interpretation of the nature of value that construes family and market both as in need of organization, coordination, and rule according to the terms and demands of the good of society as a whole.

As we have noted, government is charged with determining "the just and the unjust, the expedient and the inexpedient"—value and policy—for society as a whole. The state must make decisions about the good of the community as a whole on behalf of the community as a whole, and that perspective is very different from the perspective that thinks only in terms of the intimacy of one's immediate relationships or the perspective that thinks only in terms of impersonal "earnings." The society as a whole is a reality that is both personal and impersonal: the society as a whole has as its foundation—its "element," as Hegel puts it (*Phenomenology of Spirit*, para. 475)—groups defined by relations of intimacy, but the unification of those different groups into the society is not itself a matter of intimacy; similarly, the society as a whole depends upon alienated, economic relationships, but it does not exist for the sake of "the market." Because it is precisely charged with recognizing the needs of the society and its members, it is incumbent upon government as government to acknowledge the significance of both of these dimensions of our lives without defining itself in terms of either, and the challenge to government is thus always to mediate the conflict of family and market. Family and market each present unique needs and challenges to government.

We noted that, historically, the *polis* specifically emerged in opposition to the cultural domination of the *oikos*—the household—and this is a helpful reminder that the very meaning of government is, first, not to be "a family." The intimacy of family life, as we argued above, is integral to our human existence, but this intimacy is always a kind of "particularism"—an essential favoritism of "one's own"—and, for that reason, the intimacies of one family conflict in principle with the intimacies of another family. To the extent that the community contains more than one family, therefore, it can be a community—can be "one"—only if its nature transcends family and thus transcends the conflict that obtains in principle between different networks of intimacy. In the ancient Greek context in which the *polis* emerged, this was especially pertinent to limiting the mafia-like structures by which historically elite families tried to establish themselves in positions of power within and between the Greek cities; in our contemporary society, we recognize this issue more familiarly

in, for example, the need for the state to intervene on behalf of abused
children or abused spouses, and to protect those individuals from the
treatment they would otherwise be subjected to within their families,
or, again, in the need for the state to use force to capture and imprison
violent individuals despite the efforts of their families to shelter and
protect them from prosecution. In these and similar situations, the state
is charged with protecting the well-being of its members in opposition
to the interests of the relationships of intimacy to which they belong.
Inasmuch as government thus transcends our intimate relationships, it is
inherently a domain of alienation, in that, to participate in it, we must
renounce "our" (intimate and local) authority to settle "our" affairs in
favor of "its" authority to act on behalf of the larger "we" of the community as a whole, an alienation that must be embraced simultaneously
by members of all the other local, intimate communities that make up
the larger society. Government is thus a domain intrinsically defined by
alienation, but it is an alienated realm specially charged with caring for
the needs of the domains of intimacy that it comprises.

Because we need to sustain ourselves materially, economic life is
inescapable and inasmuch as the "division of labor" is an inherently social
matter, the care of the community's economic life is an essential focus of
government. Once economic life comes to involve us in relationships of
exchange with non-intimate others, the market itself becomes a power
that dictates its terms to intimate life and thus functions, like government itself, as a domain of alienated authority. The market, however,
is not charged with protecting the good of its community—indeed, it
precisely transcends any community and instead operates in principle as
a domain of exchange that exists between communities—but is instead
focused on the extraction of "profit" unfettered by any intimate allegiance.
Consequently, insofar as government itself has the responsibility to be the
authoritative power for caring for the communal good, the very meaning
of government is, second, not to be the market. For the market, the
human world built up through the strivings and struggles that constitute
the meaningful reality of the everyday, intimate life of a society's members
is a resource—a means—for profit: what defines economic life, in other
words, is precisely the perspective that is indifferent to the intimate, lived
significance that is in principle meaningful only to those within that
domain of intimacy. Government, however, inasmuch as it is charged
with the care of the society as a whole, is responsible in principle to
defend the integrity of the domain of intimacy against exploitation by

the indifferent perspective of the market. Just as the state must limit and manage the conflicts that naturally emerge between different networks of intimacy—different families—so, consequently, must it limit conflicts that naturally emerge between intimacy and economics—between family and market.

Government, in other words, is a matter of assessing well those particular situations in which the intrinsic demands of the family must be subordinated to the needs of economics, and when the intrinsic demands of the market must be subordinated to the needs of intimacy. In their natural functioning, both families and businesses necessarily confront the conflicting demands of intimacy and economic life, and is it the essential task of government to determine the proper extent to which each domain can encroach upon the other within the context of assessing the needs of the good of the community as a whole: government, that is, must, for example, decide the limits of the work day and the extent to which an employer must make provision for the organic and psychological health of their employees, and similarly must decide the extent to which persons and families can be held answerable for debt, the extent to which particular businesses will be allowed to operate in particular residential areas or whether or not lands shall be made available for the building of a highway, the laying of a fiber-optic cable, the installation of a pipeline, and so on. Government must ask, and answer, the question of when it is for the good of the whole to limit the interests of one of these two domains—intimate life and economics—in favor of the interests of the other.

Each of these two foundational domains—family and market—has its own raison d'être in the demands of human nature, and, in turn, has its own intrinsic needs and norms. Consequently, each domain can claim a right to exist and can complain about misrepresentation and mistreatment of its nature and needs. It is government to which these claims and complaints are naturally addressed, and government is precisely the domain of human life that is charged with adjudicating these claims. Government in this sense must carry out the essentially derivative task of "managing" the human world constituted by the intersection of the complex realities that emerge from each of the domains of intimacy and economics but, more fundamentally, must occupy the originary role of leadership in deciding, above and beyond the terms of intimacy and economics, the basic principles and terms by which this intersection of domains will be allowed to exist in the first place. The state, in short, must limit the values of intimacy and profit by the value of justice.

And, beyond limiting family and market in relation to each other, government also must determine which functions of society cannot, with justice, be subordinated to the authority of either family or market: those functions, that is, that are inherently a matter of the good of the whole. Each of medical care, public transit, sanitation, and education, for example, is integral to the health and functioning of society as such—is a matter of "the public interest"—and it is thus fundamentally irresponsible to allow these functions to be treated as matters either of private enterprise or of domestic management. Similarly, government is responsible for the management of those infrastructural dimensions of society that relate distinctly to its own distinctive functioning, such as the police, the courts, and the prisons, which are inherently and exclusively matters of the execution of justice, and the structural dimensions that are constitutive of government itself, such as the makeup of the government's legislative body, the character of its electoral system, and so on. Precisely because government is not reducible to either family or market, its existence depends upon the maintenance of this distinctive domain of social functions that embody a power superior to family and market. There is no formula that will answer the question of how these definitive decisions of governance should be made. What is determinable in advance, though, is that the disavowal of these responsibilities is bad government.

It is in considering this essential "content" that defines the fundamental role of government that we again see the distinctive challenge we face in contemporary politics: whereas it is incumbent upon government by its very nature to limit and regulate the activities of family and market in favor of the good of the community as a whole, contemporary government, by and large, has "sold out" society to the interests of the market while simultaneously "pandering" rhetorically to the interests of the institution of the family in order to maintain its ruling power, thereby manifesting a strategic disparity between "word" and "deed" that is uniquely relevant to maintaining power in a system in which the governments far removed from the vast populations they putatively "represent" are established by a popular vote.

Western governments in Europe and the United States—the contemporary descendants of the European colonial powers of the Early Modern period—have consistently abrogated their role as regulators of the market, and instead have used their power to further the independent growth of the market. Especially since the establishment of the International Monetary

Fund and the World Bank in the Bretton Woods Agreement of 1944, this practice especially installed international banking as a power capable of dictating policy to governments—the very opposite of governments regulating the market—and this situation has now developed its most extreme form yet in the establishing in 1998 of an independent "European Central Bank" that has separated the control of currency (the "Euro") from national government and that dictates financial policy to the various national governments in the European Union. This factual subordination of government to the rule of economics since the mid–twentieth century has broadly been accompanied in the West by a rhetorical—propagandistic—stance in which the realities and complexities of government are concealed and denied and, instead of defending its independent authority and educating the citizenry into its functioning, government has pretended either to be protecting the unencumbered freedom of the individual (a perspective generally of a piece with the economic interpretation of society), or to be protecting the traditional values of the family (even as the actual protection of the needs of intimate life is abandoned). Simultaneously with these developments in the West, governments in the Middle East and Asia—the contemporary descendants of societies that were dominated by European colonial powers—have in different but related ways abandoned the responsibilities of government while "pandering" to the independent interests of family or market. In India, economic profiteering has been allowed to run rampant, while government has maintained its power largely by aligning itself rhetorically with the traditionalism of family and religion. In the so-called Middle East, governments have similarly relied on family-based religious traditionalism to establish their power. China, which earlier in the twentieth century was, like Russia, a site of great peasant resistance to imperial government, has now become another massive country "sold off" to economic powers. Many nations of Africa, even in their "postcolonial" reality, have in fact been less successful than the Asian countries in establishing a meaningful independence and continue to be dominated by the economic interests of other nations. The contemporary nations of South America have often been more successful in their attempts to establish meaningful government in the wake of the European colonization that shaped their modern reality, but here too these efforts have typically been undermined by resistance from the Western powers that constitute the so-called global North.

With few exceptions, modern nation-states have abandoned the fundamental principles that define and justify government and have instead turned government into a self-serving power that has handed over its authority in word and deed to the rhetoric of "family values" and the policymaking of the market. This first dimension of the problem of the "content" of modern government—its (mis-)handling of its role in regulating the domains of intimacy and economy—is supplemented by two further dimensions that have to do with the distinctive powers of government itself.

The Limits of Government

Inasmuch as it is itself an authoritative and nonderivative reality, the state is a distinctive domain of human action and self-interpretation. This domain is defined by its authoritative role in relationship to the other domains of family and market, but the subordination of those two domains to its authority does not amount to their effacement or the disappearance of their autonomy; on the contrary, it is precisely the responsibility of the state to protect and preserve the integrity of each of those domains. The state, in other words, is both the voice of the whole and a particular voice, and this particularity must not be confused with the whole—this is the "problem of the guardians" we considered above. Consequently, just as the state must protect the rights of each of those domains against the other, so must it protect the rights of each of these domains against the overarching perspective of the government itself. The state is the domain of the self-determination of the community as such, but, as such, it is inherently charged with the task of being self-limiting, that is, of determining the limits of state intervention into family life and economics: there is, in other words, no further "check" on government, for it is by definition the voice of justice.

This necessary self-limiting of government means, for example, that the government is neither a "parent" nor a business, and consequently must not usurp from family life the properly intimate responsibilities of, for example, carrying out the upbringing of children or choosing a romantic partner, and it must not usurp from business the properly economic responsibilities of, for example, competitively pursuing individual profit. Government must determine with respect to itself the appropriate limits of its intervention into interpersonal disputes, into decisions about distribution of property, into the desiderata of hiring practices, and so on. And beyond these matters of improper transgression upon the domains of family and business as such, government must also restrict the imposition upon family and business of its own distinctive activity. We have noted some features of this distinctive activity already in noting the institutions of justice and legislation. We can grasp this issue more exactly if we recognize that the role of government as "supervisor" necessarily defines a third unique dimension to the lives of its members beyond their participation in structures of intimacy and economics. In order to lead and manage the whole society effectively, government must be cognizant of the character of the lives of its members and, consequently, it must collect information about them; subjecting its members to such "supervision," however, is not a neutral activity—on the contrary, it significantly affects the quality of life of its members—and it is consequently a significant distinctive responsibility of government as such to limit its "surveillance" appropriately.

Precisely because government is charged with being "the perspective of the whole," or, effectively, the "self-consciousness" of the society as such, its function cannot be separated from knowing the society. Consequently, methods and practices of knowing are integral to its proper functioning. It is thus essential to the functioning of government at the broadest level, for example, to conduct a regular census, both for the purpose of determining the needs and interests of its members and for the purposes of answering to its own needs of assessing taxes or calling for military service; at a structural level, records of business practices are essential to the monitoring and regulating of economic life and, at a more personal level, the ability to compel testimony is integral to the functioning of the legal system. For every essential role of government, there is a corresponding need for some form of surveillance, for it is the knowledge thus acquired that allows government to act effectively as government. Knowledge thus empowers government, but, in so doing, it simultaneously empowers government both in its particularity as a distinctive social power and in its universal role as caretaker for the society as a whole. Even when it is necessary for good governance, such surveillance of its members is invasive, in that it transgresses the limits that are intrinsic to intimate and economic life, but it is the proper reflection of the definitive subordination of family and market to the state; such surveillance is inappropriately transgressive, however, when, rather than facilitating good governance, it furthers the partisan interests of the government as an independent power. Consequently, it is incumbent upon government to establish limits to its own gathering of information, at every level, from the large-scale level of the limitation of the activities of official "intelligence agencies" to the more immediate level of the limitation of interrogation techniques; in general, good government entails the legal recognition of legitimate domains of silence and secrecy. Here, we have a second aspect to the problem of the "content" of contemporary government.

Though Western governments at least have in fact developed many protections for individual privacy—typically through the hard-won victories of citizen activist groups—those same governments have taken many opportunities to erode those protections, typically in the name of "national security," and this has been coupled with the development of huge "intelligence agencies" that, like the bureaucratic civil service in general, have been allowed to develop a massive infrastructural complexity that makes them very difficult to control or eliminate. Beyond these practices of government in its own right, governments have also allowed businesses extreme latitude in gathering and using information about their citizens. Consequently, surveillance, which is justified only by the need for the carrying-out of justice in relationship to the good of society as a whole, has become a hugely overdeveloped reality in contemporary life that is in the service, not of justice, but of maintaining the independent power of the government and of the economic interests it serves.

And, finally, the need for self-limitation by the government requires that the terms of its functioning be themselves matters of public knowledge. In other words, the norms and rules by which government is operating must be known to its membership and must be based on principles recognizable by its members. If this condition is not met, then government is no longer the self-governing of the community, but has instead become an independent body exercising coercive power over the community. This problem arises when the norm of "transparency" is abandoned explicitly, but, even in the context of contemporary governments that purport to endorse this value, transparency can be effectively undermined simply by a growth in complexity that, like the growth of the civil service, becomes overwhelming: in other words, as government itself becomes more complicated, it becomes ever less realistic that its members could grasp its workings. In fact, this is the situation of contemporary government, in which it becomes ever less plausible that individual members will understand the workings of its practical structures, whether in matters of, for example, "quantitative easement" by the central bank—which is a practice of printing currency according to the "monetarist" interpretation of economics that dominates contemporary rhetoric and practice—or of, for example, the privatized management of prisons—which, though a

DOMAINS OF SETTLEMENT AND ENGAGEMENT

matter of public record and comprehensible to the average individual, is embedded so deeply in the mass of "information" about government practice that it is not realistic to pretend that most individuals can even be aware of it, let alone reflect on it critically. This growing complexity is the third aspect of the problem of "content" in contemporary government.

Together, these problems of content and form that we have been considering define the reality of contemporary government. Growing complexity, increasing surveillance, and the self-subordination of government to economic interests are ways in which the current practices of government work against the defining value of government as such; these problems of content dovetail with the ongoing transformation of the form of government into a "machine" to produce a situation in which government, rather than being the self-determination of the people, becomes an independent power to which the members of a society are subjected. It is these problems that set the terms and tasks for responsible political engagement: they define, that is, the distinctive responsibilities that we face as citizens.

Politics and Adulthood

As we saw above, the conception of government as an essential institution goes hand in hand with the interpretation of the individual as a "citizen," and the demands of citizenship are effectively the demands of adulthood. The essential meaning of adulthood is answering to reality on its own terms, and the defining imperative of citizenship is that one take responsibility for grasping the reality of one's social situation and responding to it according to the demands of the good. One's identity as a citizen is the demand intrinsic to that identity that one grasp the reality of one's political situation and adopt an active stance toward addressing the needs of that situation; because of the tendency of contemporary government to encourage our political passivity—the infantilizing tendency of contemporary government—this imperative of citizenship is thus always a challenge, for it requires of us that we resist the smooth path of conformity that our society designs for us and instead requires of us that we take the initiative on our own for improving the form of our political life. Indeed, citizenship thus has the distinctively human meaning of calling us to adulthood.

Grasping reality—whether the reality of nature or the reality of politics—is largely a matter of understanding that environment, and understanding, as Aristotle noted, is primarily a matter of grasping the causes—the "why"—of things (*Posterior Analytics* I.2.71b8–12). The philosopher is the individual who thinks in terms of ultimate first principles, in terms of the ultimate reason "why," but most of us tend not to be thus philosophical in our affairs; on the contrary, we tend to maintain a fairly narrow horizon in our investigations about the "why" of anything. Thus, we are typically content to know that it is cold because the furnace is broken, rather than feeling any need to understand why the furnace is broken, let alone why meteorological conditions are producing these weather conditions or why there are such realities as "hot" and "cold" in the first place and, similarly, we are typically content to know that this or that investment will earn this much interest without understanding why it will "earn" interest or, indeed, why we should be seeking wealth in the first place. By limiting our investigations into the "why," we give ourselves the opportunity to "move on" with our lives, and to focus on the pressing issues that concern us more immediately. The consequence of our limited reflection on causes and reasons, though, is that it is easy for us to embrace simultaneously different beliefs or behaviors that, though superficially compatible, are at root contradictory. In other words, we can be hypocritical, imagining ourselves to be living by one set of values while our actions in fact reveal a different set of commitments. This is especially an issue in political life, in which we typically do not notice the incompatibilities of our intimate and economic behaviors with our political participation.

Even though we can be inconsistent in how we deal with the conflicting demands of the intimate and economic dimensions of our lives, at a basic level it is hard for us not to acknowledge our intimate and economic needs, even if we do not grasp either them or the conflicts between them very deeply. With politics, however, it is easy for us to live on the basis of the world it gives us without recognizing our own implication in it. In other words, we can fail to recognize that our developed social and political life is an accomplishment. Thus, while we enjoy very much the ability to choose freely for ourselves the form and content of daily life, for example, we can easily imagine this to be our "natural" situation rather than recognizing that this is a hard-won political accomplishment; indeed, we can even imagine the existence of government to be an unnecessary obstacle to our happiness. Because this reality is a political accomplishment and not a natural condition, however, its perpetuation depends upon our ongoing, active maintenance of it and, consequently, our attitude of complacency (or antagonism) makes us prone to losing our political privileges. This problematic tendency is especially exacerbated by the infantilizing governmental regime that conceals the inherent nature of government.

In fact it is up to all of us to care for our political reality, even as we take care of our personal needs for intimacy and economics. And, just as the demands of "making a living" can conflict with the demands of pursuing one's intimate life, so does owning up to our political responsibility at a minimum take time and energy that might otherwise be spent on our other life concerns and at a maximum requires us to commit ourselves to courses of action that might well jeopardize our intimate or economic existence; this latter is the case, for example, in situations of political activism that can bring one unwanted public notoriety that can result in the intrusion of the otherwise alien, public realm into one's personal life (through hate mail, violent intimidation, or incarceration, for example) or the undermining of one's career through an employer's distaste for employing a "controversial" figure. Political engagement is challenging and demanding, and typically we would prefer to be able to focus on "just living our lives," but this attitude—the very one encouraged by contemporary government—is precisely the one that will result in the loss of the "free" world in which it is possible for us to have those lives. Government is not a natural force, even though it is a natural need, and so we cannot rely upon it simply to "do what is right" on its own. We must recognize that even in our passive compliance we are being "active," that is, we are mishandling our political lives for the detriment of all.

Our adult responsibility thus requires us first to own up to our reality as citizens—simply to recognize the political character of our existence—and then to determine for ourselves how we will integrate answering to this demand while simultaneously answering to the demands of family and market. Like experiencing oneself as a family member, experiencing oneself as a citizen involves grasping oneself as a part of a larger community that is integral to one's identity; like experiencing oneself as an economic agent, experiencing oneself as a citizen involves grasping oneself as a participant in a non-intimate sphere in which one is personally called upon to act—to work—to maintain one's reality. Our challenge as citizens is to make this recognition—which is not just a conceptual affair, but a matter of practice—and to do so in a way that continues to allow us to maintain flourishing intimate lives and successful economic lives.

There is a great difference between devoting one's life to political work and minimally answering to the demands of politics, just as there is a great difference between devoting one's life to one's job and minimally doing the work necessary to sustain oneself economically, and the need to integrate our lives as citizens with our lives as family members and workers requires of each of us that we determine for ourselves how we will negotiate the intersection of these three competing interpretations of ourselves. But though there is no formulaic answer in advance to how this integration is to be accomplished, that is, though there are many responsible ways to "be political," some choices are undeniably better than others.

Direct activism—devoting one's life to being cognizant of pressing political concerns and working to address them, as we witnessed in the case of Emma Goldman—is surely the most immediate way to embrace our political identities and, like "entrepreneurship" in the context of economics, such activism is surely the *conditio sine qua non* of our political existence, that is, it is only because individuals are politically active that it is possible for a political space to exist for any of us. Velma Hopkins (1909–1996), for example, began her adult life by taking an oppressive job as a tobacco stemmer at the R. J. Reynolds Tobacco Company in Winston-Salem, North Carolina, where, because she was black and a woman, she was paid substantially less than other employees. In 1943, however, in response to the harsh working conditions, she joined with others to call for a month-long strike that led to the establishment of Local 22, the first and only union ever to exist at the company. It is because of her individual initiative that improvements in working conditions and pay equity that others relied on were won from the company and, indeed, her actions were integral to the emerging civil rights movement in the United States. A generation earlier, Bhimrao Ramji Ambedkar (1891–1956), who grew up in India as a member of an "untouchable" caste—a socially defined group so disdained that the simple touch of a member of that caste was imagined to pollute any article—endured violence and humiliation to became one of the first members of an "outcaste" to obtain a college education in India and ultimately led the movement to win separate electorates or "reservations" for otherwise excluded religious and social groups (an issue on which he and Mohandas Gandhi were opposed), and fought relentlessly to win recognition of the rights of untouchables to access drinking water. Such activism, however, comes at a cost—a cost to the most intimate dimensions of our lives—as is demonstrated, for example, in the case of Naila Ayesh (1961–). After marrying in 1986, Ayesh, while pregnant, was detained for forty-five days in 1987 for belonging to a Palestinian students' union and protesting the Israeli occupation of Gaza. In the detention camp, she miscarried after being beaten and denied medical treatment. It is to the activities of individuals such as these that we owe the development of the progressive social institutions upon whose existence we rely, but the biographies of such individuals demonstrate powerfully the tension that exists between the demands of active political engagement and the enjoyment of every-day intimate and economic life. Just as most of us do not want to take on the task of defining our own "enterpreneurial" route into economic life, most of us will want a meaningful way to be a citizen that is less challenging to our other intimate and economic pursuits.

Between direct activism—the strongest level of involvement—and voting—the weakest level—there are a range of strategies for constructive political action, for there are a variety of ways in which constructive political action is already underway in our society, thereby affording individuals routes for effective action as citizens. One can, for example, contribute time to working on behalf of progressive candidates within the context of formal elections; one can work on behalf of a particular "cause," such as promoting collective bargaining, improved public health-care, or enhanced access to childcare; one can be an educator. These are, again, "off the rack" choices, but all of them require greater agency than the extreme passivity of voting. In general, we must all work against the infantilizing character of the contemporary "political" culture that cul-tivates in us an attitude of passivity that lacks the sense that "it's up to us" to engage effectively with our (threatening) reality. In other words, effective citizenship, like adulthood more generally, always requires of us that we become active in its embrace.

5

Bearing Witness

Honesty and Wisdom

As adults, we can become trapped in the actual. In contrast, the child plays, experiencing the world as a launching pad for imagination. For the child, this is to some degree a burden, for the child would like to *engage* with the world, but she cannot, and growing into this experience will precisely be her growing out of childhood. For the adult, however, this very engagement is what becomes the burden, and often what we need is a return to an experience of play. Of course, the adult cannot and should not return to being a child *simpliciter*. Nonetheless, there is a sense in which our maturity is most fully realized in allowing a spirit of play to emerge from *within* our experience of engagement.

Play is imaginative: it is a loosening of one's engagement with what is actual in order to dwell in the possible. To some extent, this sense of play—this "loosen[ing of] the intentional threads that connect us to the world," as Maurice Merleau-Ponty describes it (*Phenomenology of Perception*, xxvii), that releases one from domination by the actual—can most immediately be maintained in adult life through the simple integration of recreational experiences, which allow one to find pleasure in "taking a break" from the demanding world of responsibility and work. More pervasively, it can be manifested in the emotional lightheartedness—the "playfulness"—with which one might take up one's serious pursuits, in an attitude, that is, that endeavors ongoingly not to be overwhelmed by the sense that the demands of daily living are what ultimately matter: they are not "the absolute." Beyond these (no doubt very important) ways of weaving an experience of play into an adult life that is in fact focused elsewhere, there are ways in which something like the experience of play—the experience of the primacy of possibility—can define the very focus of one's adult orientation.

Beyond the development of effective capacities for dealing with the actual terms of the world—the terms in which reality is "present" to us—adulthood also involves the development of receptivities for dealing with the world that is not present to us, the possibilities of the world that are not actual: what is imaginary, what is not yet, what should be, what can never be contained within the temporally and spatially finite. Our development of effective capacity is, more or less, our development of agency—our development of the ability to "do," to effect a change within the actual; we are also, however, able to hear the call of the non-actual, and it is a further dimension of our adulthood to able to be a medium for the presentation of that which is not adequately recognized in actuality. Beyond competent negotiating with the actual, in which we accept "what is" as an adequate norm for shaping our behavior, we have the capacity to recognize "what could be" and "what should be" as normative for our behavior, which is to say we can recognize "what is" to be inadequate. Whereas it is immaturity to consider actuality inadequate insofar as it does not confirm to one's immediate desires—indeed, it is precisely the work of adulthood to transcend this attitude in "owning up" to the real—it is in fact the height of maturity to recognize actuality to be inadequate to reality's own standards. Here, our maturity consists in our recognizing our responsibility to realize reality: this is the recognition of the beautiful, the good, the divine, and the true.

In fact, engaging with possibility—which is fundamentally a matter of creativity—already underlies our ability to deal competently with the actual, for it is implicit in any practice of effectively caring for a dynamic situation. But though the engagement with possibility is thus integral to our immediate practical engagement with the actual, there is also an engagement with possibility in its own right, and this is found especially in the domains of art, religion, and philosophy. In these latter domains—art, religion, and philosophy—we endeavor to engage unconditionally with reality on its own terms, that is, we endeavor to engage with what is "absolute," rather than engaging with reality only relative to our own perspective. Reflecting on these "absolute" experiences will complete our study of the occupations of adult life.

Art

Whether as an adult or as a younger person, one can feel drawn to express. One can feel drawn, that is, not simply to communicate something to someone in the course of one's everyday efforts at negotiating interpersonal life, but to give voice uniquely to something that should be brought to articulation. And "to give voice," furthermore, does not just mean speaking or singing, but is a metaphor for a very wide range of possible behaviors, whether the bodily twisting—dance—that articulates the urgency of a compelling rhythm; the inscribing on a surface of sinuous, twisting lines—drawing—that brings depth and figuration to life from ink and paper; the intoning of a sinuous line of notes—music—that carves out a landscape in our emotional world; or any other gathering up of some aspect of our sensible, bodily reality that magically realizes a meaning—a gripping presentation of the sense of our human world—that could not be apprehended in any other way. Such expressions—such works of art—are not so much objects of contemplation themselves as they are apertures: they are lenses through which one is enabled to perceive the sense of one's situation.

This artistic expression that allows us a new perspective on our situation can happen at many different levels. At perhaps the simplest level, we decorate our rooms and our bodies. When we enter a room or see a clothed individual approaching us, though we could and sometimes do explicitly notice the decorations or clothing, we typically experience an atmosphere or a character, the perception of which is prepared for us—expressed—by the decorations and clothing. Indeed, to some degree, decoration and clothing have failed if we notice them as such, rather than seeing through them to a world or a personality that they express. Beyond decoration, the presence of individual artworks can have a profound effect on how we experience the meaning—and hence the possibilities—of our environments. Indeed, we often feel the need, either through our own creation or through the acquisition of the works of others, to "furnish" (or perhaps "populate") our living environments with sculptures, paintings, or music, which, again, can be the direct objects of our perception but more often provide the supports for our experiencing our environment as a "home," or, in some cases (such as in listening to or dancing to music in a nightclub), experiencing an environment as a novel, alien world in which we can abandon our familiar identities and become "other."

And then, beyond these levels of artistic experience which have become part of the familiar paraphernalia of personal life in the modern world, there are acts of expression which aim not at satisfying these artistic needs of daily life but aim instead at grappling with the human activity of expressing on its own terms; encountering art in this sense can be a matter of deepening one's experience of the world through exposure to and engagement with the history of human artistic practice or, more directly, through engaging in creative acts of expression that endeavor to participate in and advance that historical human practice.

Like family, market, and government, art is one of the essential dimensions of the human world, a dimension that plays a fundamental role in how we perceive our world and thus how we behave, and the great history of human artistic practice has not simply been a matter of enriching personal space, but has even more fundamentally been a matter of shaping our cultures and, with that, shaping our shared perception of our very nature as humans; different artistic traditions, consequently, correspond to significantly different cultural orientations. Ancient Mesopotamian architecture, sculpture, and literature, for example, seems fundamentally expressive of a conception of humanity as essentially in relation to a form of divinity, itself identified with the power and fertility of nature, that validated a fundamental sense of the subjection of humanity to the gods and to the massively powerful kings who ruled with the perceived sanction of those gods; and this is in stark contrast, for example, to the community-empowering images of human perfection that were characteristic of ancient Greek art. Again, Italian Renaissance painting, sculpture, architecture, and literature are widely recognized as expressing an essential dignity and autonomy of the human world, in contrast to the otherworldliness associated with the medieval Christian church. And correspondingly, as Walter Benjamin demonstrates in "The Work of Art in the Age of Mechanical Reproduction," the mechanically reproducible forms of art that emerged with the modern world—especially through the invention of the printing press, photography, and, much later, sound recording—both reflected and encouraged an essentially individualistic interpretation of persons, in contrast to the communal sense of human life reflected and encouraged by, for example, highly individual religious paintings situated in public, devotional settings in the context of premodern Christianity (223–25). Historically, cultures have existed as cultures as much through their artistic traditions as through their religious beliefs and their political institutions; or, more exactly, these three—politics, art, and religion—are three facets of the single reality that is that "culture," and that is a distinctive way of interpreting the very nature of our reality as human beings. In our everyday lives, we thus live within an artistic horizon—a perspective on the world shaped by the forms of artistic expression that populate our world and through which our perspectives have been formed. In "drinking in" the existent forms of our cultural environment, we actually imbibe a perspective upon ourselves. Art, as Heidegger writes in "The Origin of the Work of Art," "first gives to things their look and to men their outlook on themselves" (168), and, without even noticing it, an attitude of social self-interpretation is cultivated within us simply through our seemingly innocent "enjoyment" of our artistic culture.

Thus, like intimacy, economics, and politics, art is for all of us a formative dimension of life that we inherit without earning. Consequently, a significant dimension of adult life is our engagement with this implicit aspect of our reality and, generally speaking, an explicit engagement with art results in a fuller and richer adulthood. For many adults, art will exist thematically only at a minimal level as a decorative backdrop to an environment or as a matter of diverting entertainment, but, though art does decorate and entertain, there are much greater rewards that art offers to the one who engages with it explicitly. Most importantly, art, itself a product of creative imagination, precisely speaks to and educates one's creative imagination. Art introduces one to different possible ways of seeing, to different ways, that is, of seeing what is possible; indeed, it was reading the novel *What Is to be Done?* by Nikolai Chernyshevsky that initially sparked Emma Goldman's imagination and set her on her dramatic life path. As with economics and politics, so with art, it is possible to take up that domain as the center of one's life or, if one's primary focus is elsewhere, to turn to prefabricated ways of taking it up: we can distinguish, that is, between such an engagement with art that takes it up "off the rack," to continue the trope I introduced in chapter 4, and an engagement that takes it up from first principles.

Taking it up from first principles—becoming an artist—is surely one of the most fulfilling of human occupations. There is, of course, a great range in the levels at which someone takes up this occupation, ranging from the popular entertainer to the world-historical creator, but at every level the artist is the person who has made this domain of creative expression their primary home, and their ongoing challenge simultaneously to push the boundaries of their capacities for creative articulation (whether in musical tones, or in painted colors, bodily gestures, improvised performances, assembled installations, and so on) and to perfect their "craft," their disciplined facility with their chosen medium of expression. Such an occupation is fulfilling because of the inherent worth of these two practices and because of the internally recognizable forms of progress one makes in each of these practices; at the same time, this can be a lonely occupation, for there is little "worldly" evidence for marking progress—especially since the most creative work precisely works against and outside of our familiar worldly terms for making sense of our experience—and there is consequently considerable psychological challenge in maintaining an artistic career, a career that typically depends upon participation in a strongly supportive community of other artists who can help one to take one's own practice seriously. And, indeed, inasmuch as, even as an artist, one must nonetheless grapple with the economic demands of everyday life, the artist's focus on their self-development as a creator is typically uncomfortably mixed with the logistical and psychological demands of "making a living": in particular, the artist in contemporary society typically faces the double challenge, first, of having to accept a near-poverty-level existence because of the large-scale lack of economic support for artists (despite the huge everyday use of, for example, musical products by the general population and the huge profits made by the massive industry that controls those products) and, second, of feeling great pressure to conform to familiar "tastes" in their artistic work for the sake of accomplishing even minimal economic success. Generally, the artist must balance these frustrations of economic life against the intrinsic reward of artistic creation and the emotional fulfillment that comes through expression and through the experience of making this experience (vicariously) possible for others.

And of course one need not become an artist to embrace art as a meaningful dimension of adult life (though that is true only if some people do embrace the artistic life). The artist, as we just noted, creates for others as much as for themself, and, consequently, we can live through artists' expressions without facing the necessity of being thus creative on our own. Regularly reading works of literature, for example, generally results in a greater understanding of, and hence greater sympathy for, the human condition, and a regular engagement with sculpture, painting, or music attunes one to the expressive qualities of stone, pigment, and sound, leading one to be more responsive in general to the ways that stone, pigment, and sound in everyday life are thus expressive—whether making one more alive to the beauty already present in things, or alerting one to the stultifying character of one's material environment. In general, engagement with artistic works exercises one in the experience of participating in the realm of possibility, thereby breaking the hegemony of prosaic actuality—the demands of family, business, and government—for determining one's perspective; indeed, it is by dwelling in the possible that we become ourselves capable of imagining a different possible world, which is itself the beginning of transforming our intimate, economic, or political existence. And, finally, whether we engage with art more passively, by responding to the works of others, or more actively, by cultivating our own capacities for artistic creation, we are in either case educating our ability to express, an education that contributes directly to our ability to enter constructively into the demands of interpersonal communication that are at the core of all of our human interactions.

Through artworks, we find ourselves in a world. They give us a way to look at the world and to look at ourselves—to find our place in it. On the one hand, this allows us to understand others: it gives us a perspective on who others are and how we fit with them, thus through taking it up explicitly, we cultivate sympathy. On the other hand, the stories thus told through art can leave us "out of the picture," so to speak, that is, we can find that the world they imagined is not sufficient to grasp our reality. This has historically been the experience of women, black people, indigenous people, workers, and other people who do not find themselves within the world imagined by artworks: people who have not been "written into" the history in a way that lets them realize their potential. To take up this side of art explicitly is to develop a critical perspective, a perspective precisely oriented to possibility, but to the possibility that is not recognized within the prevailing terms by which reality is expressed. And this critical orientation is thus a perspective that precisely needs new, creative art to give it a cultural embodiment.

Art, then, though it often appears to be something optional within one's life, is in fact inescapable: it is one of the fundamental, formative dimensions of our experience. We are always being shaped by it implicitly, and explicitly engaging with it, whether through study or through practices of expression, is one of the most liberating and most fulfilling ways of realizing the possibilities of our adult existence. Something analogous to this is true of religion.

Religion

As we noted above, art, at a cultural level, is primarily a matter of a culture's expression of its own deepest values and in that respect it is closely akin to religion. At its root, religion is not an individual affair but is a culture's expression of what it deems to be ultimate, and, consequently, what it takes itself to be in relation to that ultimate. In our contemporary culture, we often construe religion to be the institutional practices of a particular group of individuals with specific theses about, for example, "the afterlife" or "the sacred" and, especially in our diverse and multicultural society in which we recognize many such groups, we again imagine such practices to be optional—practices that, individually, we might either choose or reject—and, consequently, being "nonreligious" itself seems, similarly, to be an option. But inasmuch as religion in principle is a culture's affirmation of what is ultimate, religion is not optional but is an inescapable facet of one's living simply by virtue of the fact that one belongs to a culture: all of us live with a fundamental belief about what is ultimate, and this typically will be one of the deepest, founding views of our culture, with the result that, like art—and, indeed, in large part because of art and its formative, culturally expressive power—we will hold this belief without ever having noticed that we have adopted it, without noticing that it is "a view" at all. Thus, in our contemporary society, most of us take it for granted that "we"—human beings—just are self-responsible individuals free to think and choose our beliefs on our own, individuals who deserve to have their "intrinsic rights" recognized. Such a belief may well be true, but it is itself essentially a religious view, that is, it is a view about the ultimate nature of reality and the place of the human being within it, and it is a view that defines our culture and that came into being historically. Indeed, as we noted above in passing, in relationship to Walter Benjamin's analysis of art, the very ability to hold this view of things was something accomplished in human cultural history in part through the transformative developments in art, themselves empowered by such technological developments as the invention of the printing press and the invention of photography. Thus, like art, religion is a dimension of our lives whether we like it or not, and it is generally a form of experiencing that we have inherited, rather than one that we have deliberately cultivated or, indeed, even recognized.

Religion, therefore, should not simply be confused with the institutionalized practices with which we typically do equate it. Religion, properly speaking, as our inherited embrace of a particular mode of practically and theoretically affirming what is absolute, is, like the other definitive dimensions of our lives, one of the aspects of life to which it is incumbent upon us as adults to "own up." One essential dimension of adult life, in other words, is cultivating what we might call our "spirituality," which is to say, taking responsibility for addressing honestly the question of what is of absolute worth, and addressing this, not merely as a cognitive matter but as a way of living. Indeed, seen in this light, the difference between religion properly speaking and those institutionalized practices can, and often does, mean that those practices are precisely failures of religion, that is, as Søren Kierkegaard showed powerfully and eloquently in *Fear and Trembling*, they are often ways precisely of refusing to be responsible—refusing to be "adult"—in relationship to the real issues of religion, the real issue of recognizing what is ultimate (27–53). There is good reason, in other words, for the fact that the everyday practitioners of institutional religions are often criticized by others as carrying on dead rituals without any real appreciation of the demands of real spirituality. But though there can indeed be good reason for this criticism, it is not automatically the correct interpretation of these practices. To see how this is so, let us first consider again the familiar "secular" view.

It is inescapable that we all have "religious" views because we grow up into an embrace of a culturally transmitted interpretation of the deepest nature of ourselves and of reality as a whole, an interpretation we affirm daily both in our inconspicuous practices and in our explicit beliefs; but precisely because these views are handed down to us invisibly, we can fail to notice that those views—the views that define our fundamental sense of who we are and what the nature of reality is—are rooted in a certain faith about what is ultimate. In other words, we treat what are really matters of faith as if they were simply obvious matters of fact, thus simultaneously misrepresenting both the nature of those views and the nature of our own relationship to them: we are dogmatic in our embrace of our cultural inheritance and we live in denial of the role our own attitude of commitment plays in our experience. In other words, what, in our contemporary Western culture, is often taken to be an enlightened secularity is really itself a matter of living with the kind of dead spirituality that is imputed to "religious" others, that is, it is a living out of beliefs "mechanically" in a way that does not reflect a living commitment to a deep truth. In that way, "secular" life—a life of prosaic instrumentality—is basically the same as the life of dead ritual that "believers" are often accused of living; the secular critic, like the rule-following member of a church, accepts without question the established terms for thinking and acting, and blindly carries out these rituals without ever questioning their basis or taking on for themselves the existential weight of grappling with the deep questions of ultimate value to which these beliefs and practices are an answer. Seen in this light, then, the secular critic of institutionalized religious practices appears rather hypocritical, that is, it is this critic who apparently lives through blind faith and empty ritual.

And, indeed, from this point of view it is no longer so obvious that the everyday practitioner of institutionalized religion is guilty of that same charge. For, while it is no doubt true that the average "religious" practitioner does not deeply embrace the existential foundations of faith, the institutional practices, for many people, precisely serve, to continue the trope from chapter 4, as "off the rack" choices for meaningfully cultivating their spirituality: the regular practices can offer an opportunity to connect with a sense of the deeper purpose of life, beyond the oppressive challenges of everyday life, and the institutional character can provide the practitioner with both a community and spiritual leadership. Throughout, we have been considering adulthood in terms of whether one embraces or lives in denial of reality, and here this means that what ultimately matters in either of these two cases—"off-the-rack atheism" or "off-the-rack religiosity"—is whether one takes up one's spiritual orientation as a route into appreciating the rich complexity of our natural, interpersonal, and moral world or whether one uses it as an excuse to justify to oneself not being responsive to that complexity, two orientations that are equally possible with either case.

But one can move beyond these "off-the-rack" choices and embrace in one's own most intimate being the deep question of the ultimate nature of reality, of what is of ultimate worth. That embrace, however, requires that one has made an existential "turn," turning away from an existence that is defined by the terms of everyday actuality and turning instead toward their source. This "conversion," this living, authentic spirituality in which one asks, as one's deepest existential search, "What does it all mean?" is the introduction to philosophy.

Philosophy: Wonder, Science, and Wisdom

Embracing our own reality involves embracing that very characteristic of ourselves that we have noted from the beginning: we are the kind of beings who can experience reality as such. For that reason, there is something definitively human—and definitively fulfilling—about taking up the theme of being as such directly, that is, explicitly posing to ourselves the question of what the ultimate nature of reality is. And this can be the wholesale reflection on reality as a whole or it can also be an attitude we adopt in more specific circumstances: we adopt this perspective whenever we endeavor to put ourselves in relation to—to orient our perspective by—"first principles." To thus seek the first or ultimate "starting point" in any domain of our experience is to strive to adopt an absolute perspective rather than to rely on the relative and limited perspective in which we simply "find" ourselves; it is to endeavor, in other words, to take the responsibility for challenging our assumptions and becoming active in "earning" a point of view rather than passively living on the basis of whatever perspective we have "inherited." This pursuit of an "absolute" perspective is the practice of philosophy.

Philosophy—this questioning of the ultimate nature of reality—can rightly be identified with the attitude of wonder that we recognize so easily in children; to some significant degree, rekindling this sense of wonder in the face of reality is what an adult must do to become philosophical. At the same time, however, this attitude of wonder is just as much the foundation of an authentic artistic and religious attitude as it is the foundation of philosophy, and so that by itself does not exhaust the meaning of philosophy. Beyond living with a fundamental orientation of wonder, philosophy is also an embrace of discipline, that is, it is holding oneself answerable to what reality shows itself to be, and this is an answerability that is as much practical and affective as it is cognitive. Like art and religion, this—philosophy—is a human practice that can be taken up at many different levels and, like both art and religion again, it is also a practice that already has a highly developed history.

Philosophy and Science

First, in contrast simply to the attitude of wonder, philosophy also takes the form of science. The philosopher seeks to learn from reality what reality is, and, on the one hand, this is the attitude of "objectivity" that underlies the study of nature as that developed in Early Modern Europe through the so-called Scientific Revolution and the development of the experimental method—what we commonly nowadays call "science"—and that underlies similarly the rigorous study of history, anthropology, and so on. Indeed, commitment to the perspective of science in general is one of the most fundamental realizations of philosophy, for it is the perspective that demands of us that we be rigorous and disciplined in grasping any given domain on its own terms. But these natural and human sciences, though they themselves are a form of philosophy, do not exhaust philosophy, and the continuing, independent study of these sciences no longer occupies the "cutting edge" of philosophy, which, on the other hand, has developed as a discipline in its own right with its own distinctive set of concerns.

Just as artworks are the grasp a culture initially has of the absolute, so are the first answers to the ultimate questions a culture's first opening into science; initially recognizing that reality is "one," for example (recognizing that it is "reality"), recognizing that reality has a dynamic process of its own (recognizing it as "nature"), or recognizing the distinction within reality between what occurs on its own and what occurs only as a matter of deliberate, creative human action (recognizing the distinction within reality between the natural and the artificial) is in each case both an insight in its own right and an opening to further investigations. Consequently, the history of philosophy as wonder and the history of philosophy as science are thus paired, like question and answer: the history of all the sciences our historical human culture has developed operates within the orienting terms—the "first principles"—that initially reveal themselves in response to our questioning wonder.

This dynamic process of question and answer, however, naturally introduces new dimensions of inquiry. Science as the progressive empirical investigation into the domains of inquiry opened by philosophy begins to diverge from philosophy as the laying of foundations for inquiry: philosophical inquiry, in other words, effectively establishes the orienting hypotheses from which the empirical sciences move forward. Continuing philosophical inquiry does not itself rest with those orienting insights, however, and the questioning of the hypotheses of the developing empirical sciences becomes a study in its own right as philosophical questioning deepens its insights concerning the nature of reality and, consequently, establishes new principles for scientific inquiry. Human culture's gradually accomplished philosophical insights thus serve a twofold function: they are both the principles on the basis of which empirical inquiry is conducted and they are the points from which—the "stepping stones," as Socrates says in his discussion of the "divided line" in Plato's *Republic* (VI.511b)—further philosophical questioning is launched toward the grasp of the ultimate nature of reality as such. In this way, our sciences, like the bodies of living organisms, amount to the relatively static form—the "shell," as it were—of what is really the dynamic process of philosophy itself. In contrast to the empirical sciences to which it gives rise, then, philosophy itself thus comes to develop its own specialized fields of inquiry, namely, metaphysics (the study of reality as such), epistemology (the study of knowledge as such), and ethics (the study of right behavior as such).

Philosophy and Morality

And, on the other hand, the philosophical attitude of striving to answer to reality on its own terms is not just a "theoretical" or cognitive stance but is also a practical and especially a moral attitude. Wonder about "What matters?" naturally evolves into the discipline of attempting to be honest about what is of absolute worth—an honesty that is not so much a matter of simply asserting something to be the case as it is a matter of experiencing oneself as commanded, as "called to action," within one's individual existence. It is experiencing reality as requiring our care.

Most commonly, we think of "knowing" as a matter of detachment: to know something is to step back from immediate involvement with it and to reflect on it, disinterestedly. And, indeed, we commonly think of "knowing" something as a matter of learning how to control it, to "master" it. And yet things themselves can seem to demand of us quite the opposite: they can call precisely for our engagement rather than our detachment and for our support rather than our control. This is no doubt most evident in our dealings with other people. People, as we have considered in some detail throughout this work, depend upon their recognition by others, in the sense that they require the collaboration and confirmation of others to secure them in their perspective and, indeed, to secure them at the most fundamental level in their sense of being persons. One thus only knows a person as a person to the extent that one experiences that person as calling to one for support. And, as we have also studied throughout this work, people are also inherently open to the experience of "absolute" meanings, which prominently includes, as we are noting here, the openness to the absolute good, that is, to the imperative of morality. Thus, again, we do not recognize a person as a person unless we recognize her as such a site of moral meaning, as someone whose perspective has the capacity to be the witness to—the avatar of—ultimate value. The perspective of another thus calls for our support and it commands our respect. We are not honest about the reality of other people, in other words, unless we experience ourselves as morally answerable to them. And, though the larger world of nature is not itself a "subject" who can act morally and whose perspective needs our confirmation, it is again generally intuitively immediate for us to recognize nature as having a worth that we should honor and protect. We are not honest about nature, in other words, when, either as individuals or as a culture, we portray it as simply an instrumental resource for our own undertakings; nature, on the contrary, is both our own generative matrix—the precondition for our very being—and the original happening of whatever can be and hence whatever matters. Indeed, ultimately, we must recognize that, at the most fundamental level, it is "being itself"—the generative source and absolute context of all that is and all that matters—to which we are indebted and for which we must care. Thus, complementing and completing the realization of philosophy as science is the realization of philosophy as moral action.

Philosophy as Wisdom

Culturally, it is through the development of science and morality that philosophy has been realized, and, individually, one can be "philosophical" in taking up any of these attitudes of wonder, science, "philosophical theory," or morality. But, whether in the cognitive or the practical domain, most fundamentally philosophy is, as we noted, a matter of being honest about reality. This honesty, in its fullest development, is wisdom. In Plato's *Apology of Socrates*, which is Socrates's defense speech before the Athenian jury that ultimately sentenced him to death for "corrupting the young, not believing in the gods of the city and introducing his own divinities" (*Apology* 24b-c), Socrates describes the pursuit that has defined his life: confronted with the fact that the oracle at Delphi claimed that no one was wiser than he, Socrates devoted his life to determining what this could mean (*Apology* 21a–23b). In order to learn what wisdom is—and, indeed, in an effort to become wise, that is, in a love of wisdom or "philosophy"—Socrates first turned himself to the study of what we typically take to be wisdom: he sought out politicians, poets, and craftsmen, and tried to learn from them what their wisdom was (*Apology* 21c–22e). Socrates's turning to the traditional sources of wisdom offers an important insight.

As we have seen in our discussion here of the dynamic nature of philosophy as a cultural reality, but also in our discussions of human history and culture more broadly, we are born into a world in which the human process of questioning and answering is already well developed, and our general cultural flourishing is largely a reflection of this accumulated cultural "wisdom." Whereas a long history of trial and error was necessary for human beings gradually to learn how to deal with their surroundings and themselves, we can now generally turn to our culture's "acquired wisdom" about those things to save ourselves from having to repeat that same process; correspondingly, we take the wise to be those who have made themselves the representatives of this acquired learning. We thus appeal to "experts" in technical matters, we count on the good judgment of those in practical positions of leadership and responsibility—parents, teachers, lawgivers, priests—and we look to artists for provocative and insightful articulations of our experience. It makes sense, then, that we, like Socrates, turn to these groups of artists, lawgivers and scientists—"poets, politicians, and craftsmen"—for wisdom: it is both the case that we need there to be wisdom and, generally, we rightly imagine there to be wise people upon whom we can depend for guidance in navigating the world.

There is an important difference, however, first between science, law, and artworks, on the one hand, and scientists, lawgivers, and artists, on the other. As we noted above about the relationship between philosophy as science and philosophy as wonder, each of science, law, and art, as an established body of work is, as it were, the "shell" of the dynamic practice of scientists, lawgivers, and artists. And there is another important difference, second, within the domain of scientists, lawgivers, and artists, between those who competently represent those accumulated results of scientific, legal, and artistic practice to their surrounding worlds and those who creatively and originally generate transformative scientific, legal, and artistic work for their surrounding worlds—between those who "follow the rules," as it were, and those who open up the perspectives from which rules are derived. While the great accomplishments of our culture may rightly be called our culture's "wisdom," we truly only appreciate those products as such when we experience them as the remains of that human spirit of disciplined striving for an absolute perspective that gave rise to them. And to experience these products as such an answer to a question, we must ourselves be asking that question: we experience these products as wisdom, then, when we take up the responsibility for ourselves to commit ourselves to the pursuit of an absolute perspective. In other words, this "wisdom" by itself is only static, "dead" material: this accumulated material achieves its status as "wisdom" only when it is itself (re-)animated by the spirit that precisely is trying to be honest about the world. It is only for one who is asking the question that those "sciences" are answering that they truly amount to science, and thus their truth is not found simply in their "objective" character, but only in their being animated by subjectivity, and by the particular form of subjectivity that is the experience of being open to the revelation of transformative insight, the experience of being "called."

Thus, beyond philosophy both as wonder and as science, there is philosophy as wisdom. That wisdom is a matter of taking up our accumulated cultural learning as the living embrace of honest answerability to reality. In that case, however, these "sciences" are not experienced as rules, nor are they simply "correct answers"; rather, they are like the helpful markers one finds on a difficult path, indicating that some other traveler has been there before. Thus, as Socrates says to Cephalus, "they are like men who have proceeded on a certain road that perhaps we too will have to take, [and] one ought, in my opinion, to learn from them what sort of road it is" (*Republic* I.328d-e)

As adults, we are always dependent upon the accumulated learning—the "wisdom"—of our culture, and it is, first, important that we recognize the reality of wisdom even if only in the minimal sense of acknowledging that there are others to whom we must turn for guidance; indeed, the self-assured failure to thus acknowledge one's dependence on the insight and expertise of others is one of the most crippling forms of refusing to adopt an adult perspective. Beyond this minimal recognition, there is the more self-responsible effort to cultivate aspects of this wisdom for oneself, whether through cultivating one's sense of wonder, becoming more disciplined cognitively or morally, or explicitly studying the "first principles" of reality. And, ultimately, there is the full commitment of one's experience to honesty, which, inasmuch as it puts itself at the authentic source of art and religion as much as philosophy, is a perspective as much artistic and religious as it is philosophical.

Appendix

Notes for Further Study

This book, *Adult Life*, completes the *Human Life* trilogy, begun in *Human Experience* (2003) and continued in *Bearing Witness to Epiphany* (2009). Like those works, it is not intended as a work of academic scholarship but as a traditional form of philosophical reflection. As such, it relies not on specialized knowledge but on insight, reasoning, and the evidence of experience, all of which are resources that any reasonably well-informed and reasonably self-reflective reader can in principle bring to it. For this reason, the book does not have a substantial apparatus of footnotes and textual references, beyond the minimum necessary when particular works are quoted and so on. That said, however, this book, like the others in the trilogy, is itself deeply informed by scholarly work, in philosophy, of course, but also in psychology, sociology, history, the natural sciences, and the arts, and, in chapter 4 in particular, economics. While it would not be suitable, given the nature of the book, to incorporate more substantial discussion of scholarly work in these fields into the text, I can imagine that it would nonetheless be worthwhile for some readers to have some guidance into such work to help them further explore the themes and topics raised in that work. To that end, I append here a short discussion of some of the major works that I have found valuable in my study of these topics, which I imagine would in turn be useful to others.

My discussion of perception and action in chapter 1 is primarily informed by Merleau-Ponty's *Phenomenology of Perception* (1945) and by Henri Bergson's *Matter and Memory* (1896), and my discussions of our experiences of reality and mortality are primarily informed by two works by Martin Heidegger, *The Fundamental Concepts of Metaphysics* (1938) and *Being and Time* (1927), respectively. These works are themselves all closely related to ecological studies of animal life, most notably *A Foray into the Worlds of Animals and Humans* (1934) by Jakob von Uexküll, which is very effectively complemented by *The Ecological Approach to Visual Perception* (1979) by James J. Gibson. This chapter is also informed quite broadly by Immanuel Kant's examination of the experiences of objectivity and reason in the *Critique of Pure Reason* (1781). These are all, of course, quite challenging technical works, and the reader may desire an easier route of entry into these ideas. Technical, academic studies are not generally oriented to the beginner, and, indeed, are unfortunately of very uneven quality, while articles and websites that aim to introduce these works are often highly misleading. Nonetheless, there are still reliable works to which one can turn for introduction to these ideas (though without a doubt studying the original texts themselves is what one must ultimately do if one wants truly to understand them). For those who already have some philosophical background, *The Intercorporeal Self* by Scott Marratto, *Merleau-Ponty's Developmental Ontology* by David Morris, and *The Birth of Sense* by Don Beith are excellent presentations of Merleau-Ponty's phenomenological philosophy and its significance. There are also a number of excellent essays that offer short but compelling introductions to many of these central ideas: for an introduction to the phenomenological conception of the body, Maria Talero's essay, "Merleau-Ponty and the Bodily Subject of Learning" is a good place to start and her more technical essay "The Experiential Workspace" nicely draws out the relationship between phenomenological and ecological approaches to perception; on the theme of the "I can," Iris Marion Young's essay "Throwing Like a Girl" is a helpful introduction; and Kirsten Jacobson's "Waiting to Speak" is an excellent example of the phenomenological approach to the experience of mortality. For the relationship of Kant to these issues, I recommend two of my own essays, "The Spatiality of Self-Consciousness" and "Subjectivity and Hermeneutics."

Beyond the phenomenological background, chapter 2 draws fundamentally on three sources: the study of virtue in Aristotle's *Nicomachean Ethics* (c.350 BC), the study of "recognition" (*Anerkennung*) in G. W. F. Hegel's *Phenomenology of Spirit* (1807), and the study of "ontological insecurity" in R. D. Laing's *The Divided Self* (1955); Erik H. Erikson's *Childhood and Society* (1950) and D. W. Winnicott's *The Child, The Family, and the Outside World* (1964) are also especially relevant works for the themes in this chapter. Excellent contemporary works that take up similar ideas in relationship to phenomenology are Eva-Maria Simms, *The Child in the World*; Susan Bredlau, *The Other in Perception*; Kym Maclaren, "Intimacy as Transgression"; and any of Robert Stolorow's writings in Intersubjective Systems Theory. I have also taken up more focused discussion of some of these themes in two papers: "Personality as Equilibrium" is a phenomenological interpretation of the nature of virtue (and especially of what Aristotle calls the "mean" [*mesotēs*]) in the context of *sōphrosunē*; and "The Virtues of Agency" addresses especially the roles of trust and courage in childhood development.

The studies of the time and space of aging in chapter 3 are most fundamentally rooted in Heidegger's descriptions of "lived" time and "lived" space in *Being and Time*, in Bergson's study of time as "duration" in *Time and Free Will* (1889), and in Merleau-Ponty's analysis of situational spatiality in *Phenomenology of Perception*. For the theme of aging specifically, Simone de Beauvoir's *Old Age* (1970) is the most directly relevant philosophical text, closely followed by Heidegger's study of "being-towards-death" in *Being and Time*. My analyses in this chapter have also been prominently influenced by John Dewey, *Democracy and Education* (1916), and Michel Foucault, *Discipline and Punish* (1975). Other helpful discussions of the phenomenological approach to space and time include: Edward S. Casey, *Getting Back into Place*; David Seamon, *Life Takes Place*; Dylan Trigg, *The Memory of Place*; Iris Marion Young, "A Room of One's Own"; and Kirsten Jacobson, "The Temporality of Intimacy." I hope that the reader would also find my own discussion of "polytemporality" in chapter 1 of *Bearing Witness to Epiphany* a helpful companion text for this chapter, and, on the theme of aging, my essay "Between Two Intimacies" focuses on the changing role of formative experiences of intimacy in childhood and adult life. Francis Sparshott's *Taking Life Seriously*, which is a commentary on Aristotle's *Nicomachean Ethics*, is, I think, a very helpful text for thinking about many of the philosophical issues raised in this chapter, and Alexander Wilson, *The Culture of Nature*, is very helpful for understanding the contemporary experience of space. I have also found a number of more popular books on aging that are quite valuable: in particular Sherwin Nuland's *How We Die* and *The Art of Aging* and Nicholas Delbanco's *Lastingness* offer a wealth of provocative and insightful material.

Chapter 4 is by far the longest chapter of the book, and the topics it addresses—intimate life, economic life, and political life—have, of course, been the subject of a great deal of writing, philosophical and empirical. My philosophical orientation to these issues is shaped primarily by Hegel's notion, from the *Phenomenology of Spirit*, of "recognition" (*Anerkennung*), which is the idea that, in all of our practices, we are most fundamentally negotiating with the ways we express to each other (both personally or collectively) who we take each other to be; (for the more direct discussion of this theme, the reader can turn to any of my books on Hegel). Hegel's own *Elements of the Philosophy of Right* (1820) and, prior to that, J. G. Fichte's *Foundations of Natural Right* (1797) attempt systematically to show how this issue of recognition is worked out through the structures of family, economics, and political life. The richest phenomenological study of the dynamic relationships of recognition in intimate, interpersonal relations is in Jean-Paul Sartre's chapter, "Concrete Relations with Others," in *Being and Nothingness* (1943), and the study of character types in chapter 2 of de Beauvoir's *Ethics of Ambiguity* (1947) is similarly rich in its exploration of the implicit meaning of the forms of our interpersonal behavior; the reader might also find my essay "Why Sexuality Matters" a helpful supplement to my discussion of sexuality in this chapter. For the interpretation of family life in particular, though, it is various phenomenological psychologists and psychoanalysts whom I have found to be the most valuable guides: Laing, *Sanity, Madness and the Family* (1964), Winnicott, *Home Is Where We Start From* (1990), and especially Salvador Minuchin, *Families and Family Therapy* (1974) are among the most compelling and insightful analyses with which I am familiar. For the study of economic life, Adam Smith's *The Wealth of Nations* (1776) is without a doubt the most important text, and Smith's analysis lies at the foundation of my own thinking; beyond Smith's foundational text, the single most valuable book I have found for understanding the nature of modern money is Randall L. Wray's *Understanding Modern Money*; a close second in Bray Hammond, *Banks and Politics in America*, which is essentially a history of the emergence of modern central banking that demonstrates the inseparability of that institution from the political reality of the United States; *Other People's Money*, by Sharon Ann Murphy, is a very helpful, readable companion to Hammond's massive text. Other works I have found especially valuable are Abba Lerner, "Functional Finance and the Federal Debt"; Wendell Berry, *What Matters?*; Fred L. Block, *The Origins of International Monetary Disorder*; Geoffrey Ingham, *The Nature of Money*; William Mitchell, L. Randall Wray, and Martin Watts, *Macroeconomics*; and John Maynard Keynes, *The General Theory of Employment, Interest, and Money*. A number of works that study the relationship between household (*oikos*) and city (*polis*) in ancient Greece are also particularly illuminating regarding the nature of the family and the nature of money: Richard Seaford, *Reciprocity and Ritual* and *Money and the Early Greek Mind*, and Leslie Kurke, *Coins, Bodies, Games, and Gold*, are three such books by which my thinking has been especially influenced. Another of my essays, "The Limits of Money," might prove a helpful alternative route into understanding the relationship between intimate and economic life. On the theme of government, it is traditional works such as Aristotle's *Politics* (c.350 BC), John Locke's *Second Treatise of Government* (1689), Hegel's *Philosophy of Right*, and Jacques Derrida's *Rogues* (2003) that have most shaped my interpretation. For the distinctive (bureaucratic) character of contemporary government, Max Weber's "Politics as Vocation" (1919) is particularly helpful, and Dewey's *The Public and Its Problems* (1927) and *Individualism Old and New* (1930) are two of the most compelling and relevant works regarding the relationship of government to these issues of intimate and economic life; the *Muqaddimah* of Ibn Khaldûn (1377) is also an especially rich text for appreciating the politically enervating character of bureaucracy and institutionalization.

My discussion of art in chapter 5 draws its resources primarily from Hegel's *Aesthetics* (1835), Dewey's *Art as Experience* (1934), R. G. Collingwood's *The Principles of Art* (1938), and Heidegger's essay, "The Origin of the Work of Art" (1950). The reader might find my essay "Expressing Dwelling" a helpful introduction to these texts, and my essay "Phenomenological Description and Artistic Expression" offers an interpretation of the intrinsic relationship between art and philosophy. For Hegel, Stephen Houlgate's entry in the *Stanford Encyclopaedia of Philosophy* is very good (as is all of his writing on Hegel), and, for Dewey, Thomas M. Alexander's book, *John Dewey's Theory of Art, Experience, and Nature* is a helpful introduction. My interpretation of religion is shaped especially by Hegel's phenomenology of religious experience in his *Phenomenology of Spirit*, and by Kierkegaard's *Fear and Trembling* (1843). The reader can turn to "The Phenomenology of Religion," chapter 13 of my book *Infinite Phenomenology*, for an interpretation of Hegel's phenomenology of religion; for intelligent and insightful interpretations of religion, I have found especially useful John Dominick Crossan, *The Birth of Christianity*, Wendy Doniger, *The Hindus*, and Mark Munn, *The Mother of the Gods*. My discussion of philosophy has been most powerfully influenced by Plato's *Apology* (c. 390 BC), Book I of Aristotle's *Metaphysics* (c. 350 BC),

Kant's *The Conflict of the Faculties* (1798), and Collingwood's *Speculum Mentis* (1924). Of more contemporary work, Laura McMahon's essay, "Phenomenology as First-Order Perception," is a nice route into reflecting on the nature of philosophy.

Bibliography

Adorno, Theodor W. *Aesthetic Theory*. Translated by Robert Hullot-Kentor. Minneapolis: University of Minnesota Press, 1997.

Aho, Kevin, ed. *Existential Medicine: Essays on Health and Illness*. London and New York: Rowman and Littlefield, 2018.

Alexander, Thomas M. *John Dewey's Theory of Art, Experience, and Nature: The Horizons of Feeling*. Albany: State University of New York Press, 1987.

Alexiou, Margaret, *The Ritual Lament in Greek Tradition*. 2nd ed. Lanham, MD: Rowman and Littlefield, 2002.

Alighieri, Dante. *Inferno*. Translated by Allen Mandelbaum. New York: Bantam Classics, 1982.

Althusser, Louis. "Ideology and Ideological State Apparatuses (Notes towards an Investigation," in *Lenin and Philosophy and Other Essays*, translated by Ben Brewster, 127–86. New York: Monthly Review Press, 1971.

Alwin, Duane F. "Taking Time Seriously: Studying Social Change, Social Structure, and Human Lives." In *Examining Lives in Context: Perspectives on the Ecology of Human Development*, edited by P. Moen, G. H. Elder Jr., and K. Luescher, 211–62. Washington, DC: American Psychological Association, 1995.

Anderson, Ellie. "From Existential Alterity to Ethical Reciprocity: Beauvoir's Alternative to Levinas,." *Continental Philosophy Review* 52 (2019): 171–89.

Aristotle. *Complete Works*. 2 Volumes. Edited by Jonathan Barnes. Princeton: Princeton University Press, 1984.

Arnett, Jeffrey Jensen, "Broad and Narrow Socialization: The Family in the Context of a Cultural Theory." *Journal of Marriage and the Family* 57 (1995): 617–28.

Augustine. *The Confessions of Saint Augustine*. Translated by John K. Ryan. New York: Image Books, 1960.

Aulino, Felicity. "Rituals of Care for the Elderly in Northern Thailand: Merit, Morality, and the Everyday of Long-Term Care." *American Ethnologist* 43 (2016): 91–102.

Baars, Jan, Dale Dannefer, Chris Phillips, and Alan Walker, eds. *Aging, Global-ization, and Inequality: The New Critical Gerontology*. New York: Routledge, 2006.

Bataille, Georges. *The Accursed Share: An Essay on General Economy*. Volume I. Translated by Robert Hurley. New York: Zone Books, 1988.

Beith, Don. *The Birth of Sense: Generative Passivity in Merleau-Ponty's Philosophy*. Athens, OH: Ohio University Press, 2018.

———. "Moving into Being: The Motor Basis of Perception, Balance, and Read-ing." In *Perception and Its Development in Merleau-Ponty's Phenomenology*, edited by Kirsten Jacobson and John Russon, 123–41. Toronto: University of Toronto Press, 2017.

Benjamin, Walter. "The Work of Art in the Age of Mechanical Reproduction." In *Illuminations*, translated by Harry Zohn, 217–51. New York: Schocken, 1969.

Bergson, Henri. *Matter and Memory*. Translated by N. M. Paul and W. S. Palmer. Cambridge: MIT Press, 1990.

———. *Time and Free Will: An Essay on the Immediate Data of Consciousness*. Mineola, NY: Dover, 2001.

Berry, Wendell. *What Matters? Economics for a Renewed Commonwealth*. Berkeley: Counterpoint, 2010.

———. *What Are People For?* Berkeley: Counterpoint, 1990.

Birhan, Wohabie. "A Review of Normative and Other Factors Contributing to Africa's Adolescent Development Crisis." *Philosophical Papers and Reviews* 9 (2019): 1–9.

Blatterer, Harry. "Contemporary Adulthood: Reconceptualizing an Uncontested Category." *Current Sociology* 55 (2007): 771–92.

Block, Fred. L. *The Origins of International Economic Disorder: A Study of United States International Monetary Policy from World War II to the Present*. Berke-ley: University of California Press, 1977.

Bodenhorn, Howard. *A History of Banking in Antebellum America: Financial Mar-kets and Economic Development in an Era of Nation-Building*. Cambridge: Cambridge University Press, 2000.

Boyer-Xambeu, Marie-Thérèse, Ghislain Deleplace, and Lucien Gillard. *Private Money and Public Currencies: The 16th Century Challenge*. Translated by Azizhe Azodi. New York: Routledge, 2015.

Bredlau, Susan. *The Other in Perception*. Albany: State University of New York Press, 2018.

Bullock, Christopher. *The Cobler of Preston, a Farce: As it Is Acted at the Theatre-Royal in Lincoln's-Inn-Fields*. London: Forgotten Books, 2018.

Cairney John, and Neal Krause. "The Social Distribution of Psychological Dis-tress and Depression in Older Adults." *Journal of Aging and Health* 17 (2005): 807–35.

Carel, Havi, *Phenomenology of Illness*. Oxford: Oxford University Press, 2016.

Casey, Edward S. *Getting Back into Place: Toward a Renewed Understanding of the Place-World*. Bloomington: Indiana University Press, 1993.

Catechism of the Catholic Church. New York: Doubleday, 2003.

Center for Medieval and Renaissance Studies, University of California, Los Angeles. *The Dawn of Modern Banking*. New Haven: Yale University Press, 1979.

Clarke, Philippa, Victor Marshall, James House, and Paula Lantz. "The Social Structuring of Mental Health over the Adult Life Course: Advancing Theory in the Sociology of Aging." *Social Forces* 89 (2011): 1287–1313.

Collingwood, R. G. *Autobiography*. Revised Edition. Oxford: Clarendon, 1982.

———. *The Principles of Art*. Oxford: Clarendon, 1938.

———. *Speculum Mentis, or, The Map of Knowledge*. Oxford: Clarendon, 1924.

Collins, Amy L., and Michael A. Smyer. "The Resilience of Self-Esteem in Late Adulthood." *Journal of Aging and Health* 17 (2005): 471–89.

Costello, Peter, and Licia Carlson, eds. *Phenomenology and the Arts*. Lanham, MD: Lexington Books, 2016.

Crossan, John Dominick. *The Birth of Christianity: Discovering What Happened in the Years Immediately after the Execution of Jesus*. New York: Harper-One, 1999.

Danesi, Marcel. *Cool: The Signs and Meanings of Adolescence*. Toronto: University of Toronto Press, 1994.

de Beauvoir, Simone. *Old Age*. Harmondsworth: Penguin, 1977.

———. *The Ethics of Ambiguity*. Translated by Bernard Frechtman. New York: Citadel, 1991.

———. *The Second Sex*. Translated by Constance Borde and Sheila Malovany Chevalier. New York: Vintage, 2011.

Delbanco, Nicholas. *Lastingness: The Art of Old Age*. New York: Grand Central, 2011.

Deleuze, Gilles, and Félix Guattari. *Anti-Oedipus: Capitalism and Schizophrenia*. Translated by Robert Hurley, Mark Seem, and Helen R. Lane. New York: Viking Press, 1982.

de Roover, Raymond. *The Rise and Decline of the Medici Bank, 1397–1494*. New York: Norton, 1966.

Derrida, Jacques. *Acts of Religion*. Edited by Gil Anidjar. New York: Routledge, 2002.

———. *Aporias*. Translated by Thomas Dutoit. Stanford: Stanford University Press, 1993.

———. *Given Time I: Counterfeit Money*. Translated by Peggy Kamuf. Chicago: University of Chicago Press, 1992.

———. *Politics of Friendship*. Translated by George Collins. London: Verso, 1997.

———. *Rogues: Two Essays on Reason* Translated by Pascale-Anne Brault and Michael Naas. Stanford: Stanford University Press, 2005.

———. *The Truth in Painting*. Translated by Geoff Bennington and Ian McLeod. Chicago: University of Chicago Press, 1987.

de Tocqueville, Alexis, *Democracy in America*. Translated by Harvey Mansfied and Delba Winthrop. Chicago: University of Chicago Press, 2002.

Dewey, John. *Art as Experience*. New York: Penguin, 1934.

———. *Democracy and Education: An Introduction to the Philosophy of Education*. New York: Macmillan, 1916.

———. *Human Nature and Conduct*. New York: Modern Library, 1957.

———. *Individualism Old and New*. Amherst, NY: Prometheus, 1999.

———. *The Public and Its Problems: An Essay in Political Inquiry*. Athens, OH: Swallow Press, 2016.

Doniger, Wendy. *The Hindus: An Alternative History*. New York: Penguin, 2009.

Duby, Georges. *The Early Growth of the European Economy: Warriors and Peasants from the Seventh to the Twelfth Century*. Translated by Howard B. Clarke. Ithaca: Cornell University Press, 1974.

Eliot, George. *Middlemarch: A Study of Provincial Life*. Harmondsworth: Penguin, 2006.

Emerson, Ralph Waldo. *Essays*. New York: A. L. Burt, 1916.

Epictetus, *The Handbook (The Encheiridion)*. Translated by Nicholas P. White. Indianapolis: Hackett, 1983.

Erikson, Erik H. *Childhood and Society*. New York: Norton, 1950.

Fagan, Patricia. *Plato and Tradition: The Poetic and Cultural Context of Philosophy*. Evanston: Northwestern University Press, 2013.

Fanon, Frantz. *Black Skin, White Masks*. Translated by Richard Philcox. Revised Edition. New York: Grove Press, 2008.

Fichte, Johann Gottlieb. *Foundations of Natural Right according to the Principles of the Wissenschaftslehre*. Translated by Michael Baur. Cambridge: Cambridge University Press, 2000.

Fillion, Réal. *Multicultural Dynamics and the Ends of History: Exploring Kant, Hegel, and Marx*. Ottawa: University of Ottawa Press, 2008.

Foucault, Michel. *Discipline and Punish: The Birth of the Prison*. Translated by Alan Sheridan. New York: Vintage, 1979.

Freud, Sigmund. *Civilization and Its Discontents*. Translated by James Strachey. New York: Norton, 2010.

———. *Introductory Lectures on Psychoanalysis*. Translated by James Strachey. New York: Norton, 1977.

———. *Three Essays on the Theory of Sexuality*. Translated by James Strachey. New York: Basic Books, 1975.

Fritsch, Kelly. "Intimate Assemblages: Disability, Intercorporeality, and the Labour of Attendant Care." *Critical Disability Discourses* 2 (2010): 1–14.

Furstenberg, Frank F. "The Sociology of Adolescence and Youth in the 1990s: A Critical Commentary." *Journal of Marriage and Family* 62 (2000): 895–910.

————. "Social Class and Development in Early Adulthood." *Emerging Adulthood* 4 (2016): 236–38.

Galanaki, Evangelia. "The Origins of Solitude: Psychoanalytic Perspectives." In *The Handbook of Solitude: Psychological Perspectives on Social Isolation, Social Withdrawal, and Being Alone*, edited by Robert J. Coplan and Julie C. Bowker. Hoboken: Wiley, 2014.

Gentry, Curt. *J. Edgar Hoover: The Man and the Secrets*. New York: Norton, 1991.

Gheaus, Anca, and Lisa Herzog. "The Goods of Work (Other than Money!)." *Journal of Social Philosophy* 47 (2016): 70–89.

Gibson, James J. *The Ecological Approach to Visual Perception*. Boston: Houghton Mifflin, 1979.

Goldman, Emma. *Living My Life*. New York: Knopf, 1931.

Hammond, Bray. *Banks and Politics in America: From the Revolution to the Civil War*. Princeton: Princeton University Press, 1957.

Harvey, David, *The Enigma of Capital and the Crises of Capitalism*. Oxford: Oxford University Press, 2010.

Hegel, G. W. F. *Aesthetics: Lectures on Fine Art*. 2 vols. Translated by T. M. Knox. Oxford: Clarendon, 1975.

————. *Elements of the Philosophy of Right*. Translated by H. B. Nisbet. Cambridge: Cambridge University Press, 1991.

————. *Phenomenology of Spirit*. Translated by A. V. Miller. Oxford: Oxford University Press, 1977.

Heidegger, Martin. *Being and Time*. Translated by John Macquarrie and Edward Robinson. New York: Harper and Row, 1962.

————. "The Origin of the Work of Art." In *Basic Writings*, revised edition, edited by David Farrell Krell, 143–212. New York: HarperCollins, 1993.

————. *The Fundamental Concepts of Metaphysics: World, Finitude, Solitude*. Translated by William McNeill and Nicholas Walker. Bloomington: Indiana University Press, 1995.

————. *The Phenomenology of Religious Life*. Translated by Matthias Fritsch and Jennifer Anna Gosetti-Ferencei. Bloomington: Indiana University Press, 2004.

————. *What is Called Thinking?* Translated by J. Glenn Gray. New York: Harper and Row, 1968.

Hoff, Shannon. "Rights and Worlds: On the Political Significance of Belonging." *Philosophical Forum* 45 (2014): 355–73.

————. *The Laws of the Spirit: A Hegelian Theory of Justice*. Albany: State University of New York Press, 2014.

————. "Translating Principle into Practice: On Derrida and the Terms of Feminism." *Journal of Speculative Philosophy* 29 (2015): 403–14.

Holder, John J., ed. and trans. *Early Buddhist Discourses*. Indianapolis: Hackett, 2006.

Houlgate, Stephen. "Hegel's Aesthetics." In *The Stanford Encyclopedia of Philosophy* (Spring 2016), edited by Edward N. Zalta; https://plato.stanford.edu/archives/spr2016/entries/hegel-aesthetics/.

Howell, Whitney. "The Environmental Conditions of Agency: John Dewey and Jane Jacobs on Diversity and the Modern Urban Landscape," *Journal of Speculative Philosophy* 32 (2018): 263–84.

Husserl, Edmund. *Ideas Pertaining to a Pure Phenomenology and to a Phenomenological Psychology, First Book*. Translated Daniel O. Dahlstrom. Indianapolis: Hackett, 2014.

———. *Ideas Pertaining to a Pure Phenomenology and to a Phenomenological Psychology, Second Book*. Translated by R. Rojcewicz and A. Schuwer. Dordrecht: Kluwer, 1989.

———. *Thing and Space: Lectures of 1907*. Translated by Richard Rojcewicz. Dordrecht: Kluwer, 1997.

Ibn Khaldûn. *Muqaddimah: An Introduction to History*. Translated by Franz Rosenthal. Abridged by N. J. Dawood. Princeton: Princeton University Press, 1989.

Ingham, Geoffrey. *The Nature of Money*. Cambridge: Polity Press, 2004.

Innes, A. Mitchell. "What Is Money?" *Banking Law Journal* 30 (1913): 377–408.

Jacobson, Kirsten. "The Body as Family Narrative: Russon and the Education of the Soul." *Anekaant* 3 (2015): 49–57.

———. "The Temporality of Intimacy: Promise, World, and Death." *Emotion Space and Society* 13 (2014): 103–10.

———. "Waiting to Speak: A Phenomenological Perspective on Our Silence around Dying." In *Cultural Ontology of the Self in Pain*, edited by Siby George and Pravesh G. Jung, 75–92. New Delhi: Springer, 2016.

———, and John Russon. "Existential Medicine and the Intersubjective Body." In *Existential Medicine: Essays on Health and Illness*, edited by Kevin Aho, 191–204. London and New York: Rowman and Littlefield, 2018.

Kalaitzake, Manolis. "Central Banking and Financial Political Power: An Investigation into the European Central Bank." *Competition and Change* 23 (2019): 221–44.

———. "The Political Power of Finance: The Institute of International Finance in the Greek Debt Crisis." *Politics and Society* 45 (2017): 389–413.

Kant, Immanuel. *Critique of Pure Reason*. Translated by Norman Kemp-Smith. New York: Palgrave Macmillan, 2003.

———. *Groundwork for the Metaphysics of Morals*. Edited by Lara Denis. Peterborough: Broadview, 2005.

———. *Metaphysics of Morals*. Translated by Mary Gregor. Cambridge: Cambridge University Press, 1996.

———. *Religion within the Boundaries of Mere Reason*. Translated by Allen Wood and George di Giovanni. Cambridge: Cambridge University Press, 1998.

———. *The Conflict of the Faculties*. Translated by Mary Gregor. Lincoln: University of Nebraska Press, 1992.

Katz, Stephen. "Precarious Life, Human Development and the Life Course: Critical Intersections." In *Precarity and Ageing: Understanding Insecurity and Risk in Later Life*, edited by Amanda Grenier, Chris Phillipson, and Richard A. Settersten Jr., 41–65. Chicago: University of Chicago Press, 2020.

Kautzer, Chad. "The Occupy Movement and the Reappearance of the Polis." In *The Routledge Handbook of Philosophy of the City*, edited by Sharon M. Meager, Samantha Noll, and Joseph S. Biehl, 238–50. New York: Routledge, 2020.

Keynes, John Maynard. *The General Theory of Employment, Interest, and Money*. New York: Palgrave Macmillan, 2007.

Kierkegaard, Søren. *Concluding Unscientific Postscript*. Translated by David F. Swenson and Walter Lowrie. Princeton: Princeton University Press, 1941.

———. *Fear and Trembling* and *Repetition*. Translated by Howard V. Hong and Edna H. Hong. Princeton: Princeton University Press, 1983.

King, Andrew. "Recognising Adulthood? Young Adults' Accomplishment of the Age Identities." *Sociology* 47 (2013): 109–25.

Kraay, Colin M. "Hoards, Small Change, and the Origin of Coinage." *Journal of Hellenic Studies* 84 (1964): 76–91.

Kurke, Leslie. *Coins, Bodies, Games, and Gold: The Politics of Meaning in Archaic Greece*. Princeton: Princeton University Press, 1999.

Laing, R. D. *Sanity, Madness, and the Family: Families of Schizophrenics*. Harmondsworth: Penguin, 1990.

———. *The Divided Self: An Existential Study in Sanity and Madness*. Harmondsworth: Penguin, 1965.

Lerner, Abba. "Functional Finance and the Federal Debt." *Social Research* 10 (1943): 38–51.

Lobo, A., C. De la Cámara, P. Gracia-García. "Sociology of Aging." In *Mental Health and Illness of the Elderly*, edited by H. Chiu and K. Shulman, 1–24. Singapore: Springer, 2016.

Locke, John, *Second Treatise of Government*. Indianapolis: Hackett, 1980.

Maclaren, Kym. "Embodied Perceptions of Others as a Condition of Selfhood? Empirical and Phenomenological Considerations." *Journal of Consciousness Studies* 15 (2008): 63–93.

———. "Intimacy as Transgression and the Problem of Freedom." in *Journal of Critical Phenomenology* 1 (2018): 18–40.

Marratto, Scott. *The Intercorporeal Self: Merleau-Ponty on Subjectivity*. Albany: State University of New York Press, 2012.

Marshall, Alfred. *Principles of Economics*. Amherst, NY: Prometheus Books, 1997.

Marshall, Victor W., and Vern L. Bengtson. "Theoretical Perspectives on the Sociology of Aging." In *Handbook of Sociology of Aging*, edited by R. Settersten and J. Angel, 17–33. New York: Springer, 2011.

Marx, Karl. *Capital, Volume 1: A Critique of Political Economy*. translated by Ben Fowkes. Harmondsworth: Penguin, 1992.

———. *The Eighteenth Brumaire of Louis Bonaparte*. In *Selected Writings*, 2nd ed., edited by David McLellan, 329–55. New York: Oxford University Press, 2000.

———. *The German Ideology*. In *Selected Writings*, 2nd ed., edited by David McLellan, 175–208. New York: Oxford University Press, 2000.

McHugh Power, Joanna E., Luna Dolezal, Frank Kee, and Brian A. Lawlor. "Conceptualizing Loneliness in Health Research: Philosophical and Psychological Ways Forward." *Journal of Theoretical and Philosophical Psychology* 38 (2018): 219–34.

McMahon, Laura. "Phenomenology as First-Order Perception: Speech, Vision, and Reflection in Merleau-Ponty." In *Perception and Its Development in Merleau-Ponty's Phenomenology*, edited by Kirsten Jacobson and John Russon, 308–37. Toronto: University of Toronto Press, 2017.

———. "(Un)Healthy Systems: Merleau-Ponty, Dewey, and the Dynamic Equilibrium Between Self and Environment." *Journal of Speculative Philosophy* 32 (2018): 607–27.

Meiksins Wood, Ellen. *Peasant-Citizen, and Slave: The Foundations of Athenian Democracy*. London: Verso, 1989.

Merkur, Dan. "The Ojibwa Vision Quest." *Journal of Applied Psychoanalytic Studies* 4 (2002): 149–70.

Merleau-Ponty, Maurice. *Child Psychology and Pedagogy: The Sorbonne Lectures 1949–1952*. Translated by Talia Welsh. Evanston: Northwestern University Press, 2010.

———. *Institution and Passivity: Course Notes from the Collège de France (1954–1955)*. Translated by Leonard Lawlor and Heath Massey. Evanston: Northwestern University Press, 2010.

———. *Phenomenology of Perception*. Translated by Donald A. Landes. London and New York: Routledge, 2012.

Minkler, Meredith, and Carroll L. Estes, eds. *Critical Gerontology: Perspectives from Political and Moral Economy*. Amityville NY: Baywood, 1999.

Minuchin, Salvador. *Families and Family Therapy*. Cambridge: Harvard University Press, 1974.

Mitchell, William, L. Randall Wray, and Martin Watts. *Macroeconomics*. London: Red Globe Press, 2019.

Morris, David. *The Sense of Space*. Albany: State University of New York Press, 2004.

―――. *Merleau-Ponty's Developmental Ontology*. Evanston: Northwestern University Press, 2018.

―――. "The Open Figure of Experience and Mind." *Dialogue* 45 (2006): 315–26.

―――, and Kym Maclaren, eds. *Time, Memory, Institution: Merleau-Ponty's New Ontology of Self*. Athens: Ohio University Press, 2015.

Munn, Mark. *The Mother of the Gods, Athens, and the Tyranny of Asia: A Study of Sovereignty in Ancient Religions*. Berkeley: University of California Press, 2006.

Murphy, Sharon Ann. *Other People's Money: How Banking Worked in the Early American Republic*. Baltimore: Johns Hopkins University Press, 2017.

Noë, Alva. *Action in Perception*. Cambridge: MIT Press, 2004.

Nuland, Sherwin. *How We Die: Reflections on Life's Final Chapter*. New York: Vintage, 1995.

―――. *The Art of Aging: A Doctor's Prescription for Well-Being*. New York: Random House, 2008.

O'Dell, Lindsay, Charlotte Brownlow, and Hanna Bertilsdotter Rosqvist. "Different Adulthoods: Normative Development and Transgressive Trajectories." *Feminism and Psychology* 28 (2018): 349–54.

Ostler, Nicholas, *Empires of the Word: A Language History of the World*. New York: HarperCollins, 2005.

Patterson, Charlotte J. "Family Relationships of Lesbians and Gay Men." *Journal of Marriage and Family* 62 (2000): 1052–69.

Payer, Cheryl. *The Debt-Trap: The International Monetary Fund and the Third World*. New York: Monthly Review Press, 1974.

Pilcher, Jane, John Williams, and Christopher Pole. "Rethinking Adulthood: Families, Transitions, and Social Change." *Sociological Research Online* 8 (2003): 1–5.

Plato. *Complete Works*. Indianapolis: Hackett, 1997.

―――. *The Republic*. Translated by Allan Bloom. New York: Basic Books, 2016.

Radford, Luis. "Semiosis and Subjectification: The Classroom Constitution of Mathematical Subjects." In *Signs of Signification: Semiotics in Mathematics Education Research*, edited by N. Presmeg, L. Radford, M. Roth, and G. Kadunz, 21–35. Cham, Switzerland: Springer, 2018.

Ragep, F. Jamil. "Copernicus and His Islamic Predecessors: Some Historical Remarks." *History of Science* 45 (2007): 65–81.

Ratcliffe, Matthew. "The Interpersonal Structure of Depression." *Psychoanalytic Psychotherapy* 32 (2018): 122–39.

―――. "Selfhood, Schizophrenia, and the Interpersonal Regulation of Experience." In *Embodiment, Enaction, and Culture: Investigating the Constitution of the Shared World*, edited by Christoph Durt, Thomas Fuchs, and Christian Tewes. Cambridge: MIT Press, 2017.

Russon, John. *Bearing Witness to Epiphany: Persons, Things, and the Nature of Erotic Life*. Albany: State University of New York Press, 2009.

———. "Between Two Intimacies: The Formative Contexts of Adult Individuality." *Emotion, Space and Society* 13 (2014): 65–70.

———. "Expressing Dwelling: Dewey and Hegel on Art as Cultural Self-Expression." *Contemporary Pragmatism* 12 (2015): 38–58.

———. *Human Experience: Philosophy, Neurosis, and the Elements of Everyday Life*. Albany: State University of New York Press, 2003.

———. *Infinite Phenomenology: The Lessons of Hegel's Science of Experience*. Evanston: Northwestern University Press, 2016.

———. "On Human Identity: The Intersubjective Path from Body to Mind." *Dialogue* 45 (2006): 307–14.

———. "Personality as Equilibrium: Fragility and Plasticity in (Inter-)Personal Identity." *Phenomenology and the Cognitive Sciences* 16 (2017): 623–35.

———. "Phenomenological Description and Artistic Expression." In *Phenomenology and the Arts*, edited by Peter Costello and Licia Carlson, 3–24. Lanham, MD: Lexington, 2016.

———. *Reading Hegel's Phenomenology*. Bloomington: Indiana University Press, 2004.

———. "Self and Suffering in Buddhism and Phenomenology: Existential Pain, Compassion, and the Problems of Institutionalized Healthcare." In *Cultural Ontology of the Self in Pain*, edited by Siby K. George and P. G. Jung, 181–95. New Delhi, Springer, 2016.

———. *Sites of Exposure: A Philosophical Essay on Art, Politics, and the Nature of Experience*. Minneapolis: University of Minnesota Press, 2017.

———. "Subjectivity and Hermeneutics." In *The Blackwell Companion to Hermeneutics*, edited by Niall Keene and Chris Lawn, 205–11. London: Blackwell, 2016.

———. "The Bodily Unconscious in Freud's *Three Essays*." In *Rereading Freud: Psychoanalysis Through Philosophy*, edited by Jon Mills, 33–50. Albany: State University of New York Press, 2004.

———. "The Limits of Money: Phenomenological Reflections on Selfhood and Value." *Studies in Humanities and Social Science* 23 (2016): 55–70.

———. "The Spatiality of Self-Consciousness: Originary Passivity in Kant, Merleau-Ponty and Derrida." *Chiasmi International* 9 (2007): 219–32.

———. "The Virtue of Stoicism: On First Principles in Philosophy and in Life." *Dialogue* 45 (2006): 347–54.

———. "The Virtues of Agency: A Phenomenology of Confidence, Courage, and Creativity." In *Phenomenology and Virtue Ethics*, edited by Kevin Hermberg and Paul Gyllenhammer, 165–79. London: Continuum, 2013.

Saitabau, Henri ole. *The Role of Ceremonies in Preserving Cultural Diversity and Conserving Biodiversity for Sustainable Livelihoods: Exploring Cultural Diver-*

sity and Related Indigenous Knowledge among the Loita Maasai Community. Nairobi: Loita Hills Community Forest Association (LH-CFA), 2011.

Saner, Senem. "Migrants as Educators: Reversing the Order of Beneficence." *Journal of Global Ethics* 14 (2018): 95–113.

Sartre, Jean-Paul. *Being and Nothingness: A Phenomenological Essay in Ontology.* Translated by Hazel E. Barnes. New York: Washington Square, 1956.

———. *Critique of Dialectical Reason*, Vol. 1. Translated by Alan Sheridan Smith. London: Verson, 2004.

Schaps, D. *The Invention of Coinage and the Monetization of Ancient Greece.* Ann Arbor: University of Michigan Press, 2004.

Schelling, F. W. J. *System of Transcendental Idealism.* Translated by Peter L. Heath. Charlottesville: University of Virginia Press, 1993.

Schiller, Friedrich. *On the Aesthetic Education of Man in a Series of Letters*, German text with facing English translation. Edited and translated by Elizabeth M. Wilkinson and L. A. Willoughby. Oxford: Clarendon Press, 1967.

Schumpeter, Joseph A. *History of Economic Analysis.* New York: Oxford University Press, 1994.

Seaford, Richard. *Money and the Early Greek Mind.* Cambridge: Cambridge University Press, 2004.

———. *Reciprocity and Ritual: Homer and Tragedy in the Developing City-State.* Oxford: Oxford University Press, 1994.

Seamon, David. *Life Takes Place: Phenomenology, Lifeworlds, and Place Making.* New York: Routledge, 2018.

Seneca, Lucius Annaeus. *The Stoic Philosophy of Seneca: Essays and Letters.* Translated by Moses Hadas. New York: Norton, 1968.

Sherimani, Ferima, and Deborah L. O'Connor. "Ageing in a Foreign Country: Voices of Iranian Women Ageing in Canada." *Journal of Women and Aging* 18 (2006): 73–90.

Siebers, Tobin. *Disability Theory.* Ann Arbor: University of Michigan Press, 2008.

Simmel, Georg. *The Philosophy of Money.* London: Routledge and Kegan Paul, 1978.

Simms, Eva M. *The Child in the World: Embodiment, Time, and Language in Early Childhood.* Detroit: Wayne State University Press, 2008.

Smith, Adam. *An Inquiry into the Nature and Causes of the Wealth of Nations.* Chicago: University of Chicago Press, 1977.

Sophocles, *Antigone.* Translated by Richmond Lattimore. In *Greek Tragedies*, Vol. 1, edited by David Grene. Chicago: University of Chicago Press, 1970.

Sparshott, Francis. *Taking Life Seriously: A Study of the Argument of the Nicomachean Ethics.* Toronto: University of Toronto Press, 1996.

Stolorow, Robert D. "From Mind to World, From Drive to Affectivity: A Phenomenological-Contextualist Psychoanalytic Perspective." *Attachment: New Directions in Psychotherapy and Relational Psychoanalysis* 5 (2011): 1–14.

———. "Intersubjective-Systems Theory: A Phenomenological-Contextualist Psychoanalytic Perspective." *Psychoanalytic Dialogues* 23 (2013): 383–89.

———. *World, Affectivity, Trauma: Heidegger and Post-Cartesian Psychoanalysis.* New York: Routledge, 2011.

Struthers, Roxanne, and Felicia S. Hodge. "Sacred Tobacco Use in Ojibwe Communities." *Journal of Holistic Nursing* 22 (2004): 209–25.

Talero, Maria L. "Merleau-Ponty and the Bodily Subject of Learning." *International Philosophical Quarterly* 46 (2006): 191–203.

———. "Perception, Normativity, and Selfhood in Merleau-Ponty: The Spatial 'Level' and Existential Space." *Southern Journal of Philosophy* 43 (2005): 443–61.

———. "The Experiential Workspace and the Limits of Empirical Investigation." *International Journal of Philosophical Studies* 16 (2008): 453–72.

Trigg, Dylan. *The Memory of Place: A Phenomenology of the Uncanny.* Athens, OH: Ohio University Press, 2012.

Tymoigne, Éric, and L. Randall Wray. "Money: An Alternative Story." In *A Handbook of Alternative Monetary Economics*, edited by Philip Arestis and Malcolm Sawyer. Northampton, MA: Edward Elgar, 2006.

van den Berg, J. H. *The Psychology of the Sickbed.* Pittsburgh: Duquesne University Press, 1966.

von Reden, Sitta. *Money in Classical Antiquity.* Cambridge: Cambridge University Press, 2010.

von Uexküll, Jakob. *A Foray into the Worlds of Animals and Humans, with A Theory of Meaning.* Translated by Joseph D. O'Neil. Minneapolis: University of Minnesota Press, 2011.

Weber, Max. *Economy and Society: An Outline of Interpretive Sociology.* 2 Vols. Edited by Guenther Roth and Claus Wittich. Berkeley: University of California Press, 1978.

———. "Politics as Vocation." In *From Max Weber: Essays in Sociology*, edited by H. H. Gerth and C. Wright Mills, 77–128. New York: Oxford University Press, 1946.

Wehrle, Maren. "Becoming Old. The Gendered Body and the Experience of Aging." In *Aging and Human Nature*, edited by Mark Schweda, Michael Coors, and Claudia Bozzaro. New York: Springer, 2020.

Wilson, Alexander. *The Culture of Nature: North American Landscape from Disney to the Exxon Valdez.* Toronto: Between the Lines, 1991.

Winnicott, D. W. *Home Is Where We Start From: Essays by a Psychoanalyst.* New York: Norton, 1990.

———. *Playing and Reality.* New York: Routledge, 2005.

———. *The Child, the Family, and the Outside World.* New York: Perseus, 1992.

Wray, L. Randall. *Understanding Modern Money: The Key to Full Employment and Price Stability.* Cheltenham and Northampton: Edward Elgar, 1998.

Young, Iris Marion. "A Room of One's Own: Old Age, Extended Care and Privacy." In *Privacies: Philosophical Evaluations*, edited by Beate Rösseler, Stanford: Stanford University Press, 2004.

———. "Throwing Like a Girl: A Phenomenology of Feminine Body Comportment Motility and Spatiality." *Human Studies* 3 (1980): 137–56.

Index

Action. *See* Agency

Agency: Emma Goldman as agent, 6; action as essential dimension of experience, 19; relation of action to perception, 19–23; action as condition for our experience of time, 21; normally experienced as passivity, 22; embodied, 35, 42; cooperative, 37; product of transformative self-experience, 41; dependent on *sōphrosunē*, 41; defined and described, 42, 46, 50; as experience of being at home, 42; creative, 42–43; reliant on confirmation by reality, 42; as openness to possibility, 43; courage as recognition of, 43; encouraged in boys, 45; dependent upon habituation, 46; expressive of sense of others, 48; dependent upon support of others, 50–51; and communication, 50–51; as natural, personal, interpersonal, and impersonal, 53, 55; shaped by culture, 55; paired with participation, 70; society as agent of economics, 120; government not a normal economic agent, 130, 133, 134; banks as economic agents, 141; economic agency in money economy, 144–51; alienated economic agency, 144; government as agency of social self-responsibility, 153; passive compliance to government as, 175; and citizenship, 175–77; and possibility, 180

Activism, 3–7, 172, 175, 176–77

Adolescence: teenagers socializing, 1–3; time of recognizing subjectivity, 58; inevitable, 67; distinctive character of, 69–72; as practice for adulthood, 70–72; as experience of agency, 70; and emergence of sexuality, 70; in Western culture, 70–71; outside Western culture, 71–72; role in liberal societies, 71; and sense of individuality, 71; and experience of responsibility, 72; compared with middle adult life, 80; and sexuality, 104–107; and "narrow socialization," 105; and experimentation, 105; and getting a job, 117, 151

Adulthood: middle adulthood, 1–3, 75–81; late adulthood, 7–9, 81–82; learned by living it, 10, 73; overview of, 10, 101; as way of experiencing, 13; admits of degrees, 13, 102; as existential maturity, 28, 61; dependent upon but not defined by

Adulthood *(continued)*
  biology, 28, 61; defining norms of,
  29–30; dealing with reality as reality,
  29, 34; aging as essential condition
  of, 30; central study of stages of
  adulthood and aging, 72–82; and
  decision, 73; early adulthood,
  74–75; and independence, 81; and
  disability, 82; and sense of objective
  space, 88; and sense of place, 93;
  accomplished in dialogue with
  an environment, 93; requires our
  agency, 101; and individuality,
  103; and sense of belonging, 104;
  and sexuality, 106–107; intimacy
  essential to, 110; and family
  membership, 113; economics
  essential to, 117; and childish
  approach to economics, 119; and
  economic agency in capitalism,
  150–51; politics essential to, 152;
  and citizenship, 173–77; trapped
  in the actual, 179; and spirit of
  play, 179–80; and art, 183–85; and
  religion, 187–88; and dependency
  on others, 194; and philosophy, 194
Aging: differences in age, 1–3;
  Cephalus sheds light on, 8;
  definitive of adulthood, 13, 30; both
  physiological and psychological,
  13; as qualitative change in how we
  experience, 66, 75; analogous to
  habituation, 66–67; experienced as
  the revelation of our nature, 67; as
  change in embodied intentionality,
  67, 80–82; stages of, 67, 82; aging
  and comprehending aging, 73;
  experience of dependency in old
  age, 81–82; experience of loss in old
  age, 81
Agricultural Society, 121

Alienation: in midlife, 77; in
  immigration, 96; in old age,
  104; and Western values, 112; in
  marriage, 115; in economic agency,
  143–44; of political power, 155,
  166; and labor-saving devices, 158;
  and citizenship, 158; in voting,
  161–62; market as domain of,
  166; in money economy, 144; and
  citizenship, 158; in voting, 161–62
Althusser, Louis, 88
al-Ṭusī, Naṣīr al-Dīn, 87
al-'Urḍī, Mu'Ayyad al-Dīn, 87
Ambedkar, Bhimrao Ramji, 176
Animals, 23, 50
Antigone, 54
Anxiety, 9, 52, 55, 57, 80, 96
Aristotle: and virtue, 12–13; on
  perception in animals, 23; on being
  qua being, 24; on courage and
  moderation, 38; on courage and
  war, 43; on orientation in space,
  87; on friendship, 114; on human
  nature, 122; on knowing the "why,"
  173–74; as source for this book,
  196, 199
Art: examples of artists, 66, 76;
  distinctive nature of, 181–85;
  expression for its own sake, 181;
  as aperture, 181; degrees of artistic
  expression, 181–82; essential
  dimension of human life, 182; and
  interpretation of human nature,
  182–83; ancient Mesopotamian,
  182; Greek, 182; Italian
  Renaissance, 182; and mechanical
  reproducibility, 182; and happiness,
  183–84; challenge of living as an
  artist, 184; lack of economic support
  for, 184; and possibility, 185;
  exclusionary portrayals in, 185

"As such": experience as such, 19; distinctively human experience of, 23–29, 35, 50, 62; reality as such, 24–25, 189–91; possibility as such, 24–25; and death, 26; midlife experience of embodied temporality as such, 80; space as such, 87; value as such, 126–27; society as such, 163, 168, 170–71; person as such, 192

Autonomy: of "I," 41; never fully realized norm, 102; and relationships, 110

Ayesh, Naila, 177

Banks: integral to North American view of housing, 91; fact of contemporary life, 119; encourage misunderstanding of economics, 134; opposition to government, 136; and money, 137–40; credit (loans) as essential banking function, 137–38; coercive power of, 136, 138–39; commercial vs. central, 140; as economic agents (unlike government), 141; benefit from contemporary government, 142; Bretton Woods Agreement and European Central Bank, 168–69

Bataille, Georges, 131, 133–34

Behavior: character as behavioral readiness, 12; and nature of experience, 22; perception of reality as a matter of, 29, 101, 104; as unity of psychological and physical, 35; and passivity, 43; aging and solidified patterns of, 67; spatial interpretation in, 89, 92; and virtue, 102; and bureaucracy, 156; and voting, 161; contradictions in, 174; and morality, 191

Belonging: to a generation, 2; to a country, 91; to a place, 94–97; vs. anxiety and alienation, 96; and old age, 97, 104; child developing sense of, 103; human need for interpersonal belonging, 103–104; in intimate relationships, 110; through labor, 123, 143; in economics and intimacy, 151; in decision-making, 159–60; in religion and culture, 186

Benjamin, Walter, 182, 186

Bergson, Henri, 195, 197

Berkman, Alexander, 4–5

Bienowitch, Taube, 3

Body: root and anchor of possibilities, 20–21; must be made one's own, 35; both a physiological and a psychological reality, 35; medium for engaging with others, 37, 50, 52; transformations of in puberty, 70–71; "bodily ego," 70–71; in the eyes of others, 71; and economic need, 116

Bretton Woods Agreement, 168–69

British East India Company, 145–47

Buddha, The (Siddhatta Gotama), 74

Bureaucracy: and modern government, 156; has norms of its own, 156–57; compared to intelligence services, 172

Canadian Tire Money, 128–29

Capitalism: Emma Goldman and, 4, 6; and spatial interpretation, 90, 95, 98; and banking, 137, 140–43, 150; and subordination of impoverished working class, 142–43; and joint stock companies, 145; and inversion of economic agency, 148–50; and individualist rhetoric, 150, 186; and

modern government has ambivalent
relationship to, 155, 157; and
voting, 158–62
Derrida, Jacques, 14, 199
Dewey, John, 14, 197, 199
Disability, 9, 82
Discounting, 128–29, 135, 136, 139,
145, 147–48, 149
Division of Labor. *See* Labor

Ecclesiastes, v, 27
Economics: adults dealing with
finance, 3; distinctive nature as
domain of *sugchōrein*, 117–52;
essential domain of adult life, 117;
and entrepreneurs, 118; a collective
affair, 120; a system, 120; labor and,
123, 131–32, 146, 157–58; general
vs. restricted economy, 131, 133–34;
as interpretation of person, 151–52,
163; as challenge to authority of
state, 164; conflict with intimacy
and family life, 151–52, 166–67. *See
also* Labor
Eliot, George (Mary Anne Evans), 74
Epictetus, 39, 56
Erikson, Erik H., 196
Exchange: Cephalus's approach to
everything, 9; universal experience,
122; essential dimension of
economics, 124–25; and
intersubjective dependence, 125;
and inversion of value in money
economy, 144
Experience: of growing older, 10,
43–44, 61, 85, 92, 95–96, 179; first
principle of human life, 11; and
time, 12, 21, 61–63, 65, 73; as self-
conscious, 12, 61, 64–65; of others,
13, 37, 46, 50, 68, 70–71, 77, 105–
16, 154, 161–61, 184, 191–94; of
"calling," 14, 173, 175, 191, 194;

as perception and action, 19, 23; as
embodied, 20; and space, 20–21,
82, 88–98; definitive experience of
"as such," 23–25, 50; of finite and
infinite, 24–25; of death, 26–27, 78,
81; of reality, 29–30, 33–35, 41–42,
57, 62; of body, 33, 35–36, 37,
70–71; of pleasure and pain, 39–41;
of self, 40–41, 68–69, 70–78, 81,
88, 151–52, 154, 163–65, 173,
175, 181; of agency, 42–46, 70, 93,
103–104; of what is present, 61–63;
inaugural experiences, 64; of habit,
66, 118; of aging, 66–82, 94–98;
of choice, 73, 79, 81, 158–62; of
beginning, 105; of commitment,
110; of play, 180–81; of the
"absolute," 180–94

"Fair Labor Standards Act," 130
Family: formative base, 6; can be
oppressive, 6; parent and child
relationship, 37–38, 49, 51–52,
69, 101, 111; ancient Greek family
in *Antigone*, 54; integral to child's
development, 68; starting family
in early adulthood, 74; and midlife
crisis, 77; in Iran vs. in Canada,
96; primary sphere of meaning
for many people, 111; as essential
dimension of experience, 111–13;
and raising children, 111–12; in
Western and non-Western cultures,
112; vs. political life, 112, 153–54;
non-traditional forms of, 115–16;
basis of hunting and gathering and
pastoralist societies, 120–21; in
tension with economic life, 151–52,
166–67; as interpretation of person,
151–52, 163; as challenge to
authority of state, 164
Fanon, Frantz, 46

Market. *See* Economics

Marriage: of Emma Goldman's parents, 3; of Emma Goldman, 4; custom in Maasai culture, 71; in early adult life, 74; in middle adult life, 77; in older age, 77; defining of who one is, 77; in "narrow socialization," 105; divorce, 110; arranged marriage, 105, 110; and "what life is about," 111; as context for economic and political life, 111; and responsibility, 111; as disingenuous model of intimacy, 115

Marx, Karl, 116, 120, 142–43

Maturity: according to Cephalus, 9; existential vs. biological, 28; as living from the norm of reality, 29; as experiencing from the perspective of others, 47; vs. immature understanding of happiness, 58; and sense of time, 62, 80–81; vs. immature sense of possibility, 81; as owning up to implicit structures of *sugchōrein*, 92; role of cold space in, 92–93; vs. immaturity in interpersonal relationships, 106–107, 109; vs. immaturity in economics, 117; in politics, 173–75; and play, 179–80

Mauss, Marcel, 124

McKinley, William, 5

Mental Illness, 52, 82

Merleau-Ponty, Maurice, 14; 179, 195, 197

Method: requires phenomenon and interpretation, 1; philosophical vs. empirical, 11, 195; phenomenological, 14, 51, 179, 195–200; of collective decision-making, 158–62; experimental, 190; relies on insight, reasoning, and experience, 195

Midlife Crisis: defined and described, 75–81; as call to change relationship to meaning, 80; as embodied temporality announcing itself as such, 80

Minuchin, Salvador, 198

Moderation. See *Sōphrosunē*

Modernity: scientific revolution, 87–88, 190; conception of physical space in, 87–89; and public space, 88–89; and adolescence, 104–105, 112; and taxation, 134; failures of modern government, 168–69; in artworks, 182

Money: poverty of Emma Goldman's family, 3; Cephalus's wealth, 8–9; poverty and hardship, 9, 82; natural development of human economic life, 125–26; and commodities, 126, 127–28; function of money, 125–26; and "I can," 126; not a neutral convenience, 127, 142–43; and trust, 127; as power to engage in economic life, 129, 132–35; 136, 139–40, 142; and coercion, 129–30, 136; and government, 130–37; and sovereignty, 131; as legal tender, 132; and taxes, 132–35; division of rich and poor, 135, 142–43; foreign exchange, 136; and bank credit, 137–40; integration of government and banks in modern money, 140–43, 150; embodiment of economic order, 141–42; money and system, 143, 144; and alienation, 144; "making money" in the stock market, 147–48

Morality: Cephalus and, 9; and mortality, 10; child as moral being, 69, 111; and what should be, 180; and philosophy, 191–92

Most, Johann, 4

Navajo (Diné), 71

Public: public life, 4, 5, 26, 54,
  96, 103, 175; public space, 47,
  88–90, 95, 97; public interest,
  91–92, 142, 168, 177; public
  determination of economic value,
  125, 152; public debt, 132–37;
  publicly traded companies, 147–48;
  public transparency of government,
  172–73

Question and Answer (logic of):
  perception as, 22; agency as, 42;
  intersubjective, 48; realities not
  questioned, 119; as wonder and
  science, 190; culture as accumulated
  history of, 193; and wisdom,
  193–94

Race: and different experience of
  hardship, 9; in Fanon, 46; and lower
  pay, 176; excluded in artworks, 185
Reality: meaningful to us in terms of
  our possibilities for engagement,
  20; experienced as exceeding our
  perspective on it, 24–25; and
  Freud, 29; behavioral demands of
  recognizing it, 29, 36; demands
  objectivity, 33; defined by causality,
  33, 62; indifferent to us, 39; in
  itself vs. for us, 40; paired with
  autonomous self, 41; accommodates
  agency, 42; understanding oneself
  to be real, 51–52, 68–69; and
  intersubjectivity, 52; and Stoicism,
  56; as presence and absence,
  61–62, 180; and objective time, 62;
  experience of reality presupposes
  experience of home, 63; meaning of
  reality paired with meaning of one's
  life, 65; in the history of philosophy,
  87–88, 190; what is vs. what should
  be, 180; and art, religion, and

philosophy, 180; and philosophy,
  189; as one, natural, and open
  to human agency, 190; and care,
  191; and other people, 191–92; of
  nature, 192
Religion: and final judgment, 8–9;
  and ascetic self-discipline, 39;
  in *Antigone*, 54; spiritual crisis
  of midlife, 75, 77; and ancient
  Mesopotamian art, 182; primarily
  cultural rather than individual, 183,
  186; essential dimension of human
  experience, 186; and "human
  rights," 186; art and religion, 186;
  not to be confused with institutional
  practices, 187; and secularity, 187–
  88; and happiness, 188
Responsibility: as first norm of
  adulthood, 29–30, 101; requires
  self-effacement, 58; contrasted with
  happiness, 58–59; experience of in
  adolescence, 72; adult expectation
  of, 94; voting undermines, 162
Retirement, 96
Rights, 6, 90, 91, 97, 117, 170, 176,
  186
R. J. Reynolds Tobacco Company, 176
Roosevelt, Theodore, 5

Sartre, Jean-Paul, 198
Scepticism, 57, 62
Schiller, Friedrich, 84
Science: philosophy and, 11, 189–94;
  modern physical, 88, 102
Scientific Revolution, 87
Scrip: in coal-mining town, 129–30;
  compared to sovereign currency,
  130, 135; in competition with
  government currency, 136
Seneca, 56
Sexuality: free love advocated by
  Emma Goldman, 5; and old age,